THE CRAPS
UNDERGROUND

THE CRAPS
UNDERGROUND

• • • •

The Inside Story of How Dice Controllers
Are Winning Millions from the Casinos

FRANK SCOBLETE

Chicago and Los Angeles

07 06 05 04 03   5 4 3 2 1

Library of Congress Control Number: 2003112238

ISBN: 1-56625-217-2

Bonus Books
875 North Michigan Ave., Ste. 1416
Chicago, IL 60611

Printed in the United States of America

To Dominator

Contents

• • • •

THE CRAPS
UNDERGROUND

. . . .

1

The New Advantage Players

IT WAS 6 A.M. on September 18, 2002, at Treasure Island Casino in Las Vegas. My knees were weak and my legs were rubbery as I picked up the dice, arranged the die faces in my standard "3-V" pattern, took a deep breath, aligned the dice parallel with the back wall, and then lofted them gently toward the end of the table. The crowd at the table were as one as they watched the dice glide in a gentle arc to their final destination, the foam rubber pyramids of the back wall.

I had been shooting the dice now for about thirty minutes, hitting a half dozen points and loads of numbers. But no one was cheering. No one was shouting. The table was quiet and had been for the last couple of hours. Everyone had cheered like crazy for the first four hours, but now even the cheeriest players were fatigued. Yet no one left the table. How could they? They were watching a miracle. And they were making money—a lot of money.

But it wasn't these last thirty minutes that had me on the ropes and everyone else lead-eyed but refusing to leave the game. It had been the last *seven hours*—seven glorious hours shooting dice with a fellow dice controller and newfound friend known as the "Bodacious One," Beau Parker. Now, many gamblers have *played* craps for seven straight hours, certainly, but I was involved in something completely different that night into that morning. At a crowded table, with ten other players besides Beau and me, in the last five hours the two of us were the *only ones* who shot the dice! Every other player, when it was his turn to shoot, would indicate that he wanted to pass up his turn and pass the dice on to Beau, who stood at "stick right 1" (SR1), just to the stickman's right, and then to me, who stood on the stickman's other side at stick left 1 (SL1).

It had started around 12:30 A.M., when the kid in the corner with his girlfriend hanging all over him said: "Hell, I don't want to shoot. I want them two bearded guys to shoot," and he waved the dice away while pointing over to us. By 1 A.M., they were all doing it. Beau and I were the *official* shooters of that table.

At first, everyone screamed and cheered when Beau had one of his half-dozen fifteen-to-twenty-minute rolls. And everyone screamed and cheered when I'd match him roll for roll and minute for minute. After he shot, I'd high-five him behind the stickman. After I shot, he'd high-five me. Even the dealers were getting into the cheering, as both of us were tipping them generously.

But by 6 A.M. I could see that even the redoubtable Beau looked tired. Yet it was he who had set down the law the night before: "Frank, we don't quit as long as we keep winning."

· · · ·

WE HAD attended a party the night before thrown by the gracious George Maloof, owner of the beautiful Palms Casino Hotel in Las Vegas. The party was held at the incredible "Ghost Bar" atop his casino, which offered a 360-degree view of the entire sparkling valley of Las Vegas. This party had been arranged by Jean Scott, author of *The Frugal Gambler,* and was being held for gaming writers who happened to be in town for the Global Gaming Expo. Many of my fellow gaming writers from Bonus Books were present and partying heartily, including John Grochowski, author of the Answer Book series, Bill Burton, author of *Get the Edge at Low-Limit Texas Hold'em,* Don Catlin, author of *The Lottery Book: The Truth Behind the Numbers,* and Barney Vinson, author of *Ask Barney.* Usually casino owners don't throw parties for gambling writers—they throw fits. After all, our mission is to help the players beat the casinos, or, at the very least, cut the house edge to its bare minimum. But Maloof was different. He seemed to genuinely enjoy mixing with and meeting some of gambling's luminaries.

Beau and his lovely wife Beth were at the party, too.

Around ten thirty I decided it was time to call it a night and maybe get in some play. Beau joined me. First we shot some craps at Palms, but we weren't hot, and we stopped before we damaged ourselves. Then I said that I was thinking of going to Treasure Island, which was my favorite casino for craps in Las Vegas at the time. Beau said he'd join me.

Beth dropped us off at Treasure Island at 10:55 P.M. Beau picked up the dice for the first time at 11:10. He rolled for fifteen minutes. I picked the dice up and rolled for twenty minutes. "Maybe we should quit," I said.

"Frank, we don't quit as long as we keep winning," Beau said. . . .

• • • •

AND NOW, it was *seven hours* later. The dice I had just lofted touched down, hit a chip, and—

"Seven out!" said the stickman. "Another great roll."

I turned to Beau. "That's it," I said. "I can hardly stand."

"Yeah," he said.

The other players at the table began to clap. Not the way most players clap after a good roll but the way an audience claps after seeing a magnificent sustained performance. Beau smiled. I smiled and looked at my chip rack overflowing with a rainbow of reds, greens, blacks, and purples. It had been some performance, all right.

Over breakfast, Beau looked at me. "I made a lot of money tonight. A lot."

"I couldn't believe it when they just started passing us the dice," I said.

"And did you notice that the pit didn't give us any heat?"

"Treasure Island is a good place. We tipped, too, and the dealers made a lot of money."

"Amazing," said Beau, and he was looking far, far away.

"It's like a dream, Beau. We just experienced a dream."

"Don't wake me up," he said returning from wherever his mind had taken him. "I like this dream."

But it wasn't a dream. It was real. And it's happening more frequently to a small group of expert players: the dream of beating craps by taking your fate into your own hands and rolling "them bones" with precision.

• • • •

EVER SINCE the publication of my first book, *Beat the Craps Out of the Casinos: How to Play Craps and Win,* in which I introduced the legendary Captain of Craps and his crew of high rollers, the Captain's brilliant methods of play have been gaining more and more converts. It was the Captain who was the first to recognize that some shooters—he called them "rhythmic rollers"—could subtly influence the dice so that craps became a positive-expectation game rather than a negative-expectation game. Granted, these shooters were (and still are) few and far between. So, in order not to lose too much money waiting for such shooters to appear, or for hot rolls from random rollers (which also occur from time to time), the Captain came up with his *5-Count* principle for shooter selection. This eliminated approximately 57 percent of the shooters, all the ones who, in the long run, lost you money. It left the remaining 43 percent for you to bet on. In that remaining 43 percent would be the Holy Grail of craps players, the hot shooters and the rhythmic rollers.

Beat the Craps Out of the Casinos: How to Play Craps and Win had a profound effect on many players. It took them from looking at craps as a game that couldn't be beaten, to looking at craps as a game that could. The book could take a player from novice, teaching him the rules and bets of the game, to expert. It also introduced a host of interesting and exciting ideas and people. In addition to the *5-Count*, readers were introduced to the *Supersystem,* the *Virgin Principle,* the *High-Roller System*, the *Low-Roller System*, and *The Ten Commandments of Craps.* They read about the woman known as "the Arm," perhaps the greatest rhythmic roller of all time, whose adventures with the Captain are legendary. And they read about the Captain's Crew, a Runyonesque band of high-rolling East Coast gamblers.

In the years since that book was published thousands of players have used the Captain's methods. So have I. In my book *Forever Craps: The Five-Step Advantage-Play Method,* I took my twelve years of experience at the craps tables with the Captain's methods and developed what I consider to be the most powerful "system" for playing craps. Of course, at the heart and soul of this system are two principles: the *5-Count,* and rhythmic rolling or controlled shooting. I think it is possible for players who are disciplined to learn how to influence the dice to give themselves the edge. In fact, I *know* it is possible because I have seen and played at the same tables with the players who do it consistently.

Some go by colorful names: the uncannily focused and deadly accurate Dominator, Billy the Kid, Bucko Bob, Doc Holliday, Tenor, Jake from Pitt, Daryl "No Field Five" Henley, Wild Bill Burton, the Samurai Shooter (AKA Dr. Richard McCall), Stickman, Mr. Finesse, Howard "Rock 'n' Roller" Newman, and Street Dog (AKA Buffalo Bill). Others just quietly go about the business of winning money, and neither the public nor the casinos are any the wiser. There are the Lee brothers, Tony and Larry Lee, who travel the country making a living from craps, and there's James ("just call me James and don't write anything else about me"), who plays almost every day "on my breaks from work" and earns in "the high fives, my man." Then there is the remarkable Sharpshooter, the master craps craftsman, whose book *Get the Edge at Craps: How to Control the Dice* is the perfect companion to my *Forever Craps*.

These are the new advantage players, playing in casinos all across America even as I write this sentence, and their game is craps, a game that supposedly can't be beaten. Millions of dollars are being made by them and others like them who, through practice, discipline, and patience, have mastered a very simple concept but a highly advanced skill: if you can alter the outcome of a dice roll, if you can subtly shift the odds by your delivery of the dice, you can beat the game of craps.

It isn't easy; it isn't something anyone or everyone can learn to do. But for those savvy few, those whom I call the "Golden Touch" shooters, craps has become a moneymaker.

This book is the story of the great dice controllers of today and of days gone by. Their story takes place at the tables and behind the scenes of the latest and perhaps greatest advantage-play revolution in casino gaming history. I have

changed some of the names and identifying details of individuals at their request, but each and every person in this
book is a real flesh-and-blood human being, and I've taken
no artistic liberties for dramatic purpose with their stories.
So if something in this book seems fantastic, that's because it
damn well is!

2

The Captain I

FOR ME, everything begins with the Captain.

In 1986 or thereabouts (I'm a little fuzzy on the exact dates), I was about to star in a play titled *The Only Game in Town*. My costar was a beautiful actress named Alene Paone. This would be my fiftieth play with a traveling theater company of which I was part owner. *The Only Game in Town* is the story of a down-and-out, degenerate gambler who loves the game of craps. This guy falls in love with a showgirl who is trying to leave the business by marrying a wealthy, though pompous and boring, older gentleman. It is the classic "boy meets girl, boy loses girl, boy gets the girl in the end" type of tale.

Along the way there's a lot of gambling talk. Since I had never been to Las Vegas or Atlantic City, since I had never even been inside a casino, I thought it might be a good idea to learn what I was actually saying when my character shouted, "Hitting Hardways, yo-elevens" and the like. Yes, I could read a book about the game, but books rarely give you the feel for what it's like to actually play a game. I'd read a book later.

A trip to Atlantic City was in order.

I asked my costar Alene to go with me. Separate rooms. All on the up and up.

In Atlantic City I made two discoveries of monumental personal significance. I didn't know at the time, but they would change the course and focus of my entire life. The first and lesser of the two was a revelation that struck me when I stood at a blackjack table and watched the game being played—I realized that it might be possible to figure out a way to beat this game. If all the Aces were already in play, I thought, no one could get a blackjack. Hmmm. . . . Maybe there was a way to figure out how to win based on what cards came out. I thought I was a genius for coming up with that idea; I had no clue that others had thought that thought since as far back as the 1940s (maybe before), or that something called "card counting" already existed, had been refined, and really worked!

The second discovery, and the more important of the two, was that I met the Captain at the Claridge Casino craps tables. He was there with many of his Crew. I didn't realize how large that day would loom for me.

I was standing on the outskirts of the table watching the game. It was incomprehensible. I had no idea what was going on. I tried to take in everything at once. Chips were flying this way and that. Strange words were being spoken— words *I* would be speaking in the play. The layout looked like something from an Egyptologist's nightmare. What the heck did all those symbols and numbers mean? By comparison, blackjack looked like a walk in the park.

One guy—I would later learn he was the Captain's first mate, Jimmy P.—shouted out, "Captain! I'm getting killed! Get the Arm in here."

"She's coming down in a while," said the man to whom he had addressed his plea—the Captain.

"Hard four," a man with a gravelly voice said. This was Russ, the Breather. "Yeah, get the Arm down here, huh?" Then he coughed.

"She's coming," said the Captain.

"You're called the Captain?" I asked.

"It's an honorary title only," he laughed. At the time, he was about sixty-four years old.

Then someone yelled, "Seven out! Take the Line; pay the Don'ts."

"This game is confusing," I said.

"At first," the Captain said. "But it's very simple when you understand it. All gambling games in the casinos have to be simple, because the casinos are trying to attract the widest possible participation."

"Every idiot," I said.

"Every idiot. Step over here and watch and I'll walk you through it. A new shooter is about to shoot."

I did as I was told. I stood next to the Captain.

"The dice are now in the middle of the table. This is when people put down their initial bets. See that line that runs all around the layout? It says 'Pass.'"

"Yes."

"You put down a bet on this and the shooter over there, the one they are pushing the five dice to, he has a Pass Line bet too. Now, the shooter selects two dice—there, see—and, oh, yes, he can only touch the dice with one hand and he can't bring them off the table."

"Is that so he doesn't switch in loaded dice?" I asked. I had heard about loaded dice in some movie or other.

"Right, among other things. Now, he's going to shoot. This is called the come-out roll. He's starting a new cycle of the game now. He wants to hit a seven or eleven; those two numbers will win him even money on his Pass Line bet."

"Seven and eleven win," I repeated.

"If he rolls a two, three, or twelve, he loses."

"Seven/eleven wins; two, three, twelve loses. This is the come-out roll. What if he rolls another number? A different number?"

"That will become his 'point,'" said the Captain. "He'll have to hit that number again before rolling a seven. If he does that he wins the Pass Line bet. If the seven shows first, he loses the Pass Line bet."

"Six! The point is six!" shouted a guy holding a stick.

"The stickman does all the calling out of the numbers being hit," said the Captain. "Now they put that puck over there on the number, white side up; see it says 'On'?"

"Yep."

"Now he wants to hit that six," said the Captain.

"Uh, Captain, you don't have any bet down."

"No, I'm not risking money on this shooter yet. That's just my own personal thing; I call it the *5-Count*. It's not important for understanding how the game is played."

"So why are people putting chips in back of their Pass Line bets?" I asked.

"That's another bet. With the point established, you put money behind your Pass Line bet. It's called the 'odds' bet."

"Odd name," I said.

"It's the best bet in the game because the casino has no edge on it."

"How does the casino get its edge?"

"On the Pass Line, the casino will win more decisions overall. Since the seven is the key number, every other number is in relation to the seven," he said. "You're confused?"

"I'm confused," I agreed.

"The seven can be made six different ways with two dice.

The six that he's shooting for can be made five different ways."

"So the seven is a six-to-five favorite over the six?" I said. This I could understand. It was simple math.

"The eight has the same number of possibilities. The five and nine have four ways to be made each."

"The seven is a six-to-four favorite," I said.

"Yes, or three to two. Then the four and ten have three ways of being made each."

"Six to three or two to one."

"Right," he said. "Now, the odds bet is paid off according to the true value of the bet. Everyone has an odds bet on the six in multiples of five dollars, so, if they win, for every five dollars they bet in odds, they win six dollars. Had the point been five or nine, everyone would have had an odds bet in multiples that were even, like ten dollars or twelve dollars or twenty dollars, so they could be paid three dollars for every two dollars wagered for a winning bet."

"I got the idea," I said. "The four and ten would pay off double whatever they had bet in odds."

"Right."

"And you can bet as much as you want in odds?" I asked.

"No, they restrict you to double your Pass Line bet," said the Captain.

It was a lot to assimilate but I realized that the game was simple. Seven or 11 on the come-out roll wins; 2, 3, or 12 loses. If the shooter rolled a 4, 5, 6, 8, 9, or 10, that became his point and he had to hit that before he hit a 7 to win. If he hit a 7 it was called a seven-out and the next shooter got the dice.

The Captain then explained other bets to me. Come bets were just like Pass Line bets, only they were made after the point was established. They followed the same rules. When you first put a Come bet down, a seven or eleven won the bet for you—but the shooter had sevened out if it was a seven!—and a two, three, or twelve lost the bet for you. If a number was rolled (the 4, 5, 6, 8, 9, and 10 are called "numbers" in the game of craps, or, sometimes "point numbers"), the shooter had to hit that before a seven to win. Like Pass Line bets, you could put odds on your Come bets. Both Pass Line and Come bets were called "contract bets," because once you made them you couldn't remove them until a decision had been made. You could remove the odds from your bets at any time.

Place bets could be put right up on the numbers. These could be removed at will. For the privilege of doing that, the casino did not pay you the true odds of the Place bet. You placed the six or eight in multiples of $6 to win $7. (The true odds would be a payout of $7.20.) The house edge is 1.5 percent on this bet. You placed the five or nine in multiples of $5 to win $7. (The true odds would be a payout of $7.50.) The house edge is 4 percent on this bet. The four or ten was also bet in multiples of $5 for a payout of $9. (The true odds would be a payout of $10.) The house edge was 6.67 percent.

The Captain explained that when you look at the house edge all you have to do is think in terms of betting $100. Multiply the house edge by the $100 and you can discover what you will lose making that bet in the long run. So if the house edge were 1.5 percent, you multiply $100 by 0.015 and you come up with $1.50. That's how much you can expect to lose per $100 wagered in the long run if you bet into a house edge of 1.5 percent in a random game. So over the years, if you bet a million dollars into such an edge, you'd lose $15,000 . . . give or take.

I watched the game and started to get the hang of it. I was about to ask the Captain about all the bets in the middle of the layout when a big roar went up from the table. I didn't know what had happened. The dice were just sitting in the middle of the table; there was no action going on. But a big roar went up nevertheless.

"It's about time!" shouted Jimmy P.

"Yeah," croaked Russ.

"Help us out," said another man.

"C'mon, Arm!" shouted a short guy down at the other end of the table. This I would later learn was Vic, known as Little Vic.

"Pass the dice," said the Captain. Then he looked at me. "Everybody wants her to shoot."

The "her" he was referring to was the Arm, a woman about sixty-two years of age. She took her place to the left of the stickman, which necessitated the Captain and me moving over to give her room.

Just then Alene appeared and told me that our dinner reservations were ready. I told the Captain I'd like to talk to him after dinner, if that would be okay, to find out more about the game.

"No problem," he said. "We'll probably be right here."

"Let's go, Arm!" shouted Jimmy P.

....

ALENE AND I had dinner at the Twenties, the Claridge's gourmet room. The service was excellent; so was the food. It was a nice, leisurely dinner. We discussed what we had both learned that day. Alene's lesson was simple. "There are no showgirls in Atlantic City. They don't have the big production shows here that they do in Las Vegas. The shows in Atlantic City are just weekend things, usually star vehicles, singers, and comedians, no real big production shows. In Vegas most of the big casinos have house shows."

"Who did you talk to?" I asked.

"Oh, a dealer who used to work in Vegas."

"Ah."

"And what did *you* learn today?" she asked.

"I'm learning about craps. They call him the Captain. I'm telling you, he has all these characters around him, like a 'Damon Runyon does *The Godfather*' story."

· · · ·

AFTER DINNER, Alene and I went back down to the casino. Sure enough, the Captain and his Crew were still there. And, wonder of wonders, the Arm was still shooting the dice!

"How long were we at dinner?" I asked Alene.

Alene looked at her watch. "An hour twenty-five minutes."

I sidled next to the Captain.

"Hey," he said.

"Hey," I said. "Has she been shooting all this time?"

"Naw," he laughed. "This is her second roll. The first was about thirty-five minutes; this one is about fifty minutes. In between a couple of others shot. They aren't with us so they didn't pass the dice to her. We'll talk after she finishes shooting."

She rolled for another five minutes and then sevened out. Everyone at the table exploded into applause.

"Let's go have dinner," she said.

Everyone looked over at the Captain. He nodded, "Dinner it is," he said.

Then all but three players at the table put all their chips down on the layout in front of them. There were a lot of black and purple and some orange chips in just about everyone's stack.

"This is called 'coloring up,'" said the Captain. "We're handing in our chips and they'll count them and give us larger denominations to take to the cage."

"The cage?"

"The cashier's cage. It's easier to carry a few big denominations then a lot of little denominations. They can also figure out exactly how much we won by coloring us up."

"I don't want to stop you from having dinner. I did have some more questions."

"Come to dinner," said the Captain.

"We just ate."

"Have dessert," he said.

"Let me get Alene," I said.

"We're eating at the Twenties."

• • • •

THIS WAS the first of many occasions when I would meet, greet, and eat with Jimmy P., Russ the Breather, John the Analyzer, Phil the Forgetful, Little Vic, the Doctor, Fearful Frank, Dave, Annette, the Arm, and the Captain. In the future I would meet others of the Captain's Crew, including the wives and girlfriends, and finally write a book about the Captain's methods of play and his Crew, *Beat the Craps Out of the Casinos: How to Play Craps and Win!*

I had a second dessert; so did Alene. In the years since I started going to casinos, eating all the comped meals, drinking all that fine wine, my weight ballooned from 150 pounds in 1986 to 206 pounds by 1996. As I write this I am struggling to get under 185 and then down into the 170s (the 150s are forever gone). I used to be the leading man when I did theater; now I'd be the fat friend. Last year I was walking around a track in my neighborhood and a little kid pointed to me and said, "Look, it's Santa walking!" It must have been my white hair and beard. Okay, so I like to eat, drink, and gamble. So what? I don't happen to like little kids, though. Santa walking, indeed.

• • • •

AFTER DINNER, I asked the Captain about other bets at craps. I had a list of words that my character would be saying in the show. I took them out. I asked the Captain; he answered; I wrote down his answers.

FRANK: Hardways.

CAPTAIN: This bet is in the middle of the table, right between the stickman and boxman. You can bet a Hard four, six, eight, or ten. The bet is that the number will be made with the same face showing on both dice—two 2s for four, two 3s for six, two 4s for eight, and two 5s for ten. You have to make that before a seven and before you make the number the easy way, like a 3 and a 1 for four.

FRANK: Don'ts.

CAPTAIN: The opposite of the Pass Line. You'll notice a Don't Pass Line that goes around the table on top of the Pass Line. On the come-out, the Don't Pass loses when the seven or eleven are thrown; it wins on the two or three and pushes. . . .

FRANK: "Pushes"?

CAPTAIN: A tie or a no decision.

FRANK: Got you—twelve pushes on the Don't Pass.

CAPTAIN: When a point is established, the Don't Pass bet wins if a seven is thrown.

FRANK: Ah, so it's the favorite when the point is established.

CAPTAIN: Right, good. You're picking this up.

FRANK: Yo-eleven.

CAPTAIN: Just an eleven. They say yo-eleven so that it isn't confused with seven. Sometimes they just say yo.

FRANK: Okay, I know a twelve is called "boxcars."

CAPTAIN: Also, "midnight."

FRANK: Twelve, midnight—yes, makes sense. "Snake eyes" is the two. What are "craps"?

CAPTAIN: Craps numbers are two, three, and twelve.

FRANK: A Horn bet?

CAPTAIN: The craps numbers and the eleven.

FRANK: Whirl?

CAPTAIN: Or World. That's the Horn with a seven added to it.

FRANK: Are these good or bad bets?

CAPTAIN: Bad.

FRANK: The Field?

CAPTAIN: The box just above the Pass Line on the long side of the table. The numbers are two, three, four, nine, ten, eleven, and twelve. The two and twelve pay two to one, the rest one to one. House has about a 5½ percent edge on the bet.

FRANK: Bad?

CAPTAIN: Bad.

FRANK: That's it. Those are all the bets I need to know about.

CAPTAIN: There are more, mostly bad. You know on the Don't Pass, you can also put odds down on the bet, only you have to lay the long end of the odds. So if the point is ten, you need to put up $40 to win $20. There's a Don't Come bet, which is the opposite of the Come bet.

FRANK: And you said something about a *5-Count*?

CAPTAIN: I think your brain is loaded with enough information. Maybe some other time.

· · · ·

WHEN I returned home from Atlantic City, I bought some books on craps and studied up on the game. I thought it sounded like an interesting game, but I was all aflame with my desire to figure out if blackjack could be beaten. I couldn't see any way to beat craps (it was as if I hadn't even noticed what the Arm had done that first night I saw her!), and the books I read claimed that the game could not be a winner for the player.

So I starred in the play, fell in love with my costar, and eventually married her. And, soon after our trip, I plunged into the world of blackjack, read everything I could get my hands on about the game, sold my share of the theater company, and started my new "career" as a part-time blackjack player. (I've always been a full-time writer.) The rest, as they say, is history—a history you are about to read some significant parts of.

And boy was I wrong. I would discover not only that craps could be beaten, but also that there were—and would be—individuals who made millions from playing this game.

And it all started with the Captain.

3

The Captain II

THE YEAR 1991 was a landmark year for me. I had played craps with the Captain and the Crew for the preceding few years, absorbing everything the Captain did and said, and my book about my adventures with him, *Beat the Craps Out of the Casinos,* came out that fall. It hit a resounding note with the craps-playing and reading public. The book was—and continues to be—the best-selling craps book in the world, due in no small part to the remarkable ideas of the Captain and to the flamboyant nature of his Crew.

I don't believe there would have been a dice control or rhythmic rolling revolution in this country had it not been for the Captain's perceptive appraisal that some shooters can alter the randomness of the game by their throws. He coined the term "rhythmic rolling" and spoke of "controlled shooting" long before anyone else. Until that time, circa 1986, no one wrote or spoke about altering the game of craps through dice control—except for cheaters who utilized what was called a "blanket roll" in private games. The blanket roll, in which you slide the dice down the table, can't work on a modern craps table because right in the middle of the table is a "speed bump," a string stretched either across or under the felt. Any dice that slide across the string will catch and start to tumble, thus randomizing the roll.

The Captain discovered that careful shooters have a better chance of having good rolls, a realization that came from observation, recall, and astute supposition. The Captain is a student of human nature, and he is able to apply his insightful mind to craps in a way few others have ever done. I recall a walk I took with him in Atlantic City in the summer of 1994.

Whenever I get the chance to play craps with the Captain I jump at it. So, when he called me and asked if I'd like to join him for several days in Atlantic City, naturally I said yes. Although craps is always written about as a relatively straightforward game where the math seems to dictate the movement of wins and losses, speaking to the Captain always makes me think a little differently about craps, games of chance, and life.

"How a person plays a game," said the Captain as we walked through Showboat, "tells you a lot about his character."

"What about that guy over there, shooting—what can you tell about him?" I asked.

"He sets the dice carefully and concentrates," said the Captain. "That means he is not afraid to make it look as if he's trying. He's putting himself on the line with each roll because he is taking such care. He wants to win and he'll accept responsibility if he loses."

"Seven-out!" called the stickman.

"He looks disappointed," I said.

"He is," said the Captain, "because he wanted to win. Not just by luck but by control. Someone who feels a responsibility for his own roll, who doesn't try to pretend it's all meaningless, is someone who is worth considering wagering on."

We walked over to the Taj Mahal and watched some of the craps games there.

"What about that guy?" I said. "That shooter." I pointed.

"See how he pretends he doesn't care?" asked the Captain. "He just picks them and flings them as if he's bored that the dice have been given to him. He acts this way because, when he sevens out, he can pretend it doesn't mean anything to him. His body language says: 'See, I don't care if I win or lose. I'm not really trying.' He's a true loser, even if he has a good roll, because he doesn't want it to look as if he's serious. The guy at Showboat is my kind of player because he wants to win and he makes an effort to win."

"Do you think the guy at Showboat is a rhythmic roller?"

"I don't know," said the Captain. "I'd have to see if he sets the dice the same each time over a prolonged period and I'd have to see more than a couple of his rolls to get a sense of what kind of control he has."

"Then it doesn't matter if he concentrates or just flings the dice, if he isn't a rhythmic roller," I said, parroting gambling writers through the centuries when they speak of "independent-trial" games—those in which the result of one trial (a single roll, spin, etc.) has no impact on those that follow.

"No, no, no, it *does* matter. How you play a game is how you deal with life. We all die—that's the inevitable end of the game—and we all lose. It's a negative expectation, and how we roll the bones of life will make no difference in the outcome. Yet some of us tilt at windmills in life. We develop a style, an attitude; we play the game to the best of our ability even though we know we are going to lose. Other people, like that player who pretended he didn't care, they let the windmills smash them. I would rather fight the windmill with some thought that I can affect the current outcome, although not the future outcome, than to just stand there and let the windmill blades smash me to the ground."

We continued walking around the Taj, observing players, observing dealers.

"Have you noticed," said the Captain, "that many dealers talk about doing other things with their lives? Many dealers will say that ten years from now they won't be dealing, won't be working for a casino; they'll be doing this, they'll be doing that. You know, in ten years you'll find them still dealing. The ones who don't discuss their future plans over and over will wind up in other jobs in the casino—they'll become executives, hosts, managers—or you'll meet them in different careers outside the casino world. They'll have returned to school to get a degree. Or you never see them again. But you can assume that in the ten years between one dealer saying what he would do and another dealer actually doing it, a lot happened in both of their lives—but in some essential way one dealer acted upon life and the other dealer was acted upon by life."

We walked over to Resorts, the very first casino in Atlantic City.

"When this place first opened, you had to wait in a line that stretched down the Boardwalk. The casino gave you almost no breaks. You had to pay for parking, they almost never gave comps, the games were stingy—I think they allowed single odds, although maybe it was double, but people would line up in the wee hours of the morning to get in," he said. "You were packed in like sardines."

"There are some casinos in the country where people have to pay to get in and pay for parking," I said.

"I'd plan a trip a week to those, then not go, take the money I would have used to buy my way into the casino, and also the money I would have paid for parking, and when I had enough—I'd buy a plane ticket to Las Vegas. Charging people to get into a casino is like charging someone an entrance fee to shop at a department store."

We walked over to the Sands casino. The Captain remembered the old Sands of Las Vegas, and its famous regulars the Rat Pack.

"The best singer was Dean Martin—he was a regular knock-around guy—but Frank Sinatra always had something that put me off. I saw too many people in Brooklyn like him. With all his talent, with all his power, even when he was a legend, he was always a wannabe and he always had to show you how tough he was. Sammy Davis was the overall greatest talent of the group. But Sinatra was a great actor and I think his acting has been overlooked. In retrospect, I think we're making more out of those times than were really there."

"Who is your favorite singer of all time?" I asked the Captain.

"Nat King Cole," he said.

"Me, too," I said.

"I knew there was a reason I liked you," he laughed.

"I listen to Nat King Cole when I write." (Yes, I'm listening to him right now—he's singing "Let's Fall in Love.")

We left the Sands Hotel Casino, and we left the sands of time, and continued down the Boardwalk, chatting and watching the waves of water and the unending waves of people. And I thought, it's good to be with the Captain; I am lucky to know him.

"How many players are really rhythmic rollers, do you think?"

"I think maybe one in a hundred have the talent to control the dice to some degree. You'll see them pick up the dice, set them the same way, and loft them to essentially the same spot time and again. The dice will hit the back wall and more or less die. The shooter will look as if he's trying to win; he won't be like that guy at the Taj Mahal pretending to not care."

"That really does bother you," I said.

"Life should be lived as if it has meaning, as if it counts; dice should be rolled with seriousness of purpose. I am not saying that you should get yourself into a dither if you seven out; you have to realize that sevening out will happen and accept it as a part of the game. Even Joe DiMaggio [the Captain's favorite baseball player] struck out every once in a while. You never saw him fling the bat or make a scene or bitch and moan. He had class. He was in a league of his own."

"I can't stand people who complain too much at the table," I said. "They think they are the only ones playing. Hey, a guy sevens out, it hurts everyone, not just him."

"Some guys think the world revolves around them and that we're all interested in their personal sagas, so they moan for the benefit of the crowd. That's what babies think, too, that the world revolves around them. Growing up means you know the world doesn't revolve around you and that most of the world doesn't even know you exist and wouldn't care if it did know. The guy who constantly bitches and moans about his luck, or the seven showing, or the other shooters, or this or that, has not come to terms with real life. He also can make even a good table go sour with his constant complaining. I've seen guys bitch when a shooter sevens out after a half-hour roll. Instead of applauding the shooter, the guy will complain about him sevening out. Never blame a shooter for sevening out. Contain yourself. Play within yourself. That's important."

At the Grand (now the Hilton), the Captain stopped. "Let's see what the tables are like."

The Captain is not a believer in trends per se. His idea of

"charting" a table is more sophisticated than most charting schemes. He charts *shooters.*

"I look first to see if there are any Don't players at a table. If you see two of them you can pretty well figure the shooters at the table have been cold. That might indicate that there aren't any rhythmic rollers at that table. So I avoid those tables. Now, if I go to a table and I notice that people seem content and that my spot is open [the Captain can shoot from SR1, SR2—the first two spots on the right side of the stickman—SL1, or SL2 with equal excellence], then that's the table I'll play at."

We walked to the craps tables. Four were open. At this particular point in time I was still rolling using an underhanded lob, which I preferred to do from SR1 or SR2. One table had the SR1 position open, along with the SL1 position, into which the Captain slid. As luck would have it, the dice were immediately passed to me (often they skip a new player if he's the next to shoot). I put a $15 bet on the Pass Line. The Captain did not bet. He was waiting for the 5-Count on me. I established a point of six, put $50 in odds behind it, and then I rolled for about ten minutes. I made two points and several numbers, then sevened out. The Captain gave me a "thumbs up," which meant he made some money on my roll.

It was the Captain's turn to roll. If you ever get to see the Captain roll from any position (many readers of my books have now met him at the tables—the Captain tells me they have all been "courteous" and "curious"), you'll note several things immediately. First are his utter concentration and his equally utter *relaxation.* Concentration and relaxation personify him. Then you'll notice the absolute care he takes with his setting, his grip, and his throw. He sets the dice in a 3-V or a variation of it. He shoots the classic backhand way, three fingers on the front of the dice,

thumb behind. The dice rotate; they land, one slightly
ahead of the other (I call this the "delayed mirror" effect);
then they hit the back wall and die.

He is unflappable. Players can enter the game, leave the
game, argue over calls, throw fits; nothing bothers him. The
casino can bring chip fills in; the stickman can send the dice
to him, then suddenly take the dice back for whatever reason; hosts can come up to him to talk; the pit boss can ask
him all sorts of questions about all sorts of things, and nothing fazes him. He's in a state of total calm. He is centered.

The Captain put $60 on the Pass Line and $60 on the
Don't Pass (his *Supersystem*) and was passed the dice. His
intention would be to take maximum double odds (at that
time the only option offered at most Atlantic City casinos).
If the point was four or ten, he'd put $120 in odds; five or
nine, he'd put $160; six or eight, $200. He'd then continue
with the *Supersystem* until he had three numbers working.
Now, many critics wonder why the Captain, whom I have
proclaimed the greatest craps player of all time, would make
such an obviously high-house-edge bet as the "Doey-Don't."
After all, that twelve coming up once every thirty-six rolls
means you can't win the bet, ever. You either break even or
lose. The house edge is twice as high as it is on the Pass Line.
So why does the Captain do it?

"The Doey-Don't does two things, really. When I am
rolling, I am avoiding, or at least attempting to avoid, the
seven. I am looking to hit only point numbers from the get-
go. The power of the seven on the come-out roll or on the
initial placement of a Come bet is therefore diminished for
me. But I am not completely sure of what numbers I am
going to hit. If my throw is off just a little, I won't hit my
regular numbers [if a shooter tends to hit certain numbers,
we call these *signature numbers*—in the Captain's case four,
five, and six], but I am still avoiding the seven. So the

Doey-Don't gets me on the hot numbers I'm rolling at that time. If I find that I am hitting my [signature] numbers, then I'll place and buy them, but I have to be reasonably sure that I am on before I do that."

Sounds reasonable enough, and I know that the Captain has played this way since before 1980. I also know that the Captain has won a boatload of money from the casinos. To my knowledge no other craps player in Atlantic City history has ever had a letter circulated about his play, *warning the other casinos* about "two men" who were playing "some kind of system" that had won them over a half-million dollars each in six months, plus an enormous amount in comps. The "two men," were the Captain and his first mate, Jimmy P., back in the early 1990s. That was the notorious Tropworld (now Tropicana) memo that was sent out by shortsighted Tropworld executives and subsequently given to the Captain by the president of another Atlantic City casino who had received a copy. I got to read it, too, although I never got to make a copy.

The facts behind that memo are this: For a six-month period the Captain, Jimmy P., and the Arm, the greatest rhythmic roller of all time, hammered Tropworld three or four days a week, and occasionally on weekends. They not only won money at the tables but amassed thousands in complimentary gifts, meals, etc. (in those days Tropworld had a butcher shop where you could actually get meats as part your complimentaries; it also had an electronics store where you could purchase various electronic equipment with your comps). The Captain's Crew was going to Tropworld at that time as well, playing on the weekends, and losing even more money than the Captain, Jimmy P., and the Arm had won, but for some reason the Tropworld brain trust didn't put two and two together and realize that it was in their interests to let the Captain, Jimmy P., and the Arm continue their winning ways since the Crew would leave with the Captain should Tropworld pull the plug on him.

And, stupidly, Tropworld did pull the plug. When the Captain and Jimmy P. checked to see what they had amassed in comps one day, they found—nothing. Their player's card accounts were closed. The host who had dealt with them gave them the cold shoulder and upper management made it known that, while these two could not be "banned," they were not welcome. The upper crust even stated that the Arm and the Captain might not be allowed to shoot the dice anymore, as it was at the casino's discretion who could and could not shoot.

Jimmy P., who had a slow-to-boil but hot-as-hell temper when steamed, was ready to strangle the uppity boss with his bare hands, but the Captain just said, "We won't play here anymore." He then informed the high-rolling Crew, who by all estimates had lost well over a million dollars in that time at that particular casino, that he was moving to another casino. The Captain and the Crew left Tropworld, and not a single one of them has ever returned to play there since. "Dopes," said Jimmy P. when I talked to him about this shortly before his death in 1999. "They were dopes, Frank."

• • • •

THE CAPTAIN set the dice and then carefully lofted them to the back wall; they bounced once, hit, and died. His point was five. I was going right up on the Captain so I put $40 in odds behind my $15 Pass Line. The Captain put up $160 in odds.

And we were off to the races. He rolled for about a half-hour, calm, cool, and collected. Unlike the Arm, who had good rolls almost all the time, the Captain has good rolls only *most* of the time. If you play with him for an extended period, you make money on his rolls. It's that simple. I think in the more than dozen years I've played with him I've had only a handful of losing days when he rolled. He doesn't always have half-hour rolls, but he always seems to make his point or hit a few repeating numbers, enough to come out ahead with at least a small profit. This day, when he sevened out, he picked up his chips and said, "Let's continue our walk."

And we did.

Now, one might be tempted to ask, since we had made money on our rolls, why not hang around and roll again? First, we had walked the length of the Boardwalk from Showboat to the Grand, and we were going to walk back. Second, we had a dinner scheduled for that evening with some of the Crew who would be in town; we certainly would play after that dinner. Third, and most important, dice control or rhythmic rolling is a *physical* skill. Unlike, say, card counting at blackjack, playing long hours of craps so you can roll repeatedly is not usually in your best interests. Fatigue can wipe out your physical advantage.

Blackjack card counters can experience fatigue, too, but it is of a different kind. It takes longer to set in, too, since a card counter is not doing anything physical. Card counters are more like chess masters; the good ones can concentrate for hours and hours, getting in as many hands as possible to realize a slight mathematical advantage. The rhythmic roller is more like a well-trained pitcher who can go for only a certain number of innings before he is spent, before the curve ball doesn't quite break as he wants it to and the fast ball just doesn't rise anymore. If he stays in the game at that point, he is just asking to lose. Whereas the card counter discovers the hidden advantage that is there for any player to exploit at given moments in a deck or shoe, the rhythmic roller *creates* his advantage with his skill. One skill is passive; one is active. The active skill requires more energy, mental as well as physical.

Good rhythmic rollers have to know when they have used up their vital energy and they must take a rest. The Captain is a master at knowing that moment. If the Arm had been at the table, he would have stayed to be in on her roll (betting on others takes very little energy, after all), but, as we were playing with strangers, to the Captain the better part of valor (and value) was to assume they were just random rollers (an excellent assumption), take our profits, and go.

You have to understand that no rhythmic roller can control the dice for a sustained period of time without fatigue setting in. That's why all attempts to "prove" controlled shooting by making a real live shooter roll a million or so rolls are doomed to result in randomness—or, perhaps, the shooter's arm falling off. As in blackjack, where a computer does a simulation of millions of hands to prove that such and such a count with such and such betting can result in an edge, it is simple to figure out the edge a player has in the world of dice control by *programming* that edge in—it's just hard to determine in both blackjack card counting and rhythmic craps rolling whether this or that player actually has *the skill* to duplicate the computer's results.

You could program a computer so that a given shooter has a one-to-nine seven-to-rolls ratio (that is, instead of the seven appearing once every six rolls on average in accordance with random chance, it appears only once every nine rolls), but you wouldn't know that anyone could actually perform such a feat in a casino at an actual craps table. We would still have to essentially take on faith that real live rhythmic rollers in real live casinos have actually won money by their skill (as opposed to sustained good luck), since we only have their words and their ledgers as proof, all strictly anecdotal stuff.

It's proof enough for me! As I write this I know of at least twenty dice controllers who have kept exhaustive records of their practice throws on makeshift or real craps tables (yes, some even have regulation craps tables in their homes!), and even some who have documented their casino sessions roll by roll (by having a partner record the results). They show remarkable control and their ledgers show this. Again, this is strictly anecdotal stuff, but no different from a given card counter explaining that he has been playing the past few years with an edge and showing you his ledgers.

Even in short-term play, the card counter and rhythmic roller share a similar dilemma—how to determine whether it was luck or skill that led to them winning or losing *tonight*. Let's take a look at two scenarios: First, the card counter. The deck or shoe goes positive; the card counter ups his bet into the high count, and—loses. If asked by a skeptic whether he had an edge or not, the counter will say, "Yes, of course. Even though I lost, I had the edge at that moment. It was just the luck of the cards that failed me. But if I played that hand a million times, I'd be ahead." That is a correct statement as far as I am concerned, even though in the real world he would probably never get the opportunity to play that exact same hand at that exact same count a million times. But the totality of his decisions, in high and low counts, and the amount he bets at such times, will all lead him to eventual profit if he has the bankroll to sustain him into the long run.

Now, let's look at the question of the rhythmic roller who gets the dice and rolls for an hour, winning quite a lot of money. The skeptic will say, "You didn't have the edge; it was luck." That would be incorrect. In fact, the rhythmic roller can say, "Given the dice a million times, I will be ahead of the game. Tonight's roll might have an element of luck, but in the long run I will win." This is also a correct statement, if that particular player has been winning consistently and, better still, keeping records of his throws. The totality of his rolling will result in winning long-term play.

The major difference between a card counter and a craps player has to do with the nature of the game. In blackjack, even though every player is playing into the same dealer hands, they are not betting on the other players. In craps, you are (or are supposed to). So the rhythmic roller might get an edge for himself, but he still must contend with the other players at the table for most of his sessions. It's rare that you get to play at an empty table for prolonged periods of time.

One final analogy: I took a girl to a Yankee game in 1961, the year Maris and Mantle were locked in an incredible home-run race (and the year Maris ultimately broke the then-record of sixty home runs by belting sixty-one). I had told her that these two guys were the best home-run hitters in the league. Well, neither hit a homer that day, and Mantle, to my chagrin, struck out two or three times, looking awkward as hell. The girl was highly skeptical of both their talents after that game. In fact, she was more impressed by the guy who *had* hit a home run that day—Bobby Richardson, the least powerful hitter on the team!

Now tell me: In that year of 1961, if you were going to bet on which of any two players would be likely candidates to hit a home run when you went to a Yankee game, would you choose Maris and Mantle or would you choose light-hitting Bobby Richardson? In more modern times, would you bet on a Barry Bonds, Sammy Sosa, or Mark McGwire—or on some rookie, any rookie, picked out of a hat? I'm betting on the big three. Why? Because their past performance is an indication of their future performance. You have no idea what rookie is going to be picked out of the hat—it could be a pitcher. Still, baseball performance is merely anecdotal evidence; it doesn't *prove* that any one of them will ever hit a home run again!

The dice controller who is knocking them dead over a prolonged period of time is like the home-run hitters just mentioned. They have proven in the game that they can win, just as the card counter who has won money has proven in the game that he can also win. The computers and simulations merely give us the percentages and numbers. The casino wars give us the money—or take the money away. The counter and the dice controller have to perform in the casino; the home-run hitter has to hit in the game.

As we walked back to Showboat on that summer day in 1994, I asked the Captain about the controversy surrounding the whole idea of rhythmic rolling. He took a characteristically stoic attitude: "I really don't care if people believe it. Their beliefs have no effect on me. I'm not selling anything; it's not as if I have to convince a thousand people that rhythmic rolling is real before I die. There are people who don't think anyone can count cards, despite hundreds of players over the years writing about their experiences in the casino counting cards. Tell skeptics that there are people who can count cards at blackjack and they'll say no one can do that in a casino. Same thing with rhythmic rolling. You actually don't want too many people to gain the knowledge and not many people actually will. Although card counting has been around a long, long time, how many card counters who are any good are actually out there?"

"Not many," I said from years of experience at the blackjack tables. "Not many at all."

"Casino players in general just don't seem all that interested in learning skillful play," I said.

"And you won't ever find legions of successful rhythmic rollers, either. Anything that takes a little discipline and study, most people just aren't interested in."

"So you think they'd rather just lose their money than have a real fighting chance of beating the casinos?" I asked.

"I think they don't think about it. It's not in their field of vision as a choice. They might read a book, and say, 'Oh, that sounds interesting. Rhythmic rolling, hmmm. . . .' Then they see what it entails—practice, patience, knowledge, work—and they put the book down where it gathers dust until they have a yard sale and sell it."

"Then," I added, "they take the money from the yard sale, go to a casino, and blow it in a slot machine."

"Something like that."

4

The Arm

BACK AT Showboat, I met my wife, Alene—by this point
also known as the beautiful AP. She was sitting down at
the slots, not playing (she never plays the slots); she was
talking with the Arm. They were in animated conversation. In this summer of 1994, the Arm was turning sev-
enty and her arthritis was starting to kick in. She was
taking pills that reduced the pain, but you could see
clearly that her fingers were starting to gnarl just a little.
Although she was still rolling them bones successfully, she
couldn't shoot for as long as she had in the past; her arm
would begin to throb, and her concentration would begin
to fail as the pain set in. I didn't know it then, of course,
but she was just two years away from quitting the game
and ending one of the greatest rhythmic rolling careers of
all time. From 1978 to 1996, the Arm performed miracles
with the dice.

In retrospect, I'm not sure the Arm should be called a
rhythmic roller so much as an *eccentric* roller, someone with

a style all her own. If you happen to run across players who have taken dice-control courses, you will note that most of them have similar setting, gripping, and delivery styles. This style is very similar to the Captain's as well. It seems to be the natural and quintessential "rhythmic roll." It's the one I now use exclusively, and the one I teach to my own students.

But the Arm's mechanical technique was nothing like that. She was a "knuckleballer." That means when she released the dice there was no spin; instead, they floated. And I mean they literally *floated*. They looked more like two cubist feathers than two solid objects making their way through the air. When they landed, there was very little energy to be dissipated; they bounced once (a sickly bounce), touched the back wall, and just rested—almost as if the bottom of the wall pressed down on them so they'd stop. However, unlike the knuckleball pitchers in baseball, whose ball goes hither and yon on the wind currents, the Arm's knuckleball seemed to glide unerringly as if riding not wind currents, but a magic carpet.

She stood stick left. She would set the dice with parallel 2-spots on top and (if memory serves me right) doubles all around: two 2s on top, two 4s on the sides, two 1s and two 6s on front and/or back, and two 5s on the bottom. She gripped them over the top, so that if you were looking for the dice you could just barely see them. Her thumb was parallel with the table, not at the ninety-degree angle most rhythmic rollers use. She would make a circle with her hand and then loft the dice gently in one motion, with just enough energy to give them an arc. The dice would seem to die in midair at the top of the arc and then come down lazily. As I said, she had a "sick bounce," as if the dice just didn't have any energy left when they skidded slightly and came to rest touching the back wall.

Mentally, she was as unflappable as the Captain. It was as

if shooting dice were a leisurely walk in the park. She looked at the table and rarely even noticed when members of the Captain's high-rolling crew placed substantial bets for her. In my audiotape *Sharpshooter Craps*, I speak about the "rolling zone," a place you stick your "logical conscious-ness" so your "autonomic self" can take over; this is the place where your mind and body function smoothly together with nary a seam. Well, that's where the Arm lived—in the rolling zone! If she didn't have a half-hour to hour-long roll, she had a roll where she'd hit the same number over and over and over. I recount in *Beat the Craps Out of the Casi-nos* the time that she hit nine fours in fifteen rolls. Remark-able! But this wasn't a once-in-a-lifetime occurrence; this was like clockwork. The only reason I recount that particu-lar story in the book is that it took a weekend in which I was about to go home a loser and made it a winner for me.

This day she and AP were deep into a discussion—of what I have no idea, just the stuff women talk about in-tently that men can't fathom for the life of us. When the Captain and I approached, the Arm informed him that Jimmy P. and some of the other Crew had just checked into the hotel and were at the tables waiting for him. The Cap-tain and I headed for the tables; the Arm and AP stayed be-hind to finish their conversation.

Approaching the tables I saw a couple of Crew members, and Jimmy P., who had a rack of green, black, and purple chips in front of him. The curious thing about the Crew was that, with the exception of Jimmy P., none of them played the *5-Count* and only a couple of them took any care with their rolls. It was as if they had never noticed what the Cap-tain was doing. He was their leader; he had great rolls for them; but they didn't seem the least interested in emulating his play. I used to wonder about that. Now, I'm pretty sure I understand.

I believe they didn't actually *see* what the Captain was doing. They were into their own individual games versus the casino. When the Captain rolled then, yes, they watched, just as they watched anyone roll. They especially watched when the Arm rolled. But it was a watching without seeing, so during most of the game they just played like the happy-go-lucky guys they were. To them, playing craps was just a fun way to spend some leisure time. They had the money to sustain them; they could afford the eventual long-term losses that essentially random play would extract.

In that they were not unlike the overwhelming majority of players you'll run into at the tables. I've been at tables with some of the best rhythmic rollers in the world; I've been in games where these guys have shot the layouts off the felt and the other players *never noticed* how these great shooters rolled. It was as if the average craps player actually couldn't see that the good shooters had a distinct way about them, a form that indicated they were not your average shooters. Now, those of you who coach baseball can tell a good swing in a hitter, even if he strikes out. If you coach basketball, you can see the soft touch in a player that indicates a good eye and a deadly shot, even if he misses the particular shot he's attempting. You know what to look for and, when it's there, you *see* it. But most craps players can't see it because, I guess, they aren't looking for it.

The Captain, very early on, posed himself the question: Which shooters are having the best rolls? He answered it by observing the shooters as he played and realizing that rhythmic rollers tended to have the best rolls (not always, but more often). Now, if other players don't notice good shooters who consistently have good rolls, how can you expect them to notice something as subtle as a player utilizing the 5-Count? In fact, when *Beat the Craps Out of the Casinos* was published, one member of the Crew actually asked me,

"Hey, Frank, what is this *5-Count* stuff?" He wasn't alone. Quite a few of the Crew had no idea that the Captain was even ahead. Not being the sort to brag, the Captain never told any of the Crew of his wins. Indeed, when the Captain, the Arm, and Jimmy P. were working wonders at Tropworld, not a single member of the Crew knew about it. All they knew was that the Captain and Jimmy P. had had some kind of dispute with the Tropworld bosses and they were all going to another casino.

However, the Crew was acutely aware of the Arm's shooting ability (they thought of her as tremendously lucky as a shooter) and of the Captain's rolling prowess as well, but not one of them (again, with the exception of Jimmy P.) ever bothered to develop a rhythmic roll of his own. Some of them would set the dice, and then wing them down the felt where they careened and bounced all over the table. Some had nice soft rolls, but never set the dice. Only Jimmy P. started to set the dice and then loft them gently in a consistent manner. Only Jimmy P. actually had that burning desire to beat the house. He also used the *5-Count*. He told me: "Frank, for years I was a big loser. The key was the *5-Count;* that started me winning. I saw the Captain winning and I'm thinking to myself, 'We're playing at the same tables; why is he winning and I'm losing?' I can't believe I was such a big dope all those years."

· · · ·

AT THE TABLE, the Captain and I bought in. For about forty minutes, it was a gradual downward movement. Most shooters sevened out before the 5-Count, but enough sevened out just after the 5-Count that the Captain and I were down so far for the session. The Captain had hit two points and a couple of numbers before he sevened out, so I made a little on him (I went right up on him and didn't use the

5-*Count*), and on my own roll I made my point, hit the six and eight, then sevened out. I made a few bucks there. Otherwise, it wasn't going our way.

Then the Arm appeared. Jimmy P. yelled: "Come on, Arm, you gotta roll. We're gettin' killed." The Captain stepped back and placed a large Pass Line bet (if memory serves me right, it was $120); then Jimmy P. put down a purple, and the two other Crew members had black chips down. "*She's* shooting," Jimmy P. emphasized to the table. Now Jimmy P. was a jolly kind of guy, but when he said, "*She's* shooting," it was kind of like Wyatt Earp saying, "No guns in Tombstone." The cowboys invariably took off their guns for good old Wyatt—and thus the three people in line to shoot the dice before the Arm, including me, passed the dice.

And the Arm rolled—for forty-five minutes. We made our money back and then some. At the forty-five-minute mark I could sense something was troubling the Arm—it was her arthritis. She looked over at the Captain, who was somewhat behind her and betting for her as well as himself, and she said, "I'm not feeling right."

The Captain took the odds off his Pass Line bets and called his other bets "off." I did the same. The Arm rolled a couple of numbers, I don't remember which, and then she sevened out. The table cheered. The Arm shook her head sadly; this was not like her. She didn't seem the least bit happy, and for the first time it hit me that she was actually getting old, that it was conceivable the great rolls could end. I remember when I first realized that Muhammad Ali was just a human being and not a god. He had fought such brilliant fights, staged such great comebacks in a glorious career filled with awesome, worthy, and inspiring opponents. Then, two years after beating Leon Spinks and retiring with the championship, he made another comeback attempt, against

Larry Holmes. Ali looked spent; he looked old; he looked *mortal*.

That was the Arm at that moment. She looked mortal. She took her chips, mostly bets the Captain, the Crew, and I were making for her, and she slowly walked away from the table. The Captain was rubbing his chin and watching her slowly walk toward the cage, a spent fighter. Whether he knew that the era of the Arm was ending, I can't really say. But his look said that he was watching something sad.

As I write this, the Arm is in craps retirement. She stopped playing craps at the end of 1995, when it became evident to her that she didn't have the control anymore. Now almost eighty years old, she still goes to Atlantic City, sometimes meets up with the Captain (who is on the flip side of eighty), but her rolling days are over. She enjoys the shows, plays the slots for a few bucks, but mostly takes in the sights. Her gait is slow, she's actually shrunk a few inches, and her hands are gnarled.

But in my mind's eye, as fresh as if it happened today, I can still see the crowds part when the Arm came to a table. I can see her stride confidently to stick left; take her position; set those dice; place her hand over them; make that circle; loft them in the air to ride the magic carpet and come to rest against the back wall, to a chorus of cheers and the stickman's shouts of "Winner! Winner! Winner! Pay the Line, take the Don'ts! Same good shooter coming out. Place your bets!"

I remember that New Year's Eve at the Claridge when she was brought down from her room still in the throes of sleep to roll the dice till dawn, over and over again ("Winner! Winner! Winner!), a female Moses about to lead her people across the sea of red ink into the black. And she did, time and again. I can still feel the excitement we all had when we knew that the Arm was about to roll. It was the same excitement I used to feel when Mickey Mantle or

Willie Mays came to the plate; the same I felt when Muhammad Ali and Joe Frazier entered the ring. I was about to see the very best do her thing.

And, now, when I play in the casinos where she had some of her epic rolls and memorable evenings, I still wish—in fact I *long*—for the possibility that time might reverse itself and that I'll see her striding through the casino on the Captain's arm, smiling, ready to make the world explode with excitement. If my feelings could be made flesh, there would be no mortality, and there would never be a seven-out, for anyone, ever.

Indeed, the Arm was the very best shooter I ever saw, and I saw her enough times to know that I won't ever see her like again.

5

A "Profit" Without Honor

THE MORE I played craps, the more I became convinced that rhythmic rolling was a fact and not a superstition. Of course, in the early years of my gambling career, no one was giving courses in dice control, and as far as I knew only the Captain, Jimmy P., the Arm, and I were consciously attempting to control the dice by physical means. I personally knew of no one who was studying the game to take it to the next level, the level it's at now. And I myself still devoted more time to blackjack than to perfecting my craps game.

My book *Beat the Craps Out of the Casinos* started me down the gambling-writing road at one hundred miles per hour. In 1993, I made a long-term commitment to my publisher, Bonus Books, to come out with gambling books on all the individual games, at a rate of approximately one per year. That would mean extensive research; it would also mean I needed to play the games to get a feel for them. And that meant (hooray!) many trips to casino venues. By 1994 I had several books under my belt (which was getting substantially bigger with all the comped food and drink I was consuming!).

As my writing career accelerated I began to spend more and more time in Las Vegas, where I mostly played blackjack, and less and less time in Atlantic City, where craps had been my king. I would say that, until 1998, 90 percent of my *serious* playing time (and money!) was devoted to blackjack. In fact, since my two sons went to private high school and then on to college in those years (they are three years apart), my summers were spent in Vegas on what we called "tuition runs." My wife, the beautiful AP, and I would attempt to win the upcoming tuition by beating the house at blackjack. Talk about pressure!

But, as many expert blackjack players will attest, Las Vegas blackjack is not the golden game it once was for serious players. From the early 1990s (when the Maxim Casino Hotel dealt its legendary single-deck game) to the writing of this book in the spring of 2003, the games have become increasingly more difficult to beat with card counting, and the casinos have become, strangely, ever more paranoid of players who bet black ($100) or purple ($500) chips; some casinos even sweat green-chip ($25) action! Of course, counting cards is not the only way to get an edge at blackjack; there are other methods, some of which I perfected during these years as well. But these methods are mostly "serendipitous"—that is, they occur now and again and the astute player must take advantage of them while they last, if he knows what to look for and sees it when it's happening. (For more information on these techniques, see my book *Best Blackjack* and also John May's excellent *Get the Edge at Blackjack*.)

Now, despite the fact that very few blackjack players are actually card counters, the casinos "back off" first (that is, tell you that you can't play blackjack there) and ask questions later, if at all. AP and I had some nasty incidents during the 1990s in Las Vegas. In one downtown Vegas casino, a security guard stuck a gun in my back while the dealer pitched the cards into my face. My crime? I was ahead about $500 while spreading my bets from $25 to $125—this gradually and not in one jump, mind you. Needless to say, I picked up my chips and AP and I left that casino posthaste.

Then there was the time a pit boss from Circus Circus not only followed AP and me to the cage to make sure we cashed out, but then followed us out the door and down the Strip, attempting to intimidate us by scowling. Finally, disgusted, I turned to him and bellowed, "All right, what are you going to do, huh?" He turned and headed back to the casino. Because of incidents like these, as the 1990s were coming to a close I found that I was playing less and less blackjack—and more and more craps for more serious money than previously.

By 2000 I would say that my craps play and blackjack play were equally split. But, as I looked at my ledgers during this period, I noticed that, while blackjack was still profitable, craps was better. And that was no doubt due to the fact that I finally perfected my "new" throw. As I mentioned previously, I used to set the dice and then gently lob them underhand to the back wall. They would land gently and stop without too much bouncing around. But I realized that I still hadn't perfected an optimum roll. Every so often I would mimic the Captain's throw, an overhand, backspin method, that seemed to keep the dice from splitting and going off in different directions (dice control enthusiasts now call this "staying on axis"). By 2000 this had become my standard throw. Indeed, as soon as I worked out the kinks in my delivery, I noticed a distinct improvement in my results; whereas even in the past I had won money on my own rolls, I was now winning *more* money and having more good rolls. In fact, I started to have such confidence in my shooting ability that I began to bet "serious" money at craps—the same level of "serious" money that I had previously been betting at blackjack.

This did not sit too well with some of my dyed-in-the-wool blackjack acquaintances who, seeing my success at craps, badgered me continually, claiming it was all due to "luck." Some of my blackjack buddies went so far as to say that I had become "deluded by craps," and that the Captain was more a Svengali than a bona fide gambling genius. But these same critics never once came to a craps table with me to watch!

While it hurts to be called a fool or worse, the derision of some critics (professional writers as well as acquaintances) certainly didn't change the fact that craps was a winner for me, something I attributed to what I called my five-step method. I wrote about the method in my book *Forever Craps;* it can be summarized as follows:

1. Play the *5-Count* religiously.
2. Develop your own controlled throw.
3. Only bet those "Golden Shooters" who make it past the 5-Count and who are taking care with their rolls. Bet on no one else.
4. Make only low-house-edge bets or signature-number bets.
5. Get more comps for less action.

I was becoming disenchanted by my "semiprofessional" blackjack buddies. Some of them wouldn't tip dealers because it hurt their "edge." Others would eat one meal a day at the buffet, stuff themselves to bursting and then fill their pockets with food pilfered in baggies so they wouldn't have to spend money until the next day's orgy at the buffet. Still others refused to pay for hotel stays, preferring to freeload off friends who lived in Vegas. I found that, as I became increasingly more successful in my writing and craps-playing career, I became increasingly more uncomfortable with my blackjack acquaintances, especially those who had become obsessed with "beating Vegas" by not giving tips, buying meals, or staying in hotels.

But two events in particular really got to me, and helped to change the course of my Las Vegas gambling life.

The first took place at a book signing/talk I gave at a Barnes and Noble in Las Vegas. Some forty people showed up to hear me speak, including one of my card-counting blackjack acquaintances. In the middle of my talk, this fellow raised his hand to tell me that I had made a mistake in my play that afternoon! It rattled me to be standing there and to have someone who was supposedly a friend say something like that in front of an audience. I recovered my composure and explained that I hadn't made a mistake in the incident he was referring to—that, in fact, he had reversed his count by mistake and was playing as if he had a low count instead of a high count. The move I had made was based on a high count and was the right move. His response, after embarrassing the hell out of me, was "Oh."

The next event took place on my fiftieth birthday with a blackjack "buddy" notorious for his cheapness. Example: At gourmet restaurants he'd order rice, plain *white* rice, and then sample everyone's dinner until he was stuffed. When the time came to pay the bill, he'd whisper to me, "You know, I shouldn't have to pay more than a few dollars; I only had rice." Well, this fellow invited me out to celebrate my birthday. I agreed to go with him to a fancy gourmet restaurant, knowing full well he wasn't going to treat me.

But he did something really nice during the meal. He told the waiters to bring over a cake with candles on it and he and the waiters sang a hearty "Happy Birthday" to me. I thanked him and thought to myself that, cheap as he was, his getting me that cake was a really nice gesture. When the waiter brought us our separate bills, I noticed that my "friend" had charged the cake to *my* bill!

After that I slowly weaned myself from these acquaintances and played blackjack alone. And I played ever more sessions of craps.

In fact, as I write this, I no longer consider myself a blackjack player who plays craps; I now consider myself a craps player who, if the game conditions are right, will play blackjack. Craps has now become my game of choice. In fact, when I play blackjack and hand in a player's card, it means I am not counting cards, just playing basic strategy; if I'm going to hit a casino in blackjack, I play anonymously, for no more than forty-five minutes in any one casino during any one shift. And I play *alone*. Not so with craps. Craps is a game where you can have your "cake," your companions, and your comps, too.

And what of my wife, the beautiful AP? Has she made the journey from advantage blackjack player to rhythmic rolling craps player as I have? No, she hasn't, poor soul, because AP is the worst craps player on earth. In fact, she is an *arhythmic* roller! I say this with due respect and great love; still, not only is she a horrendous shooter but she's also quite dangerous when she gets the dice in her hands.

First, let me give you some background. My wife is an accomplished woman in every way. I say this not just because she is my wife but because the truth is the truth. She's also one of the few women I've met who hated *Seinfeld* and isn't afraid to say so. Such courage! She also hates network television. Her big show is the BBC news on PBS each night or stuff on the History Channel. She is an avid reader, and she loves to write articles on the contemporary scene, and on the religious and philosophical issues of today and of "all our yesterdays," as Shakespeare had Macbeth so aptly put it.

The beautiful AP is sharp in her critiques and has a probing mind. Of course, writing about culture, religion, and philosophy is lightweight stuff, let's be honest here. People have been writing about *those* issues for centuries and what's come of it? Nothing. The past has merely "lighted fools the way to dusty death." (Again, Shakespeare's *Macbeth*!) Ever since someone put pen to paper—or, rather, chisel to rock—we've been fascinated by the nature of life and the specter of death. But we still have no idea about the *meaning* of life and we certainly aren't any closer to solving the puzzle of death. Perhaps because these mysteries can't be solved, but merely speculated upon, thousands of religions have sprung up, riding a continuum of the sublime to the scary, all with adherents, some ready to kill you if you don't agree with their particular form of speculation.

That's why, when the beautiful AP gets really serious, she likes to delve into heavyweight matters—like casino gambling. She writes columns for several magazines and newspapers on casino games and, in one such column, she made a startling confession about something to which gaming writers should never admit—not being able to actually "do" what we write about.

I expected the wire services to pick up on this, as it was a landmark moment in gambling-writing history. But not a peep was heard. The papers were too busy covering frivolities like global warming, the war on terror, and suchlike. This shouldn't be surprising, I guess, since the mainstream press, by and large, ignores the intricacies and delights of casino gambling—or, worse, looks upon it as just several inches short of a damnable sin.

So her confession has only been seen by relatively few eyes. I think you should see it too. It might give hope to those of you struggling with the same horrible problem—crapophobia. It might also let you know that you are not alone; if the beautiful AP isn't perfect, the rest of us don't even have to pretend to be! Which is a real relief to me, I can tell you.

Here's her confession, which appeared in Larry Edell's *Crapshooter* newsletter; it's every bit as compelling as St. Augustine's—and one one-hundredth the length!

> I have a confession to make. It is a simple one, really, and not something I should really be all that ashamed of but—I am a lousy crapshooter. Literally. When I roll the dice, if roll is the right word. . . . Actually, let me change that sentence's wording to this wording: When the dice leave my hand, I really have no idea where they will wind up.
>
> I have hit more stickmen, boxmen and dealers in their eyes, ears, heads and shoulders than any dice player in history—or, as my husband says: "AP, I have never seen anyone as dangerous at a craps table as you are." I once landed a die in a person's mouth at Showboat in Atlantic City! She was busy talking and the die just went sailing right in. Thankfully, she didn't choke.
>
> I hit one stickwoman in the eye at Trump Marina in Atlantic City and I landed a die inside the blouse and bra of another female dealer at one of the Station casinos in Las Vegas. I won't say which because she gave me such a dirty look that I wished it had been her eye I had hit! I once hit BOTH the stickman and the boxman at the same time. According to Frank, that is a physical impossibility, launching two dice from the same hand and hitting two people at opposite sides of the table. Well, I did it!

Now, you might find this confession somewhat puzzling as I have written about dice control and my husband Frank has based his whole craps philosophy on the premise that some shooters, by their careful sets and deliveries, are physically changing the nature of the game. He has advocated the Captain's 5-Count as a means of eliminating bad shooters and only risking money on the potentially good shooters. He has explored the idea of rhythmic rolling. He has counseled me. Yet, here I am, having played craps for many years, having attempted to control the dice; here I am, completely out of control. I once had one die go over the boxman's head while the other die hit the floorman—at the other table! People can't do that if they try—and I wasn't trying! I only wanted to land the dice against the back wall.

I am not exactly sure why I am so horrendous. I think it is because I tend to use too much shoulder in my delivery. Or, I used to use too much shoulder. For past few years I have consistently passed up my turn to roll because what's the point? If I were to bet on myself I would not only lose money, I would probably lose the lawsuit brought by the person I injured with one of my throws. Or, worse, I might get prosecuted for a crime.

I can hear the lawyers for the prosecution now: "Your honor, this woman knew beforehand that she was a danger to all around her when she took those dice in her hands. She deliberately and with intent sent them flying into the skull of my client here who has been permanently injured. She should be found guilty of attempted murder with a deadly weapon—dice!"

So I confess. Although I, too, am a firm believer in "rhythmic rolling," I also am a firm believer that I can't and never will be able to do it. I am like a dentist that is missing some teeth, or a doctor who doesn't exercise or eat right.

AP's greatest fear, I think, is the fact that, when she is shooting the dice, other people's money is at risk. It is one thing to gamble with your own money; it is quite another to have the money of others riding on your throws. When I practice at home, AP gives me a wide berth; she does this so I won't corral her into taking practice throws. Do I think AP has a physical handicap and therefore is not capable of ever having a controlled throw? No, I don't. I just think she has gotten it into her head that she stinks and therefore she does stink. Cogito ergo sum. I think therefore I am. For AP, while she'll play craps, she just won't shoot.

6

Enter Sharpshooter and Others

IN 1996, I started to correspond with a young man who called himself Sharpshooter. He was working on a course that would teach controlled shooting to craps players, and he explained his methods and procedures to me. He also showed me the proof of his ability to change a negative game into a positive game. He had videotaped his set, grip, and rolls, and recorded the results. When he had over ten thousand rolls under his belt, he was ready to state emphatically that his seven-to-rolls ratio was somewhere around one to eight or thereabouts—on average, he only hits the seven about once every eight rolls. (Remember that random chance produces a seven once every *six* rolls.)

AP and I met Sharpshooter for lunch at Tropicana in Las Vegas later in 1996. He was part of a dice-control team that had just hammered the downtown casinos until some crews, despite generous tips from the players, started to get frisky. Sharpshooter said, "I knew it was time to leave the Golden

Nugget when the stickman swatted my dice in midair!" Effusive and enthusiastic, Sharpshooter was delighted to meet AP and me, because he felt that I "had an open mind about nontraditional methods of play." That I do. Sharpshooter said that my writing about the Captain had stimulated his interest in controlled shooting and his desire to find out if one really could get the edge at craps. He then proceeded to discuss his research and his hands-on play. Needless to say, I was impressed by his intelligence and knowledge. And I was really impressed by his results!

When we parted, I asked him to write for my (now-defunct) magazine *Chance and Circumstance*. I felt that he would have a lot to contribute in the area of "nontraditional" advantage-play techniques. I was also interested in the seminars he said that he was starting to teach. He called them PARR. It wasn't until a couple of years later that I discovered PARR stood for *Patterson Advanced Rhythm Roll*.

The "Patterson" of the acronym was Jerry Patterson, a best-selling author *(Casino Gambling* and *Blackjack's Winning Formula)* and a very controversial figure in the blackjack world. He had marketed a system called TARGET, which was supposed to alert you to tables that were player-friendly due to the nonrandom nature of the casino shuffle. Patterson's claim was that this nonrandom shuffle caused extended streaks of player-biased or dealer-biased tables. He listed certain things to look for in order to decide which tables to play at and which to avoid. TARGET was intended for shoe games (multiple-deck games in which cards are dealt face-up from a box or "shoe"), where, Patterson claimed, traditional card-counting techniques just weren't all that useful.

Patterson was one of the first book-writing card counters and was a much respected figure in the early blackjack world, but his shift of emphasis away from card counting to

TARGET caused an uproar among serious blackjack players and other blackjack authorities. Traditional blackjack authorities, while giving credence to the idea of "shuffle tracking" clumps of high cards, dismissed Patterson's claims that the nonrandom shuffle caused "predictable patterns" that could be exploited by smart players. Tracking a shuffle was one thing, they claimed; tracking *patterns* of low and high cards, chip stacks, cigarettes in ashtrays, and the like, as Patterson suggested, was quite another.

None of these battles being waged in the blackjack press had any effect on me. I was a traditional card counter, playing mostly single- and double-deck games. It seemed to me that Patterson's ideas couldn't hurt you and that the uproar in the blackjack world was much ado about nothing. (It wasn't until I started to read Internet posts sent to me by friends that I realized "uproars" are de rigueur, and ubiquitous, in the online blackjack and craps forums, and in the online gambling world in general.)

When I reviewed the TARGET claims for my book *Best Blackjack,* I figured card counters wouldn't abandon card counting, which gave them a verified mathematical edge (assuming they can perform in the casino) to pursue TARGET—and, on the flipside, following TARGET wouldn't increase the house edge for a basic-strategy player. Certainly, then, TARGET was not something over which it was worth hurling invectives. To me TARGET fell into the "all things being equal, if it doesn't hurt, and you want to do it, so what?" category of casino-gambling advice. However, there were tremendously strident anti-Patterson voices who lambasted him at every opportunity, especially when the Internet became such a staple in many gamblers' lives. Chat rooms, newsgroups, and message boards would, now and again, resound with blasts leveled at Patterson, often by former "friends" who were quick with verbal ripostes on

Patterson's ideas and his motivation for selling those ideas. Patterson was called a huckster, a fraud, a snake-oil salesman, a flimflam man, and a charlatan. He was also called much worse. He also seemed to be tremendously successful in marketing his various systems, something not lost on his loudest critics.

While I felt no animus toward the man (I met him once in 1995 at a seminar and we said hello), I also had no burning desire to get to know him. Nor had I a burning desire to get to know any of my fellow gaming authors, except through their writings. While I delighted in being a (small) part of the adventures of the Captain and his Crew, I didn't generally seek out groups to join. I preferred to make friends catch-as-catch-can—or based on, as my beautiful AP calls it, person-to-person chemistry.

And I was.

As I jettisoned those few blackjack acquaintances whose personalities were displeasing, I was also making the acquaintance of John Robison, Bill Burton, and Walter Thomason, three men who have now become good friends of mine. John is the world's foremost authority on slot machines and the author of the book *The Slot Expert's Guide to Playing Slots.* He is also my partner in *www.scoblete.com,* and he manages that Web site and the Golden Touch Web site, *www.goldentouchcraps.com.* Bill Burton is the casino guide for About.com and also the author of the excellent book *Get the Edge at Low-Limit Texas Hold'em.* Walter Thomason is the maverick of gambling writers, perhaps almost as lambasted and lacerated as Jerry Patterson, and the author of several books including the highly controversial *Twenty-first Century Blackjack.* AP and I have shared plenty of adventures with these men, although only Bill Burton is a controlled shooter at craps.

John rarely plays the game (I'm working on him, though) and Walter is, well, Walter is Walter.

Interestingly enough, I met all three at *Casino Player* Gaming Festivals where I was a featured speaker. I met John and Bill (and his lovely wife Sandy) at the Taj Mahal in Atlantic City, before either was involved in the writing/publishing end of gambling, but when both were avid, savvy players. I met Walter in Las Vegas at the Tropicana festival. The circumstances of my first meeting with Walter reinforced my growing disenchantment with certain attitudes on the part of gamblers and some gambling authors. Walter was looking to do a book titled *The Experts' Guide to Casino Games*, which was subsequently published by the Carol Publishing Group. He asked me if I'd like to contribute some chapters. I was more than happy to do so, and I was honored to be considered. At that first meeting, at the booth where AP and I were selling my books and tapes, Walter was not happy.

"I asked *Jack Smith* [a famous gaming author whose pseudonym is *not* the pseudonym I just gave him] if he'd like to contribute to the book and he looked at me as if I were a Martian. He ignored me with a sigh of disdain like, what does *this* idiot want? I asked him again and he looked down his beak at me and said, 'And *who* are *you?*'"

I laughed when Walter told me this story because I remembered how this very same snooty gaming author had just the month before gotten drunk at a party that AP and I attended and literally—and I mean *literally*—put a lampshade on his head (I'd only seen *that* in a movie before he did it) and danced around saying that his name was some other author's name: "I'm not Jack Smith, I'm Gary Jones! Ha! Ha! Ha!" The other author, let's stick with "Gary Jones," not to be outdone in the wit department, and also drunk, put a shoebox on *his* head (I guess he took it out of the host's closet) and kept saying that he was actually Buster Brown! Both these potted plants were laughing uproariously at their own humor as they stumbled around the room being witty, although I noticed that no one else found them the least entertaining. Everyone else at the party steered clear of them, which was a good thing because shoebox-on-head finally passed out in mid-dance with lampshade-on-head and both of them went headlong into the buffet table, knocking over the food and utensils.

"Well," I said to Walter, "I'm sure you'll have plenty of people who will want to contribute to the book. Jack Smith isn't the only fish in the sea."

And that's how my friendship with Walter Thomason began. I contributed chapters to his book, corresponded with him frequently, and every so often headed to Atlantic City or Las Vegas to play with him.

Walter is an *enthusiastic* gambler. He'll play craps when I go to the craps tables, but his main game is blackjack. Now, in all other casino games Walter takes the traditionalist approach. He follows the math and the computer simulations and plays the best possible strategies—or, at least, *knows* the best possible strategies. (However, in craps he's enamored of the Hardway 6 and 8—which he claims I got him "hooked on" because "you hit a lot of hard sixes when you roll.")

But, at blackjack, he is a true believer in a system of progressive betting that he calls the Four-Step Progression. His thesis is that shoe games are not randomly shuffled (sound familiar?), and that an almost equal number of player- and dealer-winning streaks will occur. He believes that you should bet into all player wins and back off all player losses. Goes like this: your first bet is $50; if you win, your second bet is $75; win that, make it $100 for the third bet; win that, your fourth bet gets capped at $125. That his

1-2-3-4 method. If you lose at $125 or at any step in the progression, you go back down to $50. (It's a two-unit, three-unit, four-unit, five-unit progression.) He also has criteria for getting out of a game that isn't going your way.

In his book *Twenty-First Century Blackjack*, Walter discusses his research of manually dealt hands. While he never makes the claim that his progressive system is better than card counting at shoe games, he does write that his system is better than flat betting at such games. His research proves his point. The only problem comes when others analyze his research, using computer simulations and recombinatorial math. Then Walter's system does not seem to work better than flat betting. There's very little difference between the two.

Still, Walter maintains that he is correct and that simulations are not reflective of the real world of casino shuffles. I do know this: Walter really believes in his system, and in his heart of hearts he not only thinks it is superior to flat betting at shoe games but also that it actually gives the player an edge equal to or greater than card counting. The reason for his belief is simple: he has been on a phenomenal winning streak since the mid-1990s. He's had losses here and there, but his wins are overwhelming in nature. Some have been absolutely spectacular.

Actually, Walter himself is absolutely spectacular. When you meet him you are struck right off by how skinny he is. Although he has gained some thirty pounds in the last two years, that just makes him this side of cadaverous. The reason he has gained so much weight has to do with his heart medications. You see Walter drinks, smokes, and eats just about everything that doesn't try to drink, smoke, or eat him first. I am fascinated by his casino visits, during which I watch him drink a steady diet of beer and smoke a steady stream of cigarettes for his fourteen-hour stints at the table. (That's right; Walter is not only a high roller, he's also a *long* roller.) At night, before dinner, he switches to gin tonics and for dessert kahlua and cream. He also drinks kahlua and cream for breakfast. Oh, and orange juice— with vodka.

All this indulgence must have had something to do with why his heart stopped beating one April day in 2000 (I say "his heart stopped beating" because that is a spectacular image considering what happens next, but in truth his heart didn't stop beating . . . *completely*), the day he was to leave for Vegas to meet me for a few days of fun. He was rushed to the emergency room, where his heart was started again. "I'm fine," he told the doctors, "and, besides, my plane is leaving for Vegas in a couple of hours." Everyone tried to persuade him to rethink his plans. But Walter was adamant; he was going to Vegas. He was given some pills and told by the doctors not to drink "too much." Walter took this to mean he could only have one beer every thirty minutes, a regimen he stuck to the way those health fiends who you see in health food stores stick to their vitamin, mineral, and herb regimens.

On the third and final day of Walter's trip to Vegas that April, we were playing in the high-roller room at Treasure Island. Walter plays right up until the moment he has to leave, so he had about two hours before he had to hightail it to the airport that night. I was at the two-deck game, getting my head handed to me; Walter was playing the shoe game. Treasure Island's shoe game had remarkable rules at the time (maybe it still does as you read this), including surrender, which significantly affects the odds in the player's favor. Walter was playing two hands of $50 and using his progression on each. In between sipping his twice-hourly beer and inhaling his once-a-minute smoke, in a two-hour time period that night, he won $20,000. Not only did I witness this incredible run, but so did gaming author Henry Tamburin, his wife Linda, Bill Burton, and John Robison—and just about every suit in the Treasure Island hierarchy. Walter was delighted with all the attention, for as he played he lectured any and all listeners on his Four-Step progressive method (he probably garnered a couple of book sales in the bargain, too). The dealers, after a while, were making sure he followed his formula to the letter. With green-chip tips coming on almost every other hand, the dealers wanted to make sure that Walter played his "A" game. He left when he had to. The Treasure Island limo pulled up, Walter cashed in his monstrous pile of chips, and off he headed home—ostensibly to enter Internet chat rooms to be told his system doesn't work!

Of course, with that kind of experience, who is going to convince him that his system is flawed and that his thinking is skewed? Internet chatters who play for red chips and scrounge out an average bet an hour counting cards? Gaming authors who don't play the game but just pontificate on their computer simulations? With a haystack of money staring him in the face, Walter doesn't see any value in the needle of criticism pointed his way, and any sharp truth that we orthodox blackjack players hold dear is blunted by the hard edge of the dollar sign. So Walter is steadfast in his system, a rock in his stand against just about every other blackjack authority (including me). He *knows* his system works and, unless he takes a sustained beating for the next decade, it will take the Second Coming to convince him otherwise.

I'm fine with that. I have no interest in ever seeing Walter lose or in seeing him turn to me one day and say, "Frank, you were right and I was wrong." I hope he keeps winning and goes to his grave (a hundred years from now) where they shower $100 bills instead of roses on his coffin. I happen to like the fact that Walter is, as John Robison puts it, "on the outermost edge of the bell curve." That's the rare terrain of unicorns, Megabucks winners, and those who win in the long run with systems that just can't work.

$\begin{array}{ccccc} \bullet & \bullet & \bullet & \bullet \end{array}$

7

$\begin{array}{ccccc} \bullet & \bullet & \bullet & \bullet \end{array}$

Dominator

THE BEAUTIFUL AP and I have several private traditions. We like to spend New Year's Eve at home watching the movie classic *It's a Wonderful Life* and reflecting on our lives in light of the movie's message. Despite the fact that we are invited to all sorts of New Year's casino parties in Vegas and Atlantic City, I just don't want to give up this most private, intimate, and important reflective experience with the woman who is most dear to me.

But we like to spend Easter in Las Vegas.

For some reason, April is our favorite time to visit. This could have something to do with the fact that my greatest roll of the 1990s occurred during that April period (I wrote about it in *Forever Craps*), but I think it really has to do with the fact that Bill and Sandy Burton, John Robison, and Walter Thomason can often get away to join us at that time.

In fact, I owe Bill Burton a "thank you very much," because he's the guy who really opened my eyes to what was happening in the dice-control world, a world of which I was only dimly aware through my contacts with Sharpshooter. We were playing at Treasure Island casino; the year was 2000, around when *Forever Craps* was published. When it came time for Bill to shoot I noticed how much his roll had improved. In fact, his set, grip, and delivery of the dice were beautifully fluid. He looked confident, calm, contained, and centered as he rolled, and the dice gently landed and just as gently died, dissipating whatever energy they had at the bottom of the foam-rubber pyramids—a magnificent throw.

"Seven out!" shouted the stickman. All right, so he had established his point and then sevened out immediately; but he looked *so damn good* doing it that I asked him, "You've been practicing?"

"Yeah," he said, "I'll tell you about it later."

Indeed, Bill's form stood him in good stead when the dice made their way back to him, after I held them for about ten minutes. He proceeded to have a nice hand, with numbers being made in bunches before he sevened out. Later, as Bill sipped his O'Doul's and as I gulped my cabernet, he told me that he had taken the PARR class given by Sharpshooter a few months before, that he had been practicing on a "rig" at home almost daily, and that he and several other players were now making weekly visits to Foxwoods, where they called themselves, ironically, "the Mohegan Mechanics." (Foxwoods is in direct competition with the Mohegan Sun casino. Both are in Connecticut, about nine miles apart.) The Mechanics' ledgers were heavily in the black.

I asked Bill what he thought of the PARR course, Sharpshooter, and Jerry Patterson. "The course is definitely worthwhile and Sharpshooter knows his stuff and is a great shooter. Jerry Patterson is a nice guy, Frank."

"You know," I said, "when Sharpshooter first started writing for *Chance and Circumstance*, I received several e-mails from someone named 'Chip' who was adamant in his condemnations of Patterson and the fact that I had a Patterson crony writing for me. I know Sharpshooter is a good guy. You didn't find Patterson to be a slick salesman or anything like that?"

"Not at all. He's really low-key. The course sells itself. I took it because a friend of mine recommended it and also to write about it for my column on About.com. You should take it. You'll find a lot of the Captain's ideas have been used. It's a very worthwhile course."

"Bill, this guy Chip called Patterson and his wife . . ."

"Nancy is his wife," said Bill.

"He called them Ma and Pa Kettle. He told me not to fall for their 'Ma and Pa Kettle routine'—that's a quote—and that Patterson was really one step ahead of everybody and was basically . . . well, I don't know if he called him a crook, but something to that effect. You don't find any of that?" Bill shook his head no. "At all?" I asked.

"Not at all," said Bill. "Sharpshooter teaches the course. Jerry just handles the setup and schedules. If PARR is any indication of anything, this guy—what's his name?"

"He said Chip."

"This guy Chip may be just one of these guys who is never satisfied with anything or maybe he has an ax to grind with Jerry."

• • • •

WE PLAYED craps quite a bit, Bill and I, that Easter trip, and I could see that he was now a shooter to be reckoned with. In the years since that trip, Bill has become not only a tremendously proficient shooter but also an excellent coach. He has been dubbed "Wild Bill" by his fellow Mohegan Mechanics—for God knows what reason, because if anyone *isn't* wild it's Bill Burton!

I asked Bill if he could set up a meeting with some of the

PARR-instructed players who might be in Vegas during our next trip. He did so. We met at the lounge at Treasure Island one afternoon. Bill introduced me to Beau and Dominator.

Both of these gentlemen were high on dice control and had been doing it for several years. What I was most impressed with was how often they play. Beau plays a few days a week, as he lives in Las Vegas, and Dominator plays several times a week either in the Midwest or in Connecticut. Dominator also makes frequent trips to Las Vegas and Atlantic City, and even gets down to Tunica every so often.

Why is it so important that individuals who practice dice control play often in real casinos? Two reasons. The first is obvious. No matter how much you practice at home on makeshift rigs or even on regulation craps tables, practice can only be so effective. A pitcher who is warming up in the bullpen is not the same as a pitcher on the mound facing an actual batter; bullpen conditions are different from the actual mound conditions. That's why when a pitcher comes out of a bullpen he must take practice pitches on the real mound so he can get the feel of it. Then he gets to pitch to the batters and, as Sherlock Holmes says, "The game is afoot."

Dice controllers have to play at real tables, under real conditions, and get a feel for each individual table, since they are all different in subtle and not-so-subtle ways. The ability to adapt quickly to different tables under casino conditions can often spell the difference between winning and losing, good throws and bad.

The second reason why extensive, *recorded* casino play is important has to do with the nature of statistics. The fact that a player goes to a casino once, twice, maybe a dozen times and is ahead of the game could just be luck. But when you play several times a week and when weeks turn into months and months into years, then being ahead means something. It isn't a fluke when you can assess your winnings and say you're ahead because of skill when you've played hundreds, if not thousands, of sessions.

Until I met Dominator, only the Captain (twenty-five years), the Arm (twenty years), and Sharpshooter (eight years) had the kind of long-term statistics to back up their contentions that their wins were due to skill more than luck. I knew that several other PARR players were sporting high seven-to-rolls ratios on their practice rigs but, again, while practice makes perfect, it only makes perfect *at practice*. The real casino game could see a perfect practice shooter lose his cool, confidence, and control, and become just another random roller, albeit with better form and flair.

Now, I was anxious to see these guys in action in the casino, and I urged them to finish up their drinks and head with me to the tables. I wasn't in a rush to play so much as in a rush to see these guys pick up the dice and show me their form.

"I'm always ready to play," said Dominator.

"Well, I am here to play," I said, but I really meant, "Come on, show me your stuff."

Bill Burton took position SL1. Beau stood at the top of the table; he didn't seem the least inclined to play. Dominator took SR1 and I took SR2. Dominator was, for some reason, the first to shoot, perhaps because he had bought in first.

Twenty-five minutes later, I had the answer to a question that had been plaguing me for years—were there any other shooters out there like the Captain and the Arm? Dominator had just answered that in the affirmative. Not only did this guy have a perfect throw, but he was also calm as could be in his demeanor at the table. His confidence in himself was evident from the moment he was passed the dice. He set them with alacrity, aimed and lofted them, and those dice obeyed his will! When he sevened out, he looked at me and said, "Not too bad."

Not too bad? The guy was phenomenal. Even had he sevened out in a flash, his form alone would indicate he was a dice controller with few peers. The fact that his performance had, on that occasion, complemented his form was just gravy—a nice fat win for all of us at the table. We made money on Bill's roll, although he didn't have a long one—singles and doubles win baseball games too; you don't always have to hit home runs. However, he did hit a few points and a few numbers before the inevitable seven. Next was Beau's turn—he passed up the dice. "I'm not in position," he said.

I offered him my position and Dominator offered him his.

"I'm not feeling just right today," Beau said. Beau won't play unless he feels 100 percent right. Since he can play every day, he is never in a rush to get into the action.

The dice were passed to me. *Please, God, just don't let me embarrass myself.* I set the dice in my 3-V, gripped them lightly and threw. Thankfully, I had a non-embarrassing roll, which is to say, I hit some numbers and made people some money before I sevened out.

Dominator said to me, "You look good."

Okay, I didn't embarrass myself; mission accomplished.

Dominator lit up a cigarette as we colored up. In time I have gotten to know Dominator quite well. We've become best of friends.

In the early seventies, he graduated college with dual degrees in biology and math, but since then has found his success in business, first as the owner of a chain of men's apparel stores and then as the owner of a software development company. As a young man, Dom loved music. "I played piano since I was eight years old and performed in bands until my twenties." He has been called the man with the "golden touch" by many of his fellow dice controllers, and he attributes his soft touch to "playing the piano."

Dom jokingly says that he started his "craps career pitching nickels against the gym wall at about eleven years old. I practiced my 'Golden Touch Delivery' of these nickels after school in the gym. It came to a point that no one wanted to pitch nickels with me any more!"

His first craps game did not go well. "I was nineteen years old and playing in the back room of a club. I didn't know anything about the game. I was with a friend and he said, 'Give me a $10 spot.' He threw it on the table, said some thing crazy about hopping something and before I knew it lost my $10. Never again, I said to myself, will I play the game of craps. Little did I know how my thoughts would change!"

Dom didn't return to the craps world again until 1997. But before that date he was an excellent card counter at blackjack and went to the casinos frequently.

"I always looked at gambling as an investment. I enjoy gambling, but I wouldn't gamble my hard-earned money unless I gave myself an advantage at winning. That is why in the eighties and nineties I was a blackjack player. I read everything I could about blackjack and learned to count cards." But gambling is not just the physical or mathematical game to Dom; there is also the inner game. "I also read books on positive thinking and how to control your emotions, because I always believed that the emotional aspect of gambling needed to be addressed to make me a better player. I tend to be emotional and sometimes that is a very bad thing for a gambler."

Dom credits his success at gambling to his burning desire to learn. "Everything I ever did I studied, from hitting a baseball to writing software, from playing blackjack to shooting craps. I read all I could on attitude of the mind, books on Zen, and I practice meditation every day, which helps me a great deal when rolling dice. Being focused during your roll is a major component of having a money roll."

Dom experienced what I experienced over the last decade with regard to blackjack, the decrease in worthwhile games. "As years went on, blackjack became a harder game to beat consistently with the advent of continuous-shuffle machines and poor rules and penetration, so I thought about other games of chance in the casino. During walks through the casinos looking for playable blackjack games, I finally stepped up to a craps table after not going near one since that night at the back room. I stepped up to the table because a blackjack-playing friend of mine, who lives in Vegas, told me he had started to play craps and talked to me about rhythmic rolling. It sounded interesting to me. As luck would have it, that very first time, I witnessed a gentleman have a long roll. He looked to be the kind of guy who could be characterized as a rhythmic roller. I said to myself, here is a game that I can beat. It brought memories of that gym wall! And so I started to practice."

His craps-playing buddies gave him his nickname, Dominator, because on most nights Dom is the one who makes the game a winner for the players. In short, he's the dominating presence at a table.

As Beau, Dom, Bill Burton, and I strolled into Treasure Island, I asked them what they thought of Jerry Patterson and the PARR course. They affirmed Bill's contention that the PARR course was a worthwhile course to take. They also agreed with Bill that Jerry Patterson was a likable guy, while both admitted that he was "a good salesman."

So I decided that I might as well look into PARR; after all, what did I have to lose? As I would find out—peace of mind!

But first I ran into the Lee brothers, and that gave me a whole other perspective on dice-control.

8

The Lee Brothers I

THEY ARE not brothers and their names aren't Lee. They are Korean or Vietnamese, or maybe they aren't; maybe they are Japanese or Chinese.

"We all look alike," laughed Tony Lee, "except to us, and so make us what you will."

"You don't make us be recognized," cautioned Larry Lee, whose name isn't Larry or anything close to Larry.

Larry Lee doesn't talk much; English isn't his first language, or his second. He was born "over there," in a poor village, and he came to America in the 1980s. He got his citizenship in 1995 and *that* he is proud of: "America is great. Casinos suck."

For a man of few words, Larry Lee sees the world clearly and in black and white. He also sees the world through a cloud of smoke; I have yet to see him without a cigarette— unfiltered, no less—dangling from his mouth, except for the times when it's in his nicotine-stained hands.

I met the Lee brothers strictly by chance. I was playing

craps at Sunset Station in Henderson, which is just outside of Las Vegas, when these two came to the table. I was all alone at the table and doing quite well, thank you, so I wasn't too thrilled to have players buying in. Tony bought in at SL1 for $500. I was on SR1 and Larry moved right in next to me, smoke billowing out of his mouth and nostrils. He crowded me and threw down $1,000.

"Hey, man, I'm shooting," I said.

Larry didn't give an inch as the boxman laid out his bills—fives, tens, twenties, fifties, and a few hundreds—counted them out and passed him his chips. He didn't put down a Pass Line bet. He just smoked. Tony didn't put out a Pass Line bet either.

"Just move over a few inches," I said to him. "We're the only ones at the table."

He didn't budge. The dice were passed to me. I had a choice. I could stop the game and complain to the pit that this idiot was crowding me, or I could concentrate on what I was doing and continue what, until then, had been a fifteen-minute roll with only me at the table. I decided to continue my roll.

I took a breath, cleared my mind, concentrated on my breathing, and then picked up the dice and set them. When Larry saw me set the dice in the 3-V, he suddenly stepped all the way back and gave me plenty of room. I then lofted them to the back wall.

Tony placed the inside numbers (five, six, eight, nine) for $110 and Larry bought the four and ten for $25 each. I rolled again. And again. And for another twenty minutes.

I totally forgot about Larry standing next to me. He had moved not only out of my way but also out of my vision; the only reason I knew he was still there, aside from his bets, was the smoke that wafted over every so often, but even this wasn't all that much. (I learned later that Larry purposely blew the smoke as far from me as possible during my roll.)

When I sevened out, Tony gave a big round of applause. I looked over at his chip rack and noticed that he had a hell of a lot more than $500 in chips after my roll. I didn't look in Larry's direction and he didn't say anything. Other people started coming to the table. Controlled shooters often like to play alone, whereas random rollers love the crowds and don't want to be the only player at the table. Unfortunately, more often than not, when a controlled shooter is playing alone it doesn't last for long. Others gravitate to the table. In a real way, we act as shills for the casinos—since we open tables and get the action going. Two of these other people bought in. One was a woman of indeterminate age, wearing sunglasses; the other was a whale of a man. The woman stood next to Larry and cashed in for $100. The whale cashed in for $2,000 and stood at the end of the table on Larry's side.

It was now Tony's turn to shoot. I played the *5-Count* on him. Larry had gone right up on him with $440 inside (that's $100 each on the five and nine, $120 each on the six and eight).

I felt a nudge on my arm. Larry was nudging me. I looked at him. "Bet," he said softly. "Good shooter." He nodded toward Tony and blew smoke out of his nose. He looked kind of like a dragon, I thought at the time.

"I will," I said, "when he gets warmed up."

Tony set the dice—in the 3-V! He gripped the dice in a very similar fashion to the Captain and had an incredibly smooth delivery and throw. The dice arced up and landed, just touching the back wall.

"Good shooter," whispered Larry in my ear. "Bet, bet."

Tony bought the four and ten for $100 each, then he turned to Larry and said, "Leave him alone; he's playing the *5-Count*."

Bowl me over with a feather! I looked over at Tony but he was busy setting the dice. His first point was a six and he made it right back. Then a beautiful young woman came to the table and stood about one person away from Tony. She bought in for $20. She placed a Hard 6 and 8 for $10 each.

"Working on the come-out," said the stickman. In Vegas, proposition bets work on the come-out roll, unless you say they don't; in Atlantic City they do not work on the come-out, unless you say they do.

Tony set the dice in the 3-V and threw an eight. This was the 3-Count and I still had to wait before going up on him. Tony's next number was a four, then he came back with another eight, his second point. The 4-Count was completed. Since he couldn't possibly seven out before the 5-Count, since he was on the come-out roll, I placed a Pass Line bet and placed the six and eight. Tony then rolled an eleven, then a Hard 6—the beautiful young woman had won her bet.

"Parlay," she said.

Now she had $100 riding on the Hard 6 and Tony had just completed the *5-Count.* I was in the action, too. Tony now hit a string of outside numbers, fours and tens, then he hit some nines, some eights, if memory serves me right about three fives in a row, and then: "Six! Hard six! Winner! Winner! Six, came the hard way!"

The young woman collected her $900 and said, "Take me down." She then left the table as the boxman said to Tony, "You have to hit the back wall." On his last throw both dice had just, well, died, *without a single bounce,* about three inches from the back wall. I was later to learn that once a session Tony Lee does his "trick-shot" Hard 6 or Hard 8—a move he has perfected and is successful with about a third of the time. The dice go up in the air and, with the backspin and trajectory just right, they land and stick to the table as if they had Velcro on them.

I would later learn that the young lady, known as Vixen (I kid you not), who had placed the Hard 6 was not all that young—and, if Tony is to be believed, was not even a woman, but "she" was a member of their five-man team, composed of Tony, Larry, the indeterminate-age woman, named Lola, and the human whale. (By the way, I am not being insensitive by calling the large man "the human whale" because that is his nickname—the "Whale"! He's a whale in stature but he's also the bankroll behind this very effective dice-control team.)

Tony rolled several more times before sevening out. The dice made their way to the Whale, who passed them up, then to the indeterminate woman, who also passed, and now to Larry, the smokestack. With a cigarette dangling from his mouth, Larry made his Pass Line bet. I moved out of his way, so that he could get as close to the stickman as possible. At this point I had an inkling that these two "Asian" guys were somehow a "team," but I had no idea about the other three.

Larry set the dice, also in a 3-V, only he inverted it, like a pyramid. He, too, had a nice soft delivery, but he sevened out rather quickly. Now it was my turn to roll. I took the dice, set the 3-V and . . .

"You guys all set the dice the same way," said the tall dealer. "Look it, all three set them with the 3-spots up." He indicated Larry, Tony, and me.

"They copied me," I said, hoping this would ease the light the dealer was shining on such a remarkable coincidence.

"He's right," said Tony. "We copied him."

The boxman waved his arm twice. "Come on, come on, get the game moving."

I set the dice and tossed—and had another great roll,

about twenty minutes. Then Tony rolled and he had an epic roll, about forty minutes. When he sevened out, I walked behind the stickman and whispered to Tony, "You are damn good."

"I know who you are," he said. "I've read all your books."

"I'm finished," I said. "When you're finished meet me for a drink in the center lounge."

Tony looked over at Whale and did some kind of gesture; I didn't catch it. Whale colored up; so did Lola, and so did Larry. They all went their separate ways.

About a half-hour later, Tony showed up in the center bar at Sunset Station. He ordered a beer; I ordered a cabernet.

"You have some nice roll," I said.

"Oh, yes, I have worked on this ever since I read your two books on the Captain. Is the Captain . . .?" He paused.

"Real?"

"Yes, I sometimes think you made him up to get out your ideas."

"No, he's real. I would have taken full credit for everything if he weren't. I wish I had come up with all these ideas, but I didn't. I would have named them after myself."

"Well, he has made me a lot of money. Me and Larry."

"Who's Larry?" I asked, but I could guess.

"The other Korean [Chinese, Japanese, Vietnamese] at the table. My brother."

"That other guy is your brother?"

"No, but I call him my brother because we are in the brotherhood of craps players."

Then Tony told me their story.

Larry Lee came over from Korea in 1980 as a ten-year-old with his mother and her brother. They settled in Brooklyn, in what is euphemistically called "a bad neighborhood." His father remained behind in their village, along with his sister who had just gotten married and his grandparents on his father's side, one of whom, grand pops, was dying of lung cancer. Larry's father joined them in 1983 upon the death of his own father. At first Larry Lee and his mother worked for several greengrocers, all relatives, and lived over the store, saving as much money as they could and working seven days a week. Larry attended school but was an unremarkable student. When Mr. Lee arrived with the family "fortune," and having amassed enough capital from several years of non-stop work, the Lee family opened their own store in Long Island, New York—in, as Larry said, "a good neighborhood, where everyone complain all the time. They drive you crazy complaining."

The Lee family built up the business, and, when Larry graduated high school in 1988, they sold it to relatives and moved to California. Larry started college but then found that he enjoyed working more than school, so he quit after his first year. He held a series of jobs, mostly with family, and in 1997 ran into Tony Lee in Las Vegas. It seems Larry had gotten the gambling bug; he played with his paychecks and was always broke. "I didn't know what I do," he said. "I play blackjack but I don't know strategy."

Tony Lee was different. A fourth-generation American who was fluent in several languages, Tony was thirty-five years old, held a masters degree in engineering, and worked for a small firm that designed shopping malls, but his real passion was gambling. However, unlike Larry, who was just throwing his money down a rat hole, Tony counted cards at blackjack, was very cautious with money, and was practicing with a "rhythmic roll" at craps. "I had read *Beat the Craps Out of the Casinos* and *The Captain's Craps Revolution*, and I knew that the Captain was on to something. I set up a half craps table in my small office and analyzing those books I was able to perfect my roll. It took me a year to have enough confidence to play craps in the casino and use my roll. But right away I saw that it worked, and I've been doing it ever since. But in 1997, I was still a small player."

Larry was watching Tony roll the dice. Tony was in the midst of a blistering roll that would last one hour; Larry was smoking incessantly and inching closer and closer to Tony to see his form and exactly what he was doing, when Tony asked him to move back. Larry said something in Korean, Tony's second language, and when Tony finally sevened out Larry asked him how he, Larry, could learn to roll like that.

Tony took Larry aside, scolded him about smoking so much. ("That was the first and only time I ever said anything about Larry's smoking. Everyone in his family smokes and all of them have died from lung cancer and the ones still alive still smoke.") Then Tony explained what he was doing.

Larry saw the possibilities immediately. Tony laughed when he remembers this: "He just said, 'We make a good living!' I don't know if he knew that I was having real problems on the job. I hated the boss; the boss hated me. I made okay money but I wasn't happy. I was only happy when I was playing craps. Once I had my roll down, I stopped playing blackjack. Craps was everything."

Larry and Tony hooked up. Since they lived some fifty miles apart, it was not hard for them to get together. Tony taught Larry his rolling technique. "Larry was very motivated. He also had great dexterity. He was a little crazy in the betting department so I had to tone him down there, but he was a natural roller. And he loved it. He was now able to make money when we went to Vegas on weekends."

It was on a trip to Vegas in 1998 that Tony and Larry, who played their own bankrolls rather than pooling their money, met Whale. Tony and Larry would use the *5-Count* on the other shooters, and this particular table had been cold. In fact, when Tony looked up, it was just Larry and he at the table. Then Whale came. A huge man, standing maybe 6'6" and weighing close to four hundred pounds, the Whale spread his $6,400 across all the numbers and threw out about $300 worth of proposition bets, as Tony picked up the dice.

"I was thinking that maybe if I had a good roll this big bettor would tip me. It had happened in the past. You have a good roll and a big player puts out some Hardways for you. You never know."

As luck would have it, Tony had one of his famous blistering rolls that lasted about fifty minutes. At one point, Whale put up a Hard 6 for $500. "Come on, kid, hit that and I'll split it with you." Tony set the 3-V and then, "I don't know, just by luck or fate or something, I lofted the dice just a little too high and I thought, 'Oh, shit, here comes the seven,' but instead the dice landed like they had a magnet on them right on the Hard six. It was incredible. But that's when I realized that hitting that Hard 6 [or its opposite side, the Hard 8] would be possible if I didn't hit the back wall and got that trajectory and spin just right. So, after that day, I went home and that's all I practiced. So now I do it once a session, not too much, and we try to get a parlay on a Hard 6 or 8 and then I do my trick shot to nail the parlay."

Whale was impressed with Tony and did indeed share his Hard 6 win with the young man. Then it was Whale's turn to roll. He established his point, hit a couple of numbers, and then sevened out. Larry was up.

Larry's set, grip, and delivery are mirror images of Tony's. He rolled for a half-hour. Whale was impressed and asked to speak with them away from the table.

Whale told them that he was a small-time movie producer of such memorable hits as *Forrest Hump*, whose publicity read, "He had a small mind but a big mind-blower!" (Note:

this is not the real name of one of Whale's movies, but it's evocative enough for you to get the picture.) He asked them if they were used to having such good rolls. "I noticed how you throw the dice. You seem to have some kind of control, right?"

At first Tony was hesitant to say anything to the big man; after all, he might be a casino spy. But finally Larry said, "Yeah, so what?"

"Here's so what," said the Whale. He took out $20,000 in $100 bills. "I'm prepared to bankroll you guys right now. I've lost millions of dollars playing craps. I love the game but I hate those fuckers," he indicated the casino and by extension the casino world, "and I want revenge. You double this $20,000 and I'll give you each $5,000 of it. What do you say?"

Larry held out his hand. "Give money," he said.

They went to the table and for two days played high-stakes craps, and not only did they double Whale's $20,000—they tripled it! Whale was delighted. He now had another plan.

"I want to form a team. I'll bankroll the whole thing; you guys get 20 percent each of what we win. I have two other people I want involved because I want us to be able to take up at least half the table so we don't have to worry about betting on these other fuckers [meaning other players]. You guys work for a living?"

Tony and Larry gave the details of their jobs.

"Quit them. They suck. The first six months, not only will I bankroll you, I'll pay all your living expenses and transportation."

Neither Tony nor Larry was married; they had nothing to lose, they figured, in accepting Whale's offer.

And that's how I found them—a five-member team,

Whale, two of his "actresses," Vixen and Lola, Tony, Larry, and a boatload of money.

The battle plan for the team is interesting. They never play the same casino more than once on the same trip. "We hit about twenty-five Vegas casinos in a month, then we go to Reno for a few days, then Tahoe, then to the South, then Atlantic City, then the Midwest, then back to Vegas. We play all the time; sometimes with Whale, sometimes without Whale." They always have the two "actresses" with them. "We are all friends. They take up space at the table, pass the dice to us, and make the Hardways bets for the team," said Tony. "They also distract people when we're really putting out big money. Today they weren't dressed up but they can be very sexy when they want to be, especially the guy." He laughed. Then he explained that one of the "actresses" was really a guy—"prettiest guy you'll ever see." She, uh, he, was beautiful and I could just imagine what (s)he looked like "dressed up."

Their bets range from $640 across to $3,200 across the numbers, between the two of them, but only when they roll. "We play the *5-Count* on everyone else. We don't bet very much on the ones that get to the 5-Count, a hundred, two hundred dollars, but it makes us look like regular players."

Because they play at least six of every seven days, they know that their rolls are fine-tuned. "This not luck what we do," Larry explained. "This skill."

I wanted to know if they had ever met any other controlled shooters or teams on their travels. Tony shook his head, "No, no teams. I haven't seen any other teams. They may be out there but I haven't met them. We have seen some good shooters like you but not many. This is not easy and not many people can do this and, you know, you don't win every day."

"What's the longest losing streak that you've had?" I asked.

"I didn't have a winning roll for four straight days; Larry went about a week once without a single winning roll. But usually one or the other of us is on even if the other one isn't."

"So what do you make?" I asked. "If you don't mind."

"Okay," said Tony, "but you must swear that when you write about us we cannot be recognized at all."

"Make us Germans," said Larry.

"No," said Tony. "Oriental."

"Chinese? Japanese? What?" I asked.

"Everything," said Larry.

"No one can know what we look like."

"Okay," I said. "No one will be able to figure out who you guys are."

"I only talked to you because you are Frank Scoobleet . . ."

"Sco-blet-tee."

"Scoblete, the great author. You are the man."

"Well," I said, "I don't think of myself as the man; the Captain is the man."

"We are making a little over $1,000 a day each; the 'actresses' make half that, and the Whale gets the rest. The Whale books our flights, pays the expenses, even now because he likes us, and we play. That's all we do is play. I never get tired of playing. And we make sure that we aren't too well known. We won't be coming back to this casino for at least a year."

I did some quick calculations: six days a week equals $6,000 a week; fifty weeks a year would be $300,000. Not bad! All expenses paid so that made their $300,000 each a pure profit, minus taxes. (Uncle Sam is the other member of the team.)

Of course, the Lee brothers are extreme examples of what

a dice controller can do in a casino. Except for Sharp-shooter's team, the Lee brothers are the only other team I have ever met in the casinos and the only full-time professional team I've encountered. True, I have read on Internet craps sites that this or that team or this or that individual is a huge long-run winner, but so much self-serving hyperbole is written on the Internet that I am skeptical of anything so publicly proclaimed. In truth, based on my calculations, even if *all* the Internet's self-proclaimed great players and teams are actually real, they still make up fewer than one in forty thousand casino craps players.

9

PARR and Patterson

IT WASN'T until the spring of 2002 that I finally attended my first PARR course. It was held in Atlantic City at the beautiful Sheraton Hotel.

The previous year had not been a good one. We ushered in the real new millennium with the beautiful AP getting very sick. Just after New Year's Eve 2001, AP came down with an awful malady that was finally diagnosed as ulcerative colitis—a chronic and, at times, crippling inflammatory disease of the colon. She missed almost three months of work. I was her caretaker.

Then there was September 11.

From a certain vantage point in my town we could see the Twin Towers burning and then, poof, vanishing, just like that. Thankfully my son Greg, who worked seventeen blocks from the Twin Towers and saw both planes hit and both buildings collapse, and my daughter-in-law, Dawn, who worked two blocks away, got out of the city safely.

AP "celebrated" Thanksgiving 2001 by getting pancreatitis and having to be hospitalized for almost a week, then getting another flare-up of her ulcerative colitis while in the hospital. Again she missed several months of work. The year ended as it began, on a low note, with the death of my cousin Bobby's twenty-year-old son in an automobile accident. In between those events, my father had a heart attack (he's fine now), two friends of mine died, one from a massive stroke while exercising (fifty-six years old), the other from lung cancer (fifty-four years old), and two lovely aunts of mine also passed away, my Aunt Mary and my Aunt Dorothy. Death, disease, and destruction characterized 2001.

The casino visits I made in 2001 were few and far between, and they were characterized by guilt for being away from AP (who was not sick at these times but just not up to traveling), and a dawning realization that blackjack was slowly fading away as my primary game and was being replaced by craps.

Sometime in February or March of 2002, I received a note from Sharpshooter asking me if I'd like to come to a PARR dice-control course that May. I told him yes. Then I received a message from Jerry Patterson, telling me that I would be comped to the PARR course in exchange for being the course's guest speaker. That was fine with me; I love to speak to groups and I rarely turn down a comp. I also thought that this class might make for an interesting article in one of the magazines for which I write. After all, I had seen several remarkable former students of PARR, including Dominator and Bill Burton; I wanted to see just how many students actually learned the technique, and how it was taught to a class full of eager novices.

Jerry announced on his Web site that I would be the keynote speaker. He also sent out a letter to his mailing list saying the same. Within several days of the announcement, a voice from the past came screaming into the present. I received an angry e-mail from "Chip," who, you will recall, had warned me about "Ma and Pa Kettle" Patterson. This time he expressed his outrage that I had "sold out to the devil" by agreeing to speak at the PARR class. He lambasted me for daring to speak to such a Satanic group, and he also assumed that I was now a partner in the PARR program.

In addition, someone just as irate sent a letter to *Casino Player* magazine, claiming that I had "sold out" to the dark side of gambling; this writer also called Patterson the "devil." The *Casino Player* letter may have been written by this same "Chip," or perhaps someone else with an equally big chip on his shoulder. The purpose of the second letter was clear—to hurt me in the eyes of the editors of *Casino Player* magazine. Of course, the breathless, end-of-the-known-world tone of both these missives precluded anyone with half a brain from taking them seriously. Perhaps Patterson was a salesman; perhaps he sold less-than-stellar systems; perhaps TARGET was not a valid system for beating blackjack—but calling Patterson "the devil" was just silly, and showed someone not in control of his or her hyperbole.

Since I had the utmost respect for Sharpshooter and for Bill Burton, both of whom assured me that PARR was on the level and that Jerry fulfilled his obligations to his students, I was not only unconcerned about speaking at the PARR seminar; I was actually looking forward to it. Since time had taken its toll on the Captain's Crew, since the Captain himself was making only weekly visits to Atlantic City, usually alone, and since the Arm was now completely out of action, I missed the camaraderie of enthusiastic and savvy craps players.

The May weekend came and I drove down to Atlantic City. I was staying at the Sands with the RFB treatment, which was in itself curious; my previous visit to the Sands had seen two very disagreeable gray-suited fellows limit my blackjack play on their six-deck games. On that last trip I handed in my card and took out some money from my line of credit. I placed my first wager, a black chip, in the betting circle. I had finished playing just two hands when two guys approached me from behind; one tapped me on the shoulder.

"Write any books lately, Mr. Scoobleet?" the tapper sneered.

"I'm always writing."

"Yeah," snarled the other guy, "well, why don't you write this down: You can't bet more than that $100 chip from now on. You can only play one hand and"—he turned to the dealer—"shuffle up on every couple of rounds, you hear me?" The dealer nodded.

The first guy, the tapper, then reached into the shoe and pulled out all the decks, and then he pulled out the cut card. "Place the cut card here," he said to the dealer. "Halfway." He shoved the card back into the deck; then he took the card out again and threw it onto the table. "Shuffle them now." The dealer did as he was told and went into his shuffling routine.

"What the fuck!" said one of the other players.

"This is none of your business," said the snarler.

"We don't like his action. Isn't that right, Mr. Scoobleet?"

"Sco-blet-tee," I corrected.

"Are you *Frank* Scobolete, the writer?" asked the other player.

"Yeah."

"Wow! I've read all your books; it's an honor to meet you." He shook my hand vigorously. Then he turned to the two casino guys. "What the fuck is wrong with you guys? This is Frank Scobolete, for Christ's sake."

"You know," I said to the tapper and the snarler, "you didn't even look at my play. You don't really know if the type of play I'm using tonight is enough to beat you."

"You got the knowledge," said the snarler. "That's all we need to know."

"You aren't making me feel very welcome at the Sands," I said.

"And you're not getting a rating for blackjack, so any action you give us here is zero, got that?" added the tapper.

"No sense playing, is there?" I said to the other player.

"You guys are fucking morons. If I was him I'd write about what a couple of shitheads you are and what a dump the Sands is. Don't Sands want good publicity? Christ, you guys are real assholes. You should *pay him* to play here, you fucking morons."

"Let me guess," I said to the other player, "You're from New York, right?"

"Fuckin'-A," he said. "But I live in Jersey now."

The reason they tolerated the badgering from the New Yorker–turned–Jerseyan was because he was betting black and purple chips and casinos will put up with a lot from such players. As for me, I just picked up my chips and walked away.

"You don't mind if I play craps?" I asked them as I parted. "I'm not going to be hassled at craps, am I?"

"Play craps all you want," said the snarler, triumphant in his knowledge that no one could beat craps.

I needed to put in four hours for my RFB, but before I went to play craps I called my parents' room and informed them that they should play craps and slots over at the Claridge. I also told them to call my aunt and uncle in the next room, two *big* slot players, and tell them to do the same thing, play at the Claridge. The Captain and some Crew members were coming down and were contemplating staying at the Sands, as it had been years since they had done so and it would be a kind of reunion for all of us. I called the Captain and told him what happened, and he took his

half-dozen Crew members, who stood to lose maybe 100K
that weekend, over to the Taj Mahal.

The Sands management had certainly made it impossible
for me to get my 1 percent edge at their six-deck blackjack
games—that is, if I had decided to count and spread my bets
from $100 to $1,200, the minimum needed to get that 1 percent edge (a spread I had no intention of making). But they
had also unwittingly blown off approximately ten other
players who would have given them edges five to ten times
greater than any I had, except for the Captain, of course. So
often casinos take precipitous actions without thinking outside the box, and the Sands was no exception. Those bosses
were "penny wise" on the money they perceived themselves
saving from my play, but they were "pound foolish" in the
amount they could have won on the slots and on the Crew's
crazy craps play had they not harassed me.

Still, a month or so later I got a call from my host, inviting me to come to Sands again. On the phone, he asked me
if I was *the* Frank Scoblete, the writer, and I said yes. "Hey,
great," he said. "I want you to know you are always welcome at the Sands." My host obviously had no idea of the
crudity of the Sands' blackjack pit personnel and their
heavy-handed and ill-conceived harassment of me—and I
wasn't going to tell him. Why should I? It would just embarrass him and create an awkward situation for me. I'd take
him up on his offer and just play craps at Sands. The Atlantic City blackjack game is not one that I like to play for
any length of time and, as I said in a previous chapter, if I
hand in my card at a blackjack game it means I'm just playing basic strategy and looking to get some comp time, so it
really isn't a winning style of play for me.

So, the Friday and Saturday of the PARR seminar, I again
took the RFB at Sands, knowing that I wouldn't even attempt
to play blackjack, and that whatever comps I received would

come from my craps play with Sharpshooter, Dominator, Bill Burton, and other PARR players. Then that Sunday I'd switch over to Bally's Park Place, where my hostess would RFB me for three more nights, so that I could hook up with the Captain on Monday and renew our playing friendship and, hopefully, hit a few casinos and win some money.

I put in some time at the Sands craps tables that Friday, but didn't really bet often since player after player sevened out before the 5-Count. The few who made it past the 5-Count would seven out on the 6- or 7-Counts, not a pretty picture at all, since I lost money on those. I had one mediocre roll and one point/seven-out roll. It certainly was not an auspicious night at the Sands craps pits for Frank *Scoobleet.*

I met John Robison for dinner and we discussed the state of affairs in Atlantic City. John is an avid slot and video poker player, writing on these subjects for my Web site *www.scoblete.com, Strictly Slots, Midwest Gaming and Travel,* and other magazines. He was lamenting the fact that Atlantic City's slot returns were comparatively quite poor, usually several percentage points behind the rest of the country.

We also discussed the impending opening of the Borgata, the massive hotel-casino complex that was a joint venture between Sam's Town and MGM-Mirage in the Marina section of Atlantic City, where Trump Marina and Harrah's are located. Everyone was looking forward to the opening, but while I figured such a new and beautiful casino would be an instant success I didn't think it would improve the gambling landscape any.

In point of fact, Atlantic City seems to be one big casino—as opposed to various competing casinos. The difference in slot returns from one casino to another is not that great; the blackjack games tend to be close to uniform throughout the casinos, with the only variation being whether you play against six decks in the high-roller rooms or eight decks on the main floor. Every once in a while an Atlantic City casino will get daring and offer surrender in blackjack or some other variation, but these options don't last long. The competition in Atlantic City is not over who can have the best games or the loosest slots, and games and slot returns as such are never advertised (there's even a silly law against doing so, which the casinos seem content not to challenge). Instead, casinos battle over who can offer the bus trade the best coin and coupon deals to get them in the door. The Atlantic City casinos must have tight slots to pay for the "freebies" they give to the day-tripping senior citizens who make their pilgrimages to Atlantic City as much to walk the Boardwalk and eat the buffets as to gamble. The typical Vegas visitor stays about four days; the typical Atlantic City visitor stays about eight hours.

Borgata might be spectacular, and it might even encourage more lengthy stays, but neither John nor I could see how it could fundamentally change Atlantic City. However, if Borgata were the first of five or six new casinos, then you might see Atlantic City become a resort destination like Las Vegas. Time would tell.

The next morning we headed over to the Sheraton Hotel. Just off the Atlantic City Expressway, it's the last hotel you see when leaving Atlantic City and the first one you see when you arrive. Although it doesn't have a casino, it is fairly large and seems to do a brisk business. As we got out of John's car, we noticed hundreds of cheerleaders waiting to cross the road to the new convention center. It was National Cheerleader Week, and schools from all over the country had sent their jumping, chanting, shimmying, singing, shouting kids to compete with each other in the cheerleading championships.

"You see, John," I said, "Jerry and Sharpshooter sent cheerleaders to welcome us!"

"That's very nice of them."

I was to speak at 3 P.M. John and I would take the PARR course with the rest of the students that morning, and then Sharpshooter, John, and I would go to Jerry's room, where we'd do *The Goodtimes Radio Show* in Memphis. This show, the longest-running casino gaming show in the nation, is sponsored by the casinos of Tunica and hosted by my good friends Rudi Schiffer and Clyde Callicott. I've been doing this show since the early 1990s, every Saturday, and it's a hoot. Despite the fact that the casinos sponsor the show, we have never been told what we can talk about, so the subjects of our gaming discussions range from slot machines to card counting. Today's topic was going to be "controlled shooting," and Sharpshooter was going to be our special guest.

As we approached the banquet hall where the PARR course was being held, I recalled the one and only time I had ever met Jerry Patterson, at a *Casino Player* gaming festival in Las Vegas. He had come to my booth and introduced himself; we shook hands, and that's all I remembered. I didn't really remember what he looked like. Then I saw him at the entrance to the banquet room at the Sheraton.

Pa Kettle!

There was Jerry Patterson standing at the door greeting people, and damned if he didn't look like Pa Kettle. He was tall and lean, with a white beard, ever so slightly stooped over; all he needed was a pitchfork and he could be one end of a pleasant-looking *American Gothic*.

I introduced myself.

"Frank," Jerry said, "glad you could come. I'll tell you, the guys have been really looking forward to meeting you, as have I. Nancy isn't going to be here today but she was look-ing forward to meeting you, too."

Well, I thought, if he was Satan, he was a hell of a per-sonable Satan.

"Nice to meet you," I said, "and this is my partner, John Robison."

"John, great you could come. I think you'll find this a very interesting day."

"I'm looking forward to it," John said.

"Sharpshooter will be down any minute. Take a seat up front and we'll begin in a few minutes."

As we made our way to our seats, I noticed that there were rigs set up all around the room. I later found out that these are called, variously, "PARR boxes," "practice boxes," "throwing stations," and "shooting rigs." This is what stu-dents can use to practice their throws during the breaks in class, and what experienced players can obtain to practice their shooting at home or in their hotel rooms. As soon as I saw the boxes I thought to myself, *ingenious!* Usually, when I go to a casino, I have to warm up at the actual tables, and it sometimes takes me a day or two to get back in the groove. These practice boxes can warm you up, like a pitcher in the bullpen, so that when you go into the casino, your arm is limber. Yes, each and every table is different, but it is much easier to adjust to different table conditions if your *arm* is already conditioned.

Dominator came up to me.

"Remember me?" he said.

"How could I forget someone who made me so much money?"

"You're going to find this course very interesting, Frank. A lot of the stuff that the Captain talked about in your books, we do in this course."

I liked Dominator right off—and not just because he was

a fan of the Captain's—and I respected him. The guy had an enthusiasm for craps and such confidence in his rolling ability that, coupled with his friendly and informal ways, made him easy to talk to and easy to get to know. He also understood the game inside and out, a true expert, and, as I saw in the next two days, a truly gifted teacher.

Dominator then introduced me to Mr. Finesse. Now, when a movie is made from this book (as it will, it will), Mr. Finesse wants Danny DeVito to play him (Brad Pitt can play me). Mr. Finesse, as I was to find out later, has one of the best "eyes" in the world and can catch a mistake in throwing form that few other coaches or players can even see. Mr. Finesse also has a beautiful throw—despite the fact that he has to stand on his tippy-toes to reach the table. (He's designing a special box to stand on, even as I write this.) He is also a highly skilled teacher and has the patience of Job with his students.

Mr. Finesse's gambling career goes all the way back to June of 1970. "My frat brother Johnny Cap and I both had the summer off from our full-time jobs, and we decided to drive cross-country. We stopped in Reno to see what a casino was all about. I don't remember the name of the casino but I do remember standing in the casino and this loud roar comes from the other side behind a few blackjack tables. I went over to see what was going on and people were everywhere standing around this table. I asked what was going on and I was informed some guy had been throwing the dice and everyone was making tons of money. This was my first experience with the game of craps. After a few minutes everyone was clapping for the guy who was throwing the dice. I kept on watching and sort of moved into the corner, close to a dealer. He asked me if I would like to play and I told him I had no idea of how to play the game. He then said, 'Stay right here and I will explain it to you.' I listened and I watched and I knew I was hooked on this game. But I still couldn't work up the nerve to actually play it.

"It was now the third week of August, and Johnny and I were on our way back from California to Connecticut. We had to be back to work for the last Monday in August, but we made a stop in Las Vegas. I was sitting at a bar in the Sands and four seats away was Jack Benny, a real live TV star; man, was I impressed. Later that night I played craps for the first time, nervous as all heck, but I won $100—talk about being on cloud nine! I could not wait to get back to Las Vegas and play again.

"When I got home I started to read about the game of craps and I couldn't wait to get back to Las Vegas. Unfortunately, life intervened and I never made it back Las Vegas until 2001! The next time I played the game was in 1985 in Atlantic City. I was going on vacation to Virginia Beach and I had to stop in Atlantic City. Well, I gave back that $100 I had won in 1970 and then some.

"I started playing regularly in the mid-nineties when Foxwoods opened in Connecticut. I lost like everyone else, but I soon became a student of the game. I read everything I could get my hands on and learned as much as I could. In the spring of 2000 I bought my first computer and I started playing craps on it. I bought software, installed it on my computer, and really learned how to bet and play.

"My only problem was in throwing the dice—I was horrible! The casino was an expensive place to practice, so I set up a few boxes on my dinning room table, bought a craps layout, and became pretty good at throwing the dice underhand and very soft from the right side of the table next to the stickman. I read more books and went on the Internet; eventually I read Larry Edell's book *How to Make Your Living Playing Craps*. I subscribed to his newsletter *The*

Crapshooter and about two months later I received a letter from Larry about a course in rhythm rolling. I ordered the course that day and I was off on a journey that is still progressing.

"I received the material the first week of July 2000, read the manual, and started practicing about two hours a day. I was in contact with the program director, Long Arm [AKA Jerry Patterson], via e-mail and he offered to meet me in Atlantic City to see how I was doing. Needless to say, the first time he saw me throw, along with another novice, he completely changed everything I was doing. I had been practicing for two months and was going nowhere.

"I made some notes and went home and started all over. It was early November 2000 and I meet Long Arm again and he had another very experienced player with him, High Five. We played in Bally's, Wild Wild West, Trump Plaza, Resorts, and Caesars that day and I had the best rolls out of the three of us. I had increased my practice to at least three hours a day and it was paying off.

"I kept on practicing and attended two weekend classes for hands-on training, and eventually became an instructor and coach for the PARR program. I finally made it back to Las Vegas in the spring of 2001. I have been back to Las Vegas six times in the last two years. I now play at least eight times a month—once or twice weekly at Foxwoods in Connecticut, and I try to get to Atlantic City once a month. I still practice four to five days a week for a minimum of forty-five minutes a day, and I always carry a pair of dice with me. I love talking about the game and also educating people about how to play it. People have different hobbies; mine is craps. Do I win all the time? No. But do I win most of the time? You bet I do!" Mr. Finesse has become so expert that he now heads the Mohegan Mechanics, the winning group of Foxwoods regulars to which Bill Burton also belongs.

Sharpshooter had entered the room. There were about twenty-five students and about eight coaches, including Jerry Patterson. A young man, Tom Iraggi, better known as the Supersonic DJ (his business name), came up to me as I was heading for my seat. I had met him on one other occasion, at Bally's Park Place. Supersonic is a perfect name for him as he is high octane all the way. He said he was delighted to see me, and he handed me one of my books to autograph.

I sat down at my table and took out my notebook; John Robison sat down next to me and took out his notebook. Sharpshooter came down the aisle, stopped at my table, shook my hand, and said, "I'm really glad you could come."

"Me, too," I said.

Then Sharpshooter started the class. The material was somewhat daunting as Sharpshooter explained the physics behind dice control. After an hour or so, some in the audience started to become fidgety. By way of analogy, they had come to learn how to drive a car, not to learn the intricacies of the combustion engine. But Sharpshooter was thorough. He wanted his students to fully understand how dice control actually worked and the scientific underpinnings that, well, underpinned it! I was fascinated for several reasons. Naturally, it's always a joy to see serious players looking to get an edge over the casinos, but, more important, what Sharpshooter was explaining to these thirty sundry folks in attendance were the physical laws that the Captain had intuitively recognized when he played craps all those years. Sharpshooter was explaining and demonstrating just how the set, grip, and delivery of the dice could turn a random game into a nonrandom game that favors the player.

I was witnessing a vindication of everything the Captain had taught me, everything I had written about in my books, everything that I had experienced at the tables. I watched as Sharpshooter explained his "perfect pitch" delivery system—it was almost the exact same as the Captain's, and Sharpshooter had *never met* the Captain; he had analyzed the best possible ways to deliver the dice, and he had settled on the essentials of the technique that the Captain had been using since the late 1970s. I was giddy and overjoyed. I wished the Captain could have seen this, seen what he had started.

When Sharpshooter's initial talk was over, students went to the throwing stations, where they attempted, under the guidance of such coaches as Dominator, Mr. Finesse, Bill Burton, and Billy the Kid, to duplicate what Sharpshooter had demonstrated. I also decided to get some practice in, especially from stick left, not my favored position. Sharpshooter worked with me. Over the course of that weekend, I started to enjoy the benefits of SL shooting: closer to the back wall, a more natural pendulum-type throw that tended to be softer, etc. Other students and teachers gathered around as I took my instruction from Sharpshooter in SL shooting. The irony was not lost on me, or on the others. Sharpshooter, who had started his musings about beating craps by reading my books, Sharpshooter, the student, was now the teacher, and this old dog (that's me) learned a new trick that day. I added SL to my shooting repertoire and it is now my favored position.

That afternoon I gave my talk to the group. Essentially I talked about what I was feeling—how joyful I felt seeing such serious players, how happy I was to see the Captain's ideas vindicated. I also explained what I considered to be some of the pitfalls of controlled shooting—not the least of which was thinking that you could overcome really-big-house-edge bets because you had gained a small edge. The talk went well, as did the entire weekend.

That Monday morning I went to Bally's Wild Wild West to practice from SL. I was the only one at the table—it must have been 6 A.M. or so—and then Howard Newman, a craps player who had just taken the PARR class for the second time, joined me. I really didn't know Howard then, so I said hello, and he said hello. Since I had just sevened out, it was Howard's turn to shoot. Howard is a big guy, and left-handed, so he prefers to shoot from SR1.

Howard had been rhythmically rolling for about two years at this point. He's a natural and has one of the softest, smoothest throws I've ever seen. ("It comes from my years of pitching soft-pitch softball in Florida," he says.) Just about every time I've been at a table with him, he's made me money. He's been a consistent money-winner for himself as well, to the point that, he says, his wife has come to expect it. "When I go to the casino, my wife tells me what she wants to buy with the winnings. She has no idea that it is also possible to lose, that controlled shooting isn't a guarantee that I'm going to win each and every time I go to a casino. I'm almost afraid to go home should I ever lose and have to face her. 'Honey, I lost.' She'll break down."

But this day was my first shoot with big Howard—and his first roll lasted twenty minutes!

"Great, great!" I said when he finally sevened out. Howard gave me his big smile, one of the most infectious smiles I've ever seen, conveying sheer joy and true warmth. "Now it's your turn," he said.

So I rolled. I wish I could say I had a monster but I didn't. I hit my point once, made a few other numbers and sevened out.

"Okay, okay, that was okay. I made some money," said Howard.

Then he shot again. Another twenty minutes!

Howard has big but highly sensitive hands—and not just from softball. Howard is a neuromuscular physical therapist who owns his own practice in Tamarac, Florida, next to University Hospital. He employs two psychologists, a medical doctor, and three therapists. "I coordinate the patients and therapists and also see many patients. I help people who are suffering muscular, joint, and nerve pain. I like to help people." But that's not the end of the Howard Newman phenomenon, because he is also a world-class artist whose paintings have appeared in such galleries as S.E. Feinman Fine Arts in SoHo, New York, and La MaMa Galleria in the East Village, New York, and in other galleries throughout America. You can see Howard's paintings on his Web site *www.newmanfinearts.com.*

"I started as an impressionist painter without ever having taken a lesson. I saw myself in a vision, perhaps a reincarnation, as a child living in France during the 1860s. When I began painting, all of my paintings were impressionistic in nature."

As a young man, Howard got into the acting field ("I was always the big guy or bodyguard or the cop") and he went to France to film a commercial. "I saw the original impressionists' works and I felt extremely moved and tears came to my eyes. Funny thing, when I signed my paintings, I never felt comfortable signing 1975; I always wanted to write 1875."

But Howard did not stay an impressionist for his whole career; instead he "decided to develop a new style for this modern time." So he began to paint New York City street scenes. "I call them nostalgic New York. These are all scenes that remind me of my happy times growing up in New York City—Coney Island, Brooklyn street corners, parks and fields, candy stores, cars, and the like."

Howard also sees dice control as "an art form." He practices every day. And it shows!

After Howard's second twenty-minute roll, Jerry Patterson and Sharpshooter came to the table, followed by Mr. Finesse, Street Dog, and Ray. Now the whole table was
composed of PARR players. So what did we all do? We took
turns shooting from the SL and SR positions, a kind of Chinese fire drill. For example, when I finished my roll from SL,
Mr. Finesse slid into my place and I went to the end of the
table. This at first confused, then amused the Wild Wild
West pit crew and dealers but, as everyone was tipping generously and most shooters were having good to great rolls,
the pit seemed quite pleased to book our action and allow
our actions. We had also heated up the atmosphere at the
casino, since most of those playing loved to cheer and shout.
Considering it was now only 9 A.M., the sounds coming
from our table had "nighttime" high energy written all over
them.

I had a late breakfast with Patterson and Sharpshooter.
Although I did not get to interact with Patterson much during the actual weekend, he seemed nothing at all like what I
expected. Even though the "Pa Kettle" comment was accurate in terms of looks, Patterson seemed a pretty straightforward and very likeable character. I complimented him on the
PARR course and what he and Sharpshooter had accomplished. I also mentioned how impressed I was with the
coaches who worked with the new players.

"And they volunteer their time, Frank," Jerry said. "They
don't get paid. But they love hanging out with the guys and
they love to teach."

"They are a real help," Sharpshooter agreed.

After breakfast, the three of us went over to the Claridge
to play. While none of us had great rolls, we consistently

made enough points and other numbers to come away with a good profit from our post-breakfast play.

I parted from them around noon and headed back to Bally's, where I was staying, to get a quick nap before meeting with the Captain for an afternoon of play and an early dinner. The Captain was coming down just for the day, all alone, with no Crew members. I couldn't wait to tell him about the PARR class I had attended.

I met the Captain outside Bally's on the Boardwalk.

"Let's take a stroll," he said. "We'll go down to Taj, play a little. If we don't do anything there, we'll go to Resorts."

As we walked I told the Captain about PARR. He was interested in the shooting technique that Sharpshooter was teaching.

"It's similar to mine because there is probably a natural way to grip and deliver the dice that serious students of the game will tend to discover or, in my case, stumble upon. So the way Sharpshooter and I do it is probably the norm for dice throws and then there are variations of it, some very close to it, some further away."

"The Arm," I said. "She's about as far away as you could get."

"There's never been anyone like her," he laughed. "She's not a variation of anything."

I explained to him my newfound enjoyment of shooting from SL1, something I only used to do in the past if I didn't have any other choice. "I've been having pretty good rolls the past few days from stick left," I said.

I also shared with him some of the betting strategies that the PARR class had discussed. The Captain is not opposed to betting systems, as long as the bets are reasonable and based on a real assessment of a shooter's skill. Still, the Captain is a realist when it comes to most bets at craps.

"Do you think anyone can overcome those Crazy Crapper

bets?" he asked. (Crazy Crapper bets are the one-roll proposition bets and the Hardways, among others.)

"I doubt it," I said. "From what I saw of the better shooters, I'd say some are playing with 5 to 10 percent edges when they shoot, although I might be overstating this based on only a few observations. I could also be seeing what I want to see. But a lot of them seem to make bad bets when they shoot and when others shoot as well."

"You can lose your edge really quick playing those bets."

Outside the Taj Mahal on the Boardwalk are food stands and an amusement park that juts out on a pier into the ocean; this park is open in the late spring and summer. Today, there were several dozen people milling around outside the Taj, not including those who were walking or running on the Boardwalk. And there was this kid, maybe twelve years old, obviously not in school; he was flipping his cap onto his head, taking it off, and flipping it on again. He had a bandana on his head so the cap could just slide on when it landed. The cap would rise into the air a couple of feet over his head, and most times he was able to get it to land square on his head—without having to move his head to meet it. At other times, a gust of wind or a bad aim would cause him to have to run the cap down. At these times, he rarely got the cap to land on his head.

"A future dice controller," said the Captain. "You can see how intense he is practicing his art."

"Too bad he's not as concerned with what's inside his head as opposed to what's on top of it," I said.

As we passed him I couldn't resist asking, "Shouldn't you be in school?"

The kid looked at me as if I were from another planet. "Fuck school," he said, and flipped his cap right onto his head.

The Captain smiled. "He'd better hope when he grows up there are jobs for hat flippers."

Inside, the Taj was crowded with the weekday crowd. The Captain and I found one table with SR1 and SL2 positions open. The Captain took SR and I took my new, preferred SL position. We each shot twice at this table before deciding to go to Resorts. The Captain had two good rolls; I had two rotten ones. The rest of the table was a nightmare for a *5-Count* player. Most of the shooters would get past the 5-Count and then seven out on the 6-Count or 7-Count. So we were both down a little when the Captain said, "Resorts."

At Resorts the tables are small and we found one that was completely empty. This was a miracle, because Atlantic City in the daytime is usually packed with the bus crowd. The Captain indicated that I should roll first. I did. I established my point and then sevened out.

"How do you like my new expertise from stick left?" I asked.

"You look good; you'll start heating up. Don't sweat it."

The Captain picked up the dice and rolled for thirty minutes. Then I got the dice. Point. Seven out!

I looked at the boxman. "This is embarrassing," I said.

We were still the only ones at the table.

The Captain now shot for fifteen minutes.

I got the dice. Point. Seven out!

"Jesus," I said.

"Maybe you should let the old guy do all the shooting," said the boxman.

"Yeah, maybe," I said.

As the Captain took the dice, I couldn't resist asking the boxman, "What do you think of his throw?"

The boxman looked at me, paused as if thinking of how to answer, then just smiled and said, "He's beautiful. I've seen him before. He does this all the time."

• • • •

The Captain was in the rolling zone. He had another big roll, maybe twenty minutes.

The dice were now passed to me. "I think I'll pass," I said.

"Let's take a break," said the Captain.

So we walked back to Bally's.

"Do you think this course you saw can actually teach rhythmic rolling?" the Captain asked.

"Yes," I said. "I think they can teach it but I'm not sure how many people who actually take the course will master it. They throw a lot of stuff at the students, stuff I wouldn't bother with. I can see changes I would make in the teaching—much more hands-on, better organization—but even so, I don't know, it takes a lot of practice to really perfect this stuff. I don't know if everyone who takes the course will really get the hang of it. Some just won't work at it; others just won't have the physical aptitude. And it could get discouraging. If I didn't know any better, I might abandon attempting to roll from stick left just because I had such awful rolls this afternoon. But I've played enough to know that this afternoon is just a blip on the long run."

"I didn't realize that there were people out there teaching rhythmic rolling. And they've had how many students?" asked the Captain.

"About six hundred or so. See what you started?"

"Maybe this will revitalize craps; bring younger players to the game. For years Atlantic City has been a craps game dominated by old-timers," said the Captain.

At Bally's Wild Wild West I finally got some hot hands from SL and rolled for twenty minutes, ten minutes, and fifteen minutes. The Captain had several more good rolls as well, and when we ended the playing day we both had made a nice profit. We then went to dinner at Arturo's, a fine gourmet Italian restaurant.

At dinner we talked politics. When the meal was over, the Captain said, "Keep me informed about these classes and any new developments in craps. With so many of the old Crew gone, your information kind of revitalizes me."

10

The Las Vegas Craps Festival

AUGUST AND September 2002 were two very interesting months for me. I spent most of both months in Las Vegas, unfortunately without the beautiful AP, who was recovering from her latest flare-up of ulcerative colitis.

August was a trip to really test out my newfound skill from stick left and to play the best blackjack games I could find. It was a *gambling* trip, reminiscent of those old "tuition runs" AP and I used to make when the kids were in school. Instead of getting comped to my rooms and going the high-roller route, I booked my own rooms in five different hotels and stayed four days in each. I paid for all my meals; I never handed in a player's card. I wanted no pressure to give any casino any given amount of action. I was anonymous. I was alone. It was the games and I.

Playing in Vegas this way is the closest thing I know to being a kid again. A kid plans his day around the games he'll be playing. These games are the be-all and end-all of a kid's existence; at least, they were when I was a kid. Well, being in Vegas, alone and anonymous, with only one thing in mind—winning money at gambling—is a rejuvenating experience. I didn't contact any of my friends who live in Vegas, or any other friends. I wanted these few weeks to be me against the house, nothing else. The only downside, a big one, to the whole experience would be not having the beautiful AP with me.

The August trip was characterized by hitting and running; I'd go to Casino Royale in the early morning, play their 100X odds game (I had one session in which I started with $1 on the Pass Line, backed it with $10 in odds, went up on two other numbers, backed them with $10 in odds, and, by the time I was finished with my roll, I had all six numbers working with $1 and $100 in odds!), then when the table filled up, as it inevitably did by mid-morning, moving on to other Strip properties such as Treasure Island, Venetian, Belaggio, Bally's, Flamingo, MGM, Mandalay Bay, and Caesars. I always looked to be the only one at the table, or, at the very least, one of only a few players. When craps conditions became too crowded and I couldn't get my spots at SL or SR, I played double-deck blackjack.

I actually prefer to play craps at a table with one other person. This way, after I roll, I get a rest. I find that, when I am the only one at the table for an extended time, I sometimes press a little too much. If I am not doing well, I tend to stay just a little too long, thinking that things will turn around. However, like a pitcher in baseball, who only pitches one-half of an inning and then gets to rest while his team is at bat, when I am with another player, be he a controlled shooter or not, that little rest sets my mind at ease, and gets me mentally ready to roll again.

On that trip, the craps crews were friendly and professional, with a few exceptions. I had only one very bad day, which had nothing to do with losing money; in fact, the worst day I had during my August trip was a winning day economically—but emotionally it was a downer. Here's what happened.

I played my usual early-morning session at Casino Royale but didn't really do much. I was behind a few dollars, the table got crowded, and I left. When you are playing at a table with twelve to fourteen people, you only get to shoot the dice once an hour, at best. That's a lot of standing around, trying to avoid the nonrandom rollers, until your turn to take the dice. So around eight-thirty I decided to go over to Bellagio, which is rarely crowded in the mornings.

This day was no exception. There were a few craps tables open, one with four players, the other with three players, and one with no players. I went to the one with no players. I bought in for a couple of hundred. When I'm being comped, I buy in for $2,000 to $4,000, mostly to get the attention of the floorperson, who will note the buy-in on my rating card. But when I'm playing A&A (alone and anonymous) I buy in for no more than $500.

The boxman counted out my money and told the dealer what to give me; the dealer counted out my chips and slid them over to me (but he didn't say, "Good luck, sir," which is a standard welcome at craps games, but it wasn't until later that I realized this), and I was off to the races . . . or so I thought.

I put down a $15 Pass Line bet, set the dice in my 3-V, and rolled. I established a point of four, put down $45 in odds (Bellagio had 3X, 4X and 5X odds); placed the six and eight for $60 each, then came right back and made the point. On the next come-out I put up a bet for the dealers, $6 on top of my six and $6 on top of my eight. By putting the dealer's bets *on top* of my bets, I controlled the bet, so that, if one or the other hit, the dealers could stay on the number instead of having to take it down with their winnings. If you have a hot streak with the dealers riding on top, they can make some nice money.

Strangely, no dealer thanked me for putting up the tip. Again, it is only in retrospect that I remember that. When I'm playing, such information is recorded but my mind is really focused on the task at hand: making the perfect throw.

I rolled for five minutes, made a point, hit a bunch of numbers, and then one of my dice failed to hit the back wall. The floorperson stormed over. "Listen, you miss the back wall one more time and we're taking the dice away from you. You got that, buddy?"

I was a little taken aback. Usually if one die fails to hit the back wall for the first time, the most a boxman might say is "Don't forget to hit the back wall." Usually, they don't caution you until you've missed the back wall a few times. I'd never had anyone react so violently to one die missing the wall the *first* time. Perhaps the floorperson saw how carefully I rolled and was worried that I had control over the dice.

Of course, if he had had any common sense or knowledge of the game, he would have realized that he had no reason to complain. If a controlled shooter intends to hit the back wall with both dice and one die doesn't do so, the roll is off—in short, when a controlled shooter misses the back wall, he's just had a *random* roll! No controlled shooter will consistently try to miss the back wall with just one die, because no controlled shooter can control both dice separately, one doing one thing, one doing another thing. Even Tony Lee's "trick shot" requires both dice to do the exact same thing.

"Sorry," I said. "Didn't do that intentionally."

I then rolled for another forty minutes. By the time I was done, the table was crowded with cheering players. I had placed a Hard 6 bet for the dealers and had hit it three times in a row! No thank-yous from them for that, either, or for any of the bets that I made and won for them.

I never missed the back wall after that, but once or twice the floorperson growled, "That *almost* missed the back wall."

The other players were acutely aware of the ill manners of this crew—and it was the whole crew, not just a given dealer or floorperson, who were nasty. When I finally sevened out, I took my chips and headed over to the cage. Several of the other players joined me.

"Great roll," one said.

"What was with that crew?" another asked.

"They had some bug up their ass," said a third.

"I have no idea," I said. "They were like that from the minute I came to the table. Maybe they had a bad night."

"Well, they certainly had a bad morning," laughed the first guy, holding up his stack of purple chips. "A real bad morning."

I never before had such an ungracious crew at Bellagio or any other casino where I've played. Sometimes you get one dealer who might be a prune, but usually the rest of the crew is fine. One thing I find is that a nice crew makes the game a pleasant experience, even if the game itself isn't going your way. Professionalism in dealers, which means not just the ability to accurately pay off bets but also the ability to relate to people, can be the difference between players developing a loyalty to a property and players avoiding the property. As I write this, my favorite places to play craps are Treasure Island in Vegas, Horseshoe in Tunica, and Claridge/Bally's/ Wild Wild West (these are all a part of one casino complex) in Atlantic City. I have found that the crews and pit personnel in these casinos just have the knack for cultivating a great gaming environment. Of course, this could change over the years as dealers and floor personnel switch jobs and are replaced, but I'm hoping it won't.

The reverse happened at Casino Royale. A few years back, I found the crews obnoxious and annoying and thoroughly unprofessional. Now they are great.

It is conceivable that the Bellagio crew I ran into that August morning had just had a bad night; still, that floorperson storming the table at the first miss of one die, and those dealers never acknowledging the hundreds of dollars in tips I gave them, leads me to conclude that this crew was just a barrel of bad apples.

In the afternoon, I decided to play blackjack at Mirage. They had one of the best double-deck games in the city that summer. Again, I was not giving in my card, and I was playing for relatively low stakes strictly according to the count, spreading from $25 on one hand to $100 on two hands. Of course, I didn't start with $25 on one hand, but varied how the bets were made. I might open with two hands of $50 or $75, then go up or down with the count. I was the smallest player at the table, bet-wise. I didn't think Mirage would even look at my action, as my expectation was not all that great. I figured mixing the bets up and being the low man on the betting totem poll at the table would make me invisible.

Boy, was I wrong. I had played for a half-hour and was down a couple hundred dollars, when I got *the tap* on my shoulder. I knew immediately what it was, because I have had this happen before. The tap is the beginning of a ritual with which many expert blackjack players have become quite familiar.

The man in the gray suit was standing there (why is it always gray suits?). "Can I speak to you away from the table for a moment, sir?"

I got up and walked over to the slot machines with him.

"We've been analyzing your play and we have come to the

conclusion that you are too strong for us. You can't play blackjack here, but you are free to play anything else."

When had they been analyzing my play? I never noticed the floorperson or pit boss looking at the game any more than casually. I never saw any phone calls to the eye in the sky. Those are the typical tip-offs that you are garnering suspicion, and they are also the signal to get the heck out of the casino. So how had they determined I was such a strong player? Probably some computer analyzing everyone's play had picked up on me, especially my insurance decisions, which had been working to perfection that session. I *hate* computers.

"Okay," I said, "I'm leaving." I went over to the table and took my chips.

In Vegas, it is no use arguing when they ask you to stop playing. It is no use explaining to them that your expectation is thus and such and that if they really look at the damage you can do, compared to the amount all your friends are losing at the other games, and blah, blah, blah. . . . It's just best to pick up your chips and leave.

Of course, emotionally it isn't an easy thing to be "asked" to stop playing blackjack or to leave the casino. After all, I'm a taxpaying American citizen playing in an American casino. I'm using my brains; I'm not cheating. I play by the rules established by the casino (except I don't agree with their "rule" that if you know how to play you aren't allowed to play). Think about it this way: I could be a war hero, a fireman who risked his life at the World Trade Center, or a cop who would put his life on the line for the family of this very casino executive, and it would make no difference. I would be "asked" to leave. Whereas a criminal or a terrorist would be allowed to play, as long as he didn't know what he was doing! I have never gotten used to the idea that American casinos can tell knowledgeable players that they can't play.

It's tantamount to advertising an all-you-can-eat buffet, then telling hearty eaters that they're "too strong" for your restaurant, and serving only anorexics.

The Bellagio crew set the tone of the day; the Mirage incident capped it. Despite the fact that I was ahead for the day, my emotions were roiled. I decided to take a break and go see the shark exhibit at Mandalay Bay.

If you have a love for fish—in tanks, that is—this is a great exhibit. Not only does it have sharks in abundance, some of them fearsome-looking, but they have all sorts of turtles and tropical fish as well. It's a relaxing environment and you can hang out there as long as you like. The shark exhibit allows you to feel as if you are right in the tank; the water is on the right and left, and below and above you. Those creatures swim all around you, yet you are safe. My kind of deep-sea diving!

I spent about an hour and a half there and it calmed me down. Then I decided to play a little craps in the casino, if I could find one of my spots open. I found a table with five guys and with an SR position open, so I bought in for $200 and played the *5-Count* until it was my turn to shoot. I was down about $40 when I got the dice. I placed the six and eight for $30 each and put $10 on the Pass Line. I established my point, a six, told the dealers to buy the four for $25, and put the remaining $5 of my previous Place 6 bet on the Hard 6 for the dealers. I put $50 behind my Pass Line in odds. I then went on to make about five points and many numbers, and the funny thing was I had a kind of split consciousness while all this was going on. I kept thinking how pleasant it was playing with a Mandalay Bay crew that was cordial compared to that morning crew at Bellagio, and all the time I was thinking this, my body was on automatic pilot, the dice landing perfectly. When the roll was over, the guys at the table applauded. "Good roll," said the boxman.

I colored up. "Thanks for the bets," said the dealers. "Good luck, sir."

As I headed for the cage, I planned my next day. I would skip blackjack and head downtown to play craps at various casinos, starting with the Golden Nugget. I was done for today; I'd go back to my room, call AP, and fill her in on the day's happenings.

I didn't play any more blackjack that August. Mirage had soured me. Besides, I was having a very good trip just playing craps. Why put a strain on myself worrying about taps on the shoulder and reminders that I'm not welcome?

I went home for the last week of August 2002, wrote some articles that were on deadline, then headed back to Vegas in September. This was more of an informational trip than a gambling trip. I was going to attend the Global Gaming Expo at the Convention Center and then be the keynote speaker at the Las Vegas Craps Festival, an event organized by Jerry Patterson and featuring some of the big names in the craps-playing community, including Dominator; Sharpshooter, whose new book *Get the Edge at Craps* had just been published; Mr. Finesse; Larry Edell, publisher of the *Crapshooter* newsletter; Bill Burton, casino guide for About.com; and Internet gurus Thom "Irishsetter" Morgan and Steve "Heavy" Haltom. In addition, there would be 170 craps players attending, many of them dice controllers or, at the very least, would-be dice controllers.

The Global Gaming Expo (called G2E) is a yearly industry convention that brings together casinos and casino-affiliated businesses, slot manufacturers, security companies, and new-game developers. It's held every September or October and there are seminars on a host of topics, from food service to player relations to security concerns, given by the experts in those fields, as well as an exhibit hall in which hundreds of casinos, manufacturers, suppliers, game developers, magazine publishers, and slot companies all vie for the attention and dollars of the casino executives in attendance. It is one huge event, for sure, with something for everyone.

For me it was a chance to see the new slot and video poker machines, the new table games, and my old friends in the gambling-writing field. I also looked forward to attending seminars about the new security procedures for catching "cheaters and advantage players"—the dishonest and honest lumped together as a "threat"—as this information would make for good articles.

The Expo did not disappoint. The exhibit hall was an *Alice in Wonderland* landscape of booths and machines and games. You got the opportunity to play tic-tac-toe against a chicken ("The Chicken Challenge"), to have your picture taken with Butterbean, the oversized heavyweight boxer, and to look at hundreds of showgirls with their big bright smiles, scrubbed faces, and self-conscious eyes hawking this or that product or casino service. I played several new versions of blackjack, craps, and stud poker—all of them, unfortunately, with very high house edges and/or fast speeds.

I also attended some very interesting security seminars. In one, an expert explained the various methods used to cheat the casinos. He showed actual eye-in-the-sky shots of dealers shoveling chips up their sleeves, dealers in collusion with players and either making false payoffs or stacking the decks so their accomplices could get the best hands. In fact, crooked dealers do most of the casino cheating. Petty theft is often against casino patrons—purse snatchings, bucket hijackings, pick pocketing, and the like—but the big scams usually have some element of insider activity, and they are invariably against the casino.

Just about everyone at the security seminars was in security and even though I was wearing a green name tag, the color of press credentials, most of the security people who spoke to me thought I was in security too. I never disabused them of that notion.

I asked one fellow from a Canadian casino if he had had any trouble with dealers stealing.

"No," he said. "We've had problems with advantage players."

"Really?"

"Oh, yeah, just the other night I booted a guy who was spreading from $10 to $100 on our shoe according to the count."

"Did you analyze what kind of edge he had? Usually one to ten isn't enough to get an edge at a six-deck game."

"What is?"

"He'd need to have at least a one to twelve spread. Double the number of decks as a baseline is about right. Did this guy have any friends with him in the casino when you asked him to leave?"

"His wife."

"What did she play?"

"Quarter slots," he said. I could see he was beginning to be uncomfortable. I think he thought I was some kind of big-shot Las Vegas security analyst.

"Well, between her and him," I said, "your casino probably had a nice-sized edge."

"You would have let him play?"

"Oh, yeah," I said. "I wouldn't have sweated it at all."

"But he knew how to count," he said.

"He wasn't betting quite enough and his wife was more than helping you guys maintain an edge over them as a couple."

"What's your philosophy?"

"Well, I see how big a threat the guy is in real dollar terms. Then I analyze if he comes to the casino with a spouse or girlfriend or other friends, what games they play—these people travel as groups, you know, and if you kick out one the others usually go too—and then I take other things into consideration. Like, oh, what if the guy is a famous writer or something [I figured I might as well help myself if I ever went to this casino]; it might be worth it to let him play if the publicity he gave my casino was positive. I wouldn't want to alienate the guy and have him write something negative about my casino in a book or article. I mean, there are so many things to analyze before you take the big step and bounce a guy."

"You've given me a lot to think about," he said.

Good, I thought. One for us!

At another seminar I learned that fifty-three million American citizens went to casinos in the year 2001 for a total of almost 350 million visits. From the Griffin detective agency I discovered that of these fifty-three million American casinogoers, only eleven hundred are skilled blackjack players. That means for every 530,000 players *only 11* have the skill to beat the casinos at their own game! If you throw in maybe a couple hundred dice controllers (if there are that many) into the mix you might find that 13 out of 530,000 players have the ability to beat the house. So what the hell are the casinos worried about? A couple hundred cheating dealers can take millions from the casinos over extended periods of time. That was theft. That was something to be concerned about. The other concern, fearing advantage players using their skills, was child's stuff, like the bogeyman under the bed or the monster in the closet. It was more a fantasy threat than an actual one.

On September 17 and 18, after the party for gaming writers at the Palms Casino Hotel, Beau and I had our epic roll at Treasure Island, described in chapter 1. That Friday, September 20, I attended the Las Vegas Craps Festival at the Mardi Gras hotel on Paradise Road, just a quarter mile south of the Las Vegas Hilton. Now, this place was an off-Strip motel with some slot machines and one meeting room. The room was packed with players; it was standing room only. There were some 170 paid attendees and about thirty coaches and teachers, including the day's speakers: Sharpshooter, Heavy, Larry Edell, Irishsetter, and me. A table had been set up near the speaker's podium to record the talks for later sale as audiocassette tapes.

Each speaker was given forty-five to sixty minutes, their talks to be followed by hands-on instruction in dice control under the tutelage of such dice greats as Dominator, Mr. Finesse, Bill Burton, Street Dog, Billy the Kid, and Howard "Rock 'n' Roller" Newman. Jerry Patterson was the master of ceremonies, and he kept the day rolling along on schedule.

Steve "Heavy" Haltom was the first speaker up. He was funny and bright, and offered amusing stories of his trip to Vegas and his playing sessions. He's a naturally gifted speaker, and the audience enjoyed every minute of his talk. As I write this, I still have not gotten the opportunity to see him roll the dice, so I have no idea of his skill level. But I do know that he has a large and loyal following, mostly people who read his posts on dice Web sites.

Sharpshooter was next up. He discussed the physics and mechanics of dice control. As an engineer, Sharpshooter is schooled in the sciences, and his lectures show this. He is acutely aware of the physical dynamics of dice control and also of the types of betting schemes that are best to utilize depending on one's throwing ability. As one of the premier dice controllers in the world, Sharpshooter not only practices what he preaches but also has perfected it. Having played with him on many occasions I can tell you—the guy is the real deal!

Thom "Irishsetter" Morgan followed Sharpshooter. Irishsetter has strong opinions. I noted right away that there seemed to be some strain between Irishsetter and Patterson. Irishsetter's talk revolved around the fact that there was so much free information on the Web that it wasn't mandatory to have hands-on instruction from dice coaches or to take classes such as PARR (although he never mentioned PARR by name). In fact, Irishsetter made a strong pitch that people shouldn't be paying or charging to learn dice control, that all the information should be free. Patterson seemed slightly uncomfortable during Irishsetter's talk, but he didn't show his annoyance, if annoyance he was feeling, when Irishsetter finished up. Patterson clapped along with everyone else.

The fourth speaker was Larry Edell, author of several books on craps, and the publisher of the popular *Crapshooter* newsletter. Larry's talk centered on how to maximize comps for your play, how to discover whether a casino comped for just Line bets or whether they also factored in odds, and whether they counted spread or just single bets.

Then it was my turn to give the keynote address. As I stood before almost two hundred people in the convention room, I knew that this was what I wanted to do—I wanted to talk about craps, about the Captain, about styles of play, and about adventure to players who wanted to listen, who wanted to learn, who wanted to win, who wanted to have adventures, too. My talk was well received (oh, to hell with humility—it was great!).

After my talk, Howard "Rock 'n' Roller" Newman, Bill Burton, and I went over to Treasure Island. Although I was paying my own way at Flamingo Hilton I decided I wanted to get some time in at Treasure Island's superior tables. We played for about an hour, with both Howard and Bill having consistently good rolls, and with me just barely breaking even on my rolls, when the pit boss, Stephen Brascia, came over to say hello and to thank me for writing in a recent article that Treasure Island was the number-one casino to play craps in Las Vegas. He arranged a comped dinner in their steakhouse for the three of us.

After dinner, I started to heat up and have good rolls. Howard, who is very big into nostalgia, described our session this way: "We were like Mantle and Maris, one of us on the stickman's left, one on the stickman's right. And we were hitting back-to-back home runs!"

11

The Lee Brothers II

AFTER MY sessions with Howard and Bill, it was time to call the Lee brothers at their hotel. They were staying at MGM but playing mostly at the downtown and off-Strip casinos this trip.

"We are giving only three Strip casinos a look," said Tony. "Bellagio, Paris, and Bally's. We are playing very early in the morning."

By early he meant 4 A.M., when the tables started to clear. I had a choice. I could stay up late and try to join them or I could go to bed and try to get up to meet them.

"Where will you be at 4 A.M.?"

"Paris," said Tony.

"See you then," I said. It was around eleven o'clock. If I went right to bed I could get four hours of sleep, shower, and be ready to play with the inimitable Lees. I put in an alarm call for 3 A.M. and went to sleep.

My adrenaline was pumping and it took me time to fall into a slumber. I was charged up in anticipation of playing with the Lees and in remembering the fun I had had talking at the Craps Festival that afternoon.

After showering, I dressed, ate a banana, and then walked the Strip from Flamingo to Paris. At 4 A.M., the Strip still has loads of people walking or, rather, staggering around. The younger casino patrons, often loud and intent on showing everyone within earshot what a great time they are having in Party Central, U.S.A., dominate the early-morning crowds. As I walked past the Barbary Coast to get to the overpass escalators that would allow me to cross Flamingo Road without becoming roadkill, a young lady got in my way.

"Hi," she said. "Want a blow job?"

"Huh, are you talking to me?" I asked.

"Yeah, honey, do you want . . .?"

"No, no, thanks." I tried to walk by her.

"No charge," she said, blocking my way.

"No."

"What are you, gay?" she said.

"I love my wife and you, young lady, should be doing something more productive with your time."

Like playing craps, I thought to myself.

She looked at me askance as I strolled around her and headed toward the escalator. Evidently she was drunk or high on something. Then she propositioned the next middle-aged guy who walked past her. For all I knew, she might be setting up people for a drug and mug. Drug and mugs go something like this: A pretty young woman approaches a middle-aged or older man who looks as if he has some money and invites him to have sex with her. They go to his hotel room, where she orders drinks and, when the older gentleman goes to the bathroom, she pours one of several knockout drugs in his drink. He comes back, sips his drink, and wham!—down for the count. The young lady then lifts his wallet and jewelry and anything else of value, and off she goes into the Las Vegas night looking for another guy who feels flattered by her attentions.

When I arrived at Paris, there was still a crowd at the tables. The Lees were just standing around, waiting for their spots to open.

"Hey," I said.

"Hey, the man is here," said Tony.

"What happened to your eye? And your cheek?" Tony had a slight shiner and a small scratch on his cheek.

"Vixen in love with him," laughed Larry.

"Really?"

"She . . . he had a little too much to drink and . . ." started Tony.

"He fight her off," said Larry.

"She doesn't look it but she is strong," said Tony.

"I helped or he be raped," said Larry.

"She's not with you guys anymore?" I asked.

"No, no, they kiss and make up," said Larry.

"We didn't *kiss* and make up. We shook hands. You know, things got a little out of hand. We've been traveling together for a very long time."

"He irresistible," said Larry.

Just then an entire table suddenly became available. This happens every so often. A table is crowded; there are a few awful rolls and people flee. Larry immediately took SR1, Tony SL1, and I took SL2. A moment later Vixen arrived, smiling, and cashed in for $100. She stood next to me. I took a quick look at her face. She had a slight shiner under her eye as well. Then Lola appeared and stood next to Larry. The only one missing was Whale.

"He's making a movie," said Tony after I whispered, "Where is he?" to him. "I think it's called *Saving Ryan's Privates*." Tony laughed at his own joke.

. . . .

Then the game began.

And we got killed. It was a rare performance by the Lees, a rare *awful* performance. I did much better, which is to say that I made money on my rolls, but none were extraordinary. I started the session by going right up on the Lees, but they sevened out early so many times that I started to use the *5-Count* on them. It helped, but only a little. We ended the session at 6 A.M. I was down some money but happy as always to watch such a skillful team in action.

The Lees decided to take a break and go back downtown around 10 A.M. The fatigue of the week was beginning to get to me. Between the G2E events, the party at the Palms, the seven-hour session at Treasure Island, my talk at the Craps Festival, and my continuous play, I was worn out. I told the Lees that I wasn't going to hook up with them downtown that day. I was bushed.

I wanted to get home to the beautiful AP and resume a somewhat more normal life.

It's funny, but when I'm in Vegas I usually think, "I don't ever want to leave this place," but sometime toward the end of my trip I begin to get homesick and also tired of my gambling high-wire act.

Speaking to an assemblage of savvy, competent craps players had gotten my blood pumping with excitement, and then playing with the redoubtable Lee brothers that weekend had my blood roaring. Playing as I had been for almost two straight months, I was hot, I was on; my throw was just about as good as I've ever seen it. Practice makes perfect and playing daily makes perfecter!

But it was time to go home.

12

Positive Thinking and
Negative Results

WHEN I returned to New York, I had a lot of mail, articles, and book editing to catch up on. I was scheduled to give a couple of talks, one at a bookstore in New Jersey, not far from Jerry Patterson's home.

Jerry said that he had an idea he wanted to run by me, and suggested we get together for dinner. I wondered if he was thinking of bringing me into PARR, perhaps as a partner. I had done two events with Jerry, the PARR class in May and the Las Vegas Craps Festival, and both went extremely well. Jerry had mentioned several times in my presence that he was ready to retire from the gaming business. Maybe he wanted me to take his place in PARR?

Patterson's other systems might be controversial, but PARR wasn't. It was the real deal, as was Sharpshooter, who taught the course. Although I realized that many PARR students would never get the edge at craps, mainly due to their own lack of practice, poor concentration, or physical ineptness, I also knew that I had seen some pretty awesome displays of controlled shooting on the part of several former PARR students, now coaches in PARR: Dominator, Mr. Finesse, Billy the Kid, Bill Burton, and Howard Newman, among others.

I'm no stoic, so I told the beautiful AP what I was thinking and hoping.

"Do you really want to get involved in business arrangements with him?" she asked. "Will you have the time with all your books and writing?"

She had a point there. I had just signed a contract with Bonus Books for three books (this one is the second), and I had several more books coming out under my Scoblete Get-the-Edge Guide imprint. Did I have the time?

"Besides," said AP, "why would he want to bring you in as a partner? He seems to be doing just fine without you."

"My name?" I said.

AP looked at me with *that* look, which meant, do you really believe what you're saying?

"I didn't say I thought I was a big name, but some people think I am."

Which is true. I've never been all that sure just how big a name I am, how much of a draw I am. I've done seminars and book talks where it was standing room only. I've spoken before audiences of five hundred to fifteen hundred people. Those talks have made me puff up with pride. But I've also arrived at bookstores for book signings and had only a handful of people wander over to talk to me. I did one book signing where only one poor soul showed up and he came over "because I didn't want you to feel bad that no one wanted to attend your book signing." Whatever hubris might have ballooned in me over the standing-room-only crowds was quickly deflated when I experienced someone taking pity on me. I once was in a bookstore and offered to autograph one of my books for a patron. He looked at me deadpan and said: "No. You'll ruin the book that way."

"Okay, so maybe Patterson doesn't want me for my big name," I said to AP.

But I still had some hope, because "hope is the thing with feathers," to quote Emily Dickinson; hope is lightweight and easy to carry with you.

So I drove out that day to Jersey to give a book signing/talk, but first I had dinner with Jerry Patterson. After some chitchat about the Las Vegas Craps Festival and how we should make that an annual event, Jerry said, "The reason I wanted to talk to you is, have you ever thought of getting into the business end of this?"

"Yes," I said, "I have."

"You have a big name [oh, stroke my ego, baby!] and you probably can do quite well. You have a pretty extensive mailing list from Paone Press?"

"Yes, about five thousand names and another twenty-five hundred who used to subscribe to my magazine." Paone Press is the mail-order publishing company owned by my wife, and the magazine I was referring to was *Chance and Circumstance*, which is no longer being published.

"Here's what I'm thinking," said Patterson. "Sharp-shooter, you, and I become partners. I'm thinking a third, a third, a third for each of us. We mail to your list, use your contacts as well, and publicize the PARR home-study course and the seminars. We could do a Tunica seminar where you have your radio show."

He did want to make me a partner!

"Well, it isn't my radio show. It's Rudi Schiffer's show. Tunica would be interesting and I'm sure Rudi would get behind us 100 percent; he's a great guy. It's a big slot town; about 90 percent of the players play the machines. But I think we could promote a craps festival and a PARR class down there. I could take some ads out in the papers that I write for in the South. We might be able to pull it all off."

"All right. I'll go home and write up a proposal for you to look over, and I'll send it to you."

"Great," I said.

"I think this will work out for all of us," said Patterson.

"You know, I have some ideas for making PARR even better—not that it isn't great already, but I think I can improve on it, make it tighter, without so much wasted time. Also more focused. Also address some things that haven't been addressed, like how to play when others are shooting."

"Great," said Patterson.

When I was finished with dinner and parted from Patterson, I immediately called AP.

"He wants to make me an equal partner with him and Sharpshooter," I said. "He figures I have a big name. We split everything a third, a third, a third."

I was riding high until I got to the bookstore and discovered that they were only displaying one of my books, *Guerrilla Gambling,* and not all fourteen. I was to give a little talk at 7:30. It was now 7:20 and three people were present, a husband, wife, and their preteen son. I had brought one hundred copies of *The New Gambling Times* magazine to give out to those who attended, plus a list of all my books and publications, in case people were interested in reading my articles or subscribing to the magazines for which I write.

By 7:30 I had exactly twelve people present and I gave my talk. I learned many years ago when I was an actor that it doesn't matter how many people are in an audience; you give it your all because the audience has come to see you and deserves your best. I spoke for about an hour and fifteen minutes on all aspects of casino gambling—how the house gets its edge, what strategies to use at various games, how to manage your money—essentially all the material that they could find in much greater detail in *Guerrilla Gambling*.

But, even with the small turnout, I was still feeling great. The thought of being involved in the teaching aspect of controlled shooting had me on fire. I knew exactly what changes I wanted to see in PARR. I knew I could make it the best dice-control course on the planet. Actually, it probably was already the best course on the planet, but I still could see plenty of things to improve, and I couldn't wait to get started. I outlined what I considered to be a more efficient and powerful method of teaching the physical and mental aspects of the game. I looked at the amount of time PARR was spending on information and activities that did not really advance a student's learning of the dice-control technique. I even started to write a complete curriculum for the course.

A couple of days later, while I was fleshing out the curriculum, Jerry sent me an e-mail outlining our agreement. He had changed the percentages to give me 25 percent, Sharpshooter 25 percent, himself 25 percent, and JPE, Inc., his business, 25 percent. His reasoning was that JPE would be doing all the booking, organizing, and selling of the course (the "dog work," as I called it), and it should therefore get an equal percentage. It didn't seem an unreasonable request, so I went along with it.

One other thing struck me, and that was a paragraph that described the nature of our business relationship. It was strictly to market his PARR home-study course and seminars to my mailing list. There was no mention of me being an actual partner in the whole PARR setup. I was just being asked to market PARR to my mailing list and to help set up a big Tunica festival. I should have realized this when Patterson talked about my mailing list at dinner, but I was blinded by my own desire to be a part of an organization that would take what were essentially all the methods the Captain discussed and teach the world. How grandiose my dreams! How big my ego! Mr. Big Name, indeed.

Pop went the overweening pride. I was back on planet Earth.

Of course, why would Patterson want me to have one-third or even one-quarter of his PARR classes? He was a businessman and he had a very successful thing going. Why bring in another partner? Why change anything?

When I settled down from my disappointment, I asked myself a very simple question: "Would people who bought books and tapes from Paone Press benefit by taking PARR?" The answer was obvious: yes. So I agreed to the deal with Patterson.

As I did so, I recalled Chip writing about "deals with the devil." That, of course, had been long before I made any deal or thought of any deal. Could Chip be psychic? Was Patterson the devil? No. He was just an astute businessman. In fact, despite my disappointment over our agreement, I still happened to like the man. After all, it was I who had misunderstood the nature of the offer he was tending. He wasn't responsible for that. I was.

A few weeks later, I had dinner with Jerry Patterson and his wife Nancy at Arturo's at Bally's Park Place. That night I was to be in my first baccarat tournament and, after the tournament, I was supposed to hook up with the Lee brothers at Wild Wild West casino.

It was about a half-hour before dinner when Jerry and his wife Nancy saw me at the craps table. I had been rolling for a few minutes. There was no space at my table so Jerry went to a table just across from me. Jerry Patterson doesn't just sell the PARR course; he does play craps himself, and the times I have played with him I've made money from his rolls. He uses what is called a "suitcase roll." Instead of setting the dice parallel to the back wall, he sets them at a ninety-degree angle to the wall, one die behind the other. His delivery looks as if he's bowling the dice down the felt. The idea behind the suitcase roll is to freeze the first die with the second die against the back wall, thereby limiting its possible movements.

With Patterson occasionally glancing over at me, I rolled for twenty minutes on that occasion and just about all my decisions were numbers. When I sevened out, I had a rack full of chips and it was time for dinner.

If Jerry Patterson was Pa Kettle, Nancy Patterson was anything but Ma Kettle. In fact, Nancy was more tuned in to the psychic hotline than the *Farmer's Almanac*. During dinner Nancy discussed her psychic "healing" vocation and her communion with spirits and ghosts. Jerry was not the least bit skeptical or condescending toward his wife's claims; in fact, he called her "gifted" time and again. Nancy also did remote healing and past life regressions.

When it comes to psychic phenomena I am on the fence, although I tend to lean toward the side that claims to have made inroads into the great unknowns of life. This leaning is from predilection, upbringing, desire, and hope, and from many unexplained, downright weird occurrences in my own life. However, I am not gullible and I have studied stage magic, so I know when a "psychic" is actually using classic magicians' tricks in his or her conjuring.

One of my best friends is like that kid in *Sixth Sense*. He "sees ghosts"; in fact, he helps ghosts to realize they are dead and to move on. I do not dispute him in this—hell, maybe he does just what he says he does. He, too, has been involved in some remarkable occurrences. I have another friend who doesn't believe in anything other than chance, the big bang, and oblivion after death. I can understand the reasoning behind each of my friends' positions. If you see dead people, you are going to believe in the afterlife, even if those dead people might be, as my second friend says, "manifestations of a slight schizophrenia." If you don't see dead people, if you've never had a truly weird occurrence in your life, then everything is what it appears to be—pretty much mundane, mechanical, and deterministic.

So Nancy Patterson was a psychic healer. Good. My left shoulder had been killing me for several months now, from either tendinitis or some kind of rotator cuff problem, and I told her that I could use her powers. She offered to help me right after dinner, before my baccarat tournament.

After polishing off two bottles of Pouilly Fuisse, Jerry, Nancy, and I headed for my room. Some of the most incredible views of ocean and city can be found at Bally's Park Place. I happened to have a wraparound corner room, so I had a full view of the ocean and an almost equally good view of the city and many of the other casinos. Jerry took in the sights, while Nancy had me standing up straight and closing my eyes. I could hear her rubbing her fingers together and then feel her lightly touching my shoulder. She did this for about five minutes and then said, "Open your eyes and see how you feel."

I opened my eyes. I raised my arm. Even though I couldn't get my arm all the way up in the air, I was raising it more than I had previously. Either Nancy Patterson had the power of healing, or the placebo effect was in full force that night. Or the wine was acting as an anesthetic.

"Much better," I said. Nancy seemed pleased. It could have been that I was trying to please her; after all, she was a sincere woman who was trying to help me. Then again, damned if my shoulder didn't feel at least 50 percent better. Placebo or psychic healing or wine—you choose.

Nancy gave me some parting advice about my upcoming

baccarat tournament. "Don't think, 'I hope I win it.' Don't think, 'I will win it.' Say to yourself, 'I am winning it.'" I said my goodbyes to the Pattersons and was off to the convention rooms for the tournament.

I am winning it. I am winning it. I am winning it.

I was one of three hundred players invited to participate in the Bally's $40,000 Invitational Baccarat (pronounced *bah-cah-rah*) Tournament, which was held that Saturday evening, with the finals on Sunday at high noon. Now, the key word here is "invitational"; this was an *invitation-only* event. That's for big shots (as opposed to "big names")—you know, like me.

An invitational tournament for big shots like me means no buy-in. That is, you get a chance to win $25,000 without putting up a penny. No risk is my kind of gambling! The prize structure called for that big $25,000 first-place prize, followed by $5,000, $4,000, $3,000, $2,000, and $1,000 for places two through six, respectively.

Now, even though I'm such a big-shot player, and a big-shot gambling author to boot, that doesn't mean I am a hands-on expert in every arcane aspect of gambling. I have not, for example, had much tournament experience, except for a couple of low-stakes blackjack events, which I lost, probably because my opponents didn't realize what a big shot I was. I had no experience with baccarat tournaments.

But, when I realized that I was going to be in Atlantic City that weekend anyway, to hook up with the Lee brothers and then with my buddy Walter Thomason, author of *Twenty-first Century Blackjack*, I figured I had nothing to lose and everything to gain by participating in the invitational baccarat tournament for big shots. So I signed up.

Signing up was easy. We big shots just call our hosts and say, "Sign me up, Pierre, my man." Of course, my host's name was Susan, but that's beside the point.

• • • •

So I was in.

Now, unlike the players against whom I would be competing, who would probably just be yukking it up and playing for fun and the outside chance of winning some money, I figured I'd quickly become an expert in baccarat tournament strategy and give myself an outstanding chance to brag to my fellow big-shot gambling authors. "Oh, yes, and, by the way, I won that $25,000 baccarat tournament at Bally's. Ho hum."

You see, tournaments are not like regular casino gambling. In regular casino gambling you go up against the house edge; that's why players lose in the long run. In a tournament, you go up against your fellow players, almost all of whom are not big-shot gambling authorities like me. You don't even have to necessarily *win money* in a tournament to win the tournament; you just have to win more or lose less than the other players at your table. And there are gambling strategies you can use to increase the likelihood that you'll win your table and the tournament.

So I studied the strategies for baccarat tournaments. Unlike blackjack tournaments, in which every player plays his own cards, in baccarat all the players are betting on only three propositions, Bank, Player, and Tie, and they all play against the same exact hands. There are no choices to make, just which of the three propositions you'll be betting on and for how much.

I found a wealth of information on tournament baccarat, which I boiled down to six basic principles:

1. If the tournament bet-to-bankroll ratio is small—that is, if you are given $10,000 as your stake but the minimum bet is, say, $1,000—you can take your time in putting out your big bets, since you'll have between forty and eighty decisions to face. You have time to analyze the

other players before you go for the lead in the last ten hands or so.

2. If, however, the tournament bet-to-bankroll ratio is large—that is, if you have a stake of $10,000 but a minimum bet of $100—you must try to take the lead early and fend off all comers in your forty to eighty decisions.

3. Bet Bank for all hands, with a few exceptions, because most tournaments don't take a commission out of the Bank bet and the Bank bet has a slightly greater chance to win.

4. At times, you'll do opposition betting to get the lead; that is, if your nearest opponents are betting Bank, you'll bet Player.

5. In the last round only, put a maximum bet out on Bank and Tie (which pays eight to one) if you need this to win the table.

6. Never let anyone get too far ahead of you. Don't be afraid to bust out—you *have* to win your table, or at least be in a position to advance if more than one player moves on.

Okay, six simple principles memorized. I was ready to rumble and win that $25,000 prize.

I am winning it. I am winning it. I am winning it.

Now, according to the pre-tournament instructions, there would be only two rounds, one preliminary and one final. Since there were three hundred players, I couldn't see how Bally's brain trust was going to get one table for the finals when there would be twenty tables for the preliminary round. Even if you only took the winner from each table, you'd still wind up with twenty players and only fifteen spots at the final baccarat table. But that was their problem. My problem was sizing up my opponents at my table.

When I sat down, I checked them out. I knew I would

have to beat each and every one of them to advance. There was a Chinese woman with dyed blonde hair, a lot of jewelry, and even more makeup. She affected boredom, but her appearance indicated that she was used to playing for big stakes; she'd be dangerous. There were several guys with backward baseball caps on their heads. No problem. Most guys who wear baseball caps backward on their heads are not deep thinkers but slavish followers of pop culture and sports, and these guys had probably never read a single thing on baccarat tournament strategy. There were several other Asians, neatly dressed; they might cause me some difficulty. One annoying woman kept saying to anyone who would listen: "I never played *back-a-rat* before. I play slots. But I figured, what did I have to lose?" *Sucker!* She'd be a piece of cake!

In fact, I wasn't too impressed with the majority of the players at my table. I figured my competition would be coming from the Asians. I kept repeating to myself: "You don't have to win a ton of money; you just have to beat everyone at your table. Beat the people at your table and you advance to the finals and that $25,000." Then I said to myself: "I'm prepared. I know what to do. *I am winning it. I am winning it. I am winning it.*"

Then the host got on the microphone. "Ladies and gentlemen, welcome to the Bally's $40,000 Invitational Baccarat Tournament. The rules are simple. The top twelve moneymakers in the first round go on to the final table. You are not competing with the players at your table; you are just trying to win as much money as you can. You each have $10,000 starting stake; you can bet $100 to $10,000 on a hand. You will play eleven hands. Good luck!"

What? What? My carefully laid strategy? My cunning appraisal of my fellow players? Eleven stinking hands? What the heck was going on?!

"Hey, this *back-a-rat* tournament is just like a slot tournament," said the annoying woman. "I know how to play this," and she put up a hefty bet on Player. She was told she had to wait her turn to bet.

I was in the second seat. There was no real strategy to this game; only the top 3 percent would advance to the final round, which meant it was theoretically possible that no one at my table might advance. So I made a quick estimate of what I—the big-shot *bah-cah-rah* player and big-shot gambling authority—should do . . . and I put up my whole $10,000 on Bank. I figured I'd take my shot at Bank at max bet all the way and hope I could make as much money as I possibly could in eleven hands. Since you could only bet $1,200 on Tie, I was better off just letting it all hang out on Bank.

I am winning it. I am winning it. I am winning it.
Come on, Bank!

"Player wins," said the dealer.

I blinked as Player won and I found myself getting up from the table. On the first hand, I was through, finished, a loser. Everyone in the room looked up as I got up. I thought for a moment I had the word "big shot" printed on my forehead as everyone just stared at me. I thought I could hear some snickers, but I might have been paranoid. Luckily, another guy at another table who had obviously stumbled upon my "big-shot gambling authority" strategy soon stood up. The attention of the room turned to him.

In the hall outside the baccarat tournament room, the other loser looked at me and said: "Crazy. Man, that was one crazy tournament." And then he put his baseball cap on, backward.

So I headed over to Wild Wild West Casino, which is a part of the Bally's complex that also includes Claridge, Park Place, and Caesars. Wild Wild West has the feel of a locals' casino in Vegas, similar to Texas Station or Sam's Town, and because of that I like to play there. I also like to play there because their craps tables, all short, give you a very close to true bounce.

The Lee brothers were not yet there and one table had only a couple of players at it. I took my position at SL and bought in.

"Table has been ice cold," said a man at the end. "He's made a mint," indicating the guy at SR3, an obvious Don't bettor.

I will confess that I am an inveterate "right bettor" at craps. A right bettor is one who bets with the shooter or the dice and, in the point cycle of the game, against the seven. That means I make Pass Line or Come bets, perhaps Place the six or eight, and buy the four or ten. I don't want the seven (except on the initial come-out roll). I don't *like* the seven.

And, despite my recognition that "wrong bettors" or "Don't players" or "darksiders" are not really playing against me but against the house, I just can't make myself believe it on a deep emotional level. As far as I'm concerned, when they win, I lose. If we're on the come-out and the two or three rolls, they win and I lose. On the point cycle, if the shooter sevens out, they win and I lose.

So, yes, I do take it personally when a Don't player is glaring down the felt at some shooter who is beginning to have a hot hand. I do take it personally because I can read his nasty little thoughts: "Come on, seven! Come on, seven!" I do take it personally when a shooter sevens out and that same Don't player gets a smug look.

One thing about Don't players, or at least most Don't players; they are usually very quiet at a table. They know that, in the pantheon of craps castes, they rate under the foot of the offal digger. So at least they know their place.

But that night at Wild Wild West Casino in Atlantic City I experienced one of the most sublime, beautiful, thrilling, funny, wonderful, and amazing spectacles—a Don't player getting *his* . . . and getting it with a vengeance. But it did take awhile.

The man at the end of the table had accurately assessed not just the past of this particular table but its immediate future. It was cold; that meant most of the shooters were sevening out before the 5-Count. So these shooters weren't hurting me. However, enough shooters, myself included, had sevened out just after the 5-Count that I was losing money and, naturally, I was *not* happy about that.

And there was this Don't bettor with two filled racks of green chips in front of him. He was about my age, around fifty-five or so, thin; he looked like a leftover from the radical sixties, although he was relatively clean-shaven with maybe a day's growth of stubble. He had some kind of fishermen's cap or painter's cap pulled down low over his forehead. His graying hair came down on either side of his cap. He was wearing a green army jacket and baggy army pants, and he was betting $50 on the Don't Pass for each and every shooter. And he was cleaning up. He had this little permanent sneer, as if he was saying: "Look at you, you fools, playing the right side. And look at me, and how much I'm making. You are *all* fools." *Sneer.*

Now, many of you Don't players don't realize that we "Do players" are acutely aware of your presence at *our* tables—just as we are aware of a mote in our eyes or a paper cut or hemorrhoids. Don't players are *that* irritating, and this guy was irritating me and irritating the guy next to me, a young fellow who had been taking a shellacking.

And now the dice were being passed to the Don't player— just as Tony and Larry Lee and their entourage arrived. There was enough room at the table for the Lee brothers but that was all. Tony managed to get next to me at SL2. Larry squeezed in at SR1.

Usually Don't players aren't arrogant enough to pick up the dice and shoot; instead they pass the dice on to the next right player while hoping their wicked hopes and dreaming their deadly dreams. Not *this* guy. He picked up the dice, looked right (he was on stick right, so he was looking away from where he was shooting the dice) and he flung them with disdain.

"Seven! Winner seven! Pay the Line, take the Don'ts."

"I hope he keeps this up," I said to Tony Lee and the kid next to him.

"Yeah," the kid said. "I hope he kills himself."

"That would be nice," said Tony.

The Don't player was passed the dice again and this time he rolled a four. He looked at the rest of us at the table and put $200 in odds on his four. The only time he took odds was if the point was four or ten—the longest shots at the table when it comes to point numbers. So he was a two-to-one favorite to hit a seven before a four.

He looked away and disdainfully flung the dice.

"Four, winner four! Pay the Dos, take the Don'ts!"

"Yahoo!" yelled the kid next to me.

The Don't player just kept that sneer on his craggy face. He put out another $50 Don't Pass bet.

"Winner eleven! Yoooooo-eleven!"

"Yahoo!" yelled the kid.

Mr. Don't flung the dice again.

"Seven, winner seven!"

"Yahoo!"

"Oh, God, let this last forever!" I said to Tony and the kid.

"This is great," Tony said to me. Then to the shooter: "Keep up the good shooting!"

The Don't bettor's jaw started to twitch. He was grinding his teeth.

He flung the dice down the table, sneering, not looking.

"Nine, Nina, nine is the point!"

The Don't bettor didn't lay odds on his nine. He flung the dice.

"Nine! Nina! Nina! Winner! Nine! Pay the Dos, take the Don'ts."

"Yahoo! A nine!"

"Good shooting, good shooting," clapped Larry Lee at SR1. The Don't player's jaw was really twitching now.

For a about forty minutes this Don't player stubbornly, persistently, dog-headedly, *gloriously* made those $50 Don't Pass bets and hit sevens and elevens on his come-out rolls—or, when he established a point, he *made* the point! Players were cheering wildly—led by the Lees and the kid. "Ya-hoooo! Keep up that hot hand, shooter!"

Finally, with the table hooting, jeering, sneering, and cheering, with chip racks filled to overflowing, the Don't bettor looked at the table layout with a dead look on his face. He was busted, broke; he didn't have a single chip left! He had just rolled his umpteenth seven on the come-out and was finished.

He stormed off.

"Wait! Wait!" yelled the kid. "Come back! You didn't finish your roll!"

Tony Lee shouted, "I'll put up a bet for you so you can keep shooting!"

Whether the Don't player heard this, I don't know, but I do know he had one heavenly roll—and he was damned because of it.

Many of the players at the table colored up after the Don't player's fantastic roll. Larry was the next to shoot (the player at SR2 was coloring up), which meant Larry was

taking over the roll from the Don't player who had not sevened out but had snuffed it. Normally in a case like this I
would take all my bets down and begin the *5-Count* over
again with the new shooter. However, I let my bets stay up
because, after all, this was Larry Lee shooting, not just any
old random roller.

Larry established his point, a six, and then rolled. Seven
out!

Ah, well. Even Barry Bonds has been known to strike out
on occasion.

Once all the players had colored up and left, there was
room at the table for the two "actresses," so Lola slid in
next to Larry and Vixen slid in next to Tony.

It was my turn to shoot. I set the dice in the 3-V and proceeded to hit five sixes in a row. Since three were on the
come-out rolls, I didn't win any money on those, but for the
next fifteen minutes I went six-crazy. It seemed that every
second or third number was a six. I even toyed with the idea
of letting my six work during the come-out rolls because I
was hitting it so frequently, but I just couldn't bring myself
to do it; old habits die hard, and I was in the habit of keeping my bets off during the come-out.

After my seven-out it was Tony's turn to roll. Vixen put
up a $10 Hard 6 and Hard 8. Tony established his point, an
eight, and then proceeded to hit an easy six. Vixen again put
up another $10 Hard 6. This time Tony rolled consecutive
nines, then a ten, then made his point, eight, the easy way.
She put up another $10 Hard 8.

"My Hardways are working," said Vixen.

The dealers put an "on" button on her chip.

(Once again, in terms of the Hardways, Atlantic City and
Las Vegas have two sets of rules. In Vegas all Hardways are
working during the come-out roll unless the player turns

them off; in Atlantic City all Hardways are off unless the player calls them on.)

Tony set the dice in the 3-V and carefully lofted them down the table.

"Six, the *hard* way. Point is six!" cried the stickman.

"Let it ride," said Vixen.

The dealers put her $90 win on top of her $10 Hard 6 bet. She now had $100 riding on Tony's trick shot.

Tony set the dice and lofted them. They just missed the back wall and landed like they were magnetized.

"Winner! Winner! Six, came the *haaarrrd waaay!*"

Vixen was paid $900 and told the dealers to take down her $100 Hardways bet and her $10 Hard 8. From that point on she just placed the six and eight for $12 each (it was a $10 minimum table). Lola would buy either the four or the ten for $35. However, as usual, Tony and Larry were betting big bucks. When either of them shot, they had several thousand at risk; when others shot, they had several hundred at risk on those who made it through the *5-Count*.

I played for about three hours with the Lees before I was just too tired to play anymore. I didn't do very much on my subsequent rolls, although they were minor moneymakers for me. But both Tony and Larry were on and they were consistently having good rolls. When I left them, I added up what I had won thus far this weekend at Bally's. Despite my disgrace in the baccarat tournament, I was a big, *big* winner going into my next two days, when I'd be moving over to the Claridge and playing with my buddy Walter Thomason.

13

The Old Men and the Claridge

I SHOULDN'T have moved to the Claridge!

Playing blackjack for the first time in several months during my first session at Claridge, I hit a bad streak that all but wiped out what I had won at craps. Walter, too, had a bad time of it at the Claridge's six-deck game, but he was dogged. He stayed and played, trying to recoup his losses (which he did!). I moved over to craps.

I have a certain soft spot for the venerable Claridge. I was conceived there in September of 1946. I first played serious craps with the Captain there in 1986. I witnessed some of the Arm's greatest rolls there.

In fact, my father still plays at the Claridge, and when I hand in my player's card invariably someone in the pit says, "Say hi to your father for us!" And I do, since it makes him feel good to be remembered and it makes me feel good to know the pit personnel and dealers make a point of remembering.

Time. Time and memories.

The Captain is now over eighty, and the Arm is in permanent craps retirement, but the Claridge still stands strong, its brick and mortar a distinct paean to a day that now crawls toward the dusty pages of history texts and hardly visited sites on the World Wide Web. And the Claridge must have a special place in the hearts and memories of the rapidly dwindling World War II generation and of the legions of Korean War veterans who come to Atlantic City to renew their life's juices at the craps tables—because, per square foot of table space, there are more old guys playing craps at the Claridge than at any other Atlantic City casino.

Go to Atlantic City in the weekday daylight hours and you'll see the old guys playing craps in every single casino venue along the Boardwalk. Go to the Claridge and, if you are sixty or younger, you'll be the "kid" at the table by a considerable number of years. The Claridge pit personnel and dealers have become experts in handling the senior crowds, as they are unlike any craps-playing crowd you're likely to meet in Vegas or other parts north or south. They are enthusiastic, cantankerous, deaf, savvy, forgetful, argumentative, eclectic, and idiosyncratic. Some are insane. And they all know each other! The Claridge pit crews and dealers remember their names, say hi to them like they are old, old friends (which in a way they are) and treat them with respect and dignity—no matter how exasperating they can be.

Here's a scene from the Claridge craps tables after I left Walter, when I was the "kid" at the table—by at least fifteen years!

STICKMAN: Shooter on the come-out. Place your bets.

OLD GUY WITH HAT: Where's my Pass Line bet?

BOXWOMAN: You lost it.

OLD GUY WITH HAT: How could I lose it? The shooter's just shooting.

DEALER: That was the other shooter, sir.

OLD GUY WITH HEARING AID: Who's the other shooter? I thought that guy was shooting?

BOXWOMAN: He is.

OLD GUY WITH BANDAGE ON FACE: Can we get these dice moving? I don't have much time left!

OLD GUY WITH DARK CIRCLES UNDER EYES: I thought you were dead already. You weren't moving there for a while.

OLD GUY WITH BANDAGE ON FACE: I was just napping.

OLD GUY WITH HAT: Him? He's like a horse. He can sleep standing up.

STICKMAN: Dice are out. Watch your hands.

OLD GUY WITH DARK CIRCLES UNDER EYES: See how carefully he sets them? He was a bricklayer. Pete the bricklayer. See, one on top of the other.

STICKMAN: Five, point is five. Place your bets. Place the nine. Nine goes with the five. Hardways, anyone?

OLD GUY WITH HEARING AID: What's the point?

STICKMAN: Five, sir.

OLD GUY WITH HEARING AID: I thought you said nine. You put the puck on five.

OLD GUY WITH HAT: Do I have a Hard 8? Where's my Hard 8?

DEALER: You don't have a Hard 8, sir.

OLD GUY WITH HAT: So where's my Hard 8? I had a Hard 8.

BOXWOMAN: That was the last shooter sir. He, uh, didn't make his point.

OLD GUY WITH DARK CIRCLES UNDER EYES: His point is five! Can we get the game moving, here? Come on, Petey, lay some bricks.

OLD GUY WHO LOOKS LIKE A RODENT: Whoof. Ooo. Smell that? Whew! Who did that? Hee, hee, hee. Who? Ha!

STICKMAN: Dice are—oh, Jesus, what the hell? Oh, man. God. (holding his nose) Dice are out. God.

OLD GUY WHO LOOKS LIKE A RODENT: Hee, hee, hee.

BOXWOMAN: *Point is five.*

STICKMAN: Sorry. God. Point is five.

OLD GUY WITH HEARING AID: I thought it was nine. Didn't he say it was nine?

OLD GUY IN WINDBREAKER: Chrissake! Will ya listen, for chrissake?

OLD GUY WITH DARK CIRCLES UNDER EYES: What'cha building, Petey? Go, Petey!

STICKMAN: Six, six, came easy.

OLD GUY WITH HAT: Don't I get paid? Where's my six?

DEALER: You don't have a six, sir.

OLD GUY WITH HAT: I had a six and eight!

DEALER: Do you want a six and eight, sir?

OLD GUY WITH HAT: Yeah, give me a six and eight and don't forget!

DEALER: I won't, sir. Could I have your chips, sir? Your chips . . . sir?

STICKMAN: Dice are out.

OLD GUY IN WINDBREAKER: That's my Come bet! Isn't that my Come bet?

STICKMAN: Watch your hands.

OLD GUY IN WINDBREAKER: That's my Come bet.

OLD GUY WITH HAT: He says that's his Come bet. That's *my* Come bet.

OLD GUY IN WINDBREAKER: That's *my* Come bet.

BOXWOMAN: You don't have a Come bet, sir. That *is* his Come bet.

OLD GUY WITH HAT: I had a Come bet.

DEALER: You didn't have a Come bet, sir.

OLD GUY WITH DARK CIRCLES UNDER EYES: Petey, the bricklayer.

STICKMAN: Seven out! Take the Line, pay the Don'ts.

OLD GUY WHO LOOKS LIKE A RODENT: Whoops! Hee, hee, hee. Whoopsie! Ha!

STICKMAN (HOLDING HIS NOSE): Oh, God. Oh, Christ.

OLD GUY WITH BANDAGE ON FACE: That's how we won World War I, don't you know? Mustard gas.

OLD GUY WITH DARK CIRCLES UNDER EYES: That was the Germans.

OLD GUY WITH HAT: Where's my Pass Line bet?

And so it goes. Those men, hard of hearing, somewhat forgetful, exhibiting all the foibles of remorseless age, had fought the wars that kept my generation free, built the economies that kept my generation materially contented. For some, their manhood may have begun in Atlantic City, where many World War II soldiers received their training, and now it culminates in Atlantic City as the dice roll down the table awaiting the stickman's final call. I was proud to be in their company. I was happy to be at the Claridge, despite the fact that I had taken a beating.

14

Trouble in PARR-a-dice?

THE CRAP started to hit the fan on the weekend of November 15–17, 2002, at the Taj Mahal PARR weekend in Atlantic City. As I was soon to learn, disaffection with Jerry Patterson was widespread among the coaches. Bill Burton, Mr. Finesse, and Dominator wanted to speak with me privately about their concerns. None knew of my deal with Jerry and Sharpshooter to do several seminars in Tunica, Atlantic City, and Vegas.

While each and every one of them liked Jerry, they all felt he was a bit of a "user." The primary gripe concerned the amount of work they had done with Jerry for the past few years without ever being offered some form of payment. As they were speaking, I recalled an e-mail exchange I'd had with Jerry: We'd agreed to pay the coaches for their efforts during our joint seminars. Yet we had never established the amount we would pay them, since that money would come out of the JPE, Inc., share of the seminars, controlled by Patterson. I wish I had known the gripes before I got involved. This was shaping up to be a messy interpersonal, well, *mess*.

"We travel all over the country at our own expense," said Mr. Finesse. "We make ourselves available to coach students individually in our own areas. Jerry never even offers us a token payment, a sense of appreciation. It gets to you."

One coach said: "You'd think he'd offer us a black chip or something on a weekend where we work like crazy to shape up the students. Nothing. He even makes us buy our own sandwiches at lunch."

When the coach made this complaint, it dawned on me that the mailing Jerry, Sharpshooter, and I had sent to my mailing list promised that students could get one-on-one instruction with the coaches in their area. Well, what if the coaches didn't want to do that anymore? We were promising a service that depended on someone doing something for nothing. That's bad business.

Dominator was the most forceful in his disenchantment. He had taken out ads in the *Robb Report* at over $350 a month for one year in order to publicize what he thought would be the new PARR Platinum course that he, Jerry, Sharpshooter, and the coaches would give. He even wanted me involved ("However you want to be involved," he told me), although I knew Jerry preferred to keep me out of PARR Platinum. Dominator's view of the current PARR course was dim. "We don't run a professional seminar. We have shitty handouts; we do things on the cheap. We don't even have a PowerPoint presentation and when we set up the practice boxes in the room they look like crap. I think, when you attend a seminar where you're paying good money, you should feel that you are in an atmosphere of quality and class. We should have a full fold-out craps table to demonstrate on."

Dominator also felt that Jerry had seriously used him.

"He has taken every one of my ideas and incorporated them into the PARR course. I didn't even get credit, much less a thank-you or an offer of some money. I now think the things that were said about Jerry, about how he uses people, are absolutely true. I like the guy but I really have a bad taste."

I wasn't ready to write off Jerry. I, too, liked the man. I liked his wife, Nancy. But I recalled Chip's admonition not to fall for the "Ma and Pa Kettle" routine. I was wondering whether I was actually a big sucker.

Whatever the truth about Jerry Patterson, the truth about dice control was not in doubt. The PARR course, for whatever its shortcomings, was a legitimate course. There were many things I would change about it, areas I felt needed shoring up, but a student taking the course with Sharpshooter and the current coaching team would learn a valuable skill. When I got involved with the actual teaching, I would incorporate my ideas and I would make it a truly intense hands-on experience—which, as of yet, it was not.

I asked Bill Burton, Mr. Finesse, and Dominator if they were the only three who felt this way or if the other coaches did, too. They rattled off a list of nine of the best coaches, who were ready to quit PARR. The consensus among the coaches was that they would not work with PARR Platinum, that instead a new organization was called for, one that equitably distributed the money from the seminars. Not one of the guys I talked to was looking to get rich off the dice-control seminars, since they knew that only a narrow band of dedicated craps players would be interested in learning controlled shooting. No, they wanted a piece of the action for a sense of recognition and worth, a monetary pat on the back for a job well done. Interestingly enough, most of the coaches made money in the casinos during these festivals and seminars, and not one of them was looking to make a living by the teaching of the skill.

I did get to speak to some of the other coaches after the Taj weekend. There seemed to be widespread agreement with what Bill Burton, Mr. Finesse, and Dominator had told me. The ideas for a new organization were not fully formed at the moment; essentially, the coaches were in the angst zone—pissed off, hurt, but not clear as to where they were going or what they were going to do. I suggested that maybe they should form a corporation. You'd have several big-money people to invest who would get the lion's share of the profits, but every coach would get a piece of the pie as well, and a stipend for their teaching time. I also thought that it was important to include Jerry and Sharpshooter in the new organization. After all, splitting off into different competing groups was not a good idea. The powerhouse coaches— Dominator, Mr. Finesse, Bill Burton, Billy the Kid, and Sharpshooter (among others)—were also the powerhouse players who, in a casino, walked the walk as well as talked the talk. The best course of action for everyone, and the best opportunity for new students of dice control, was for these powerhouses to all be a part of one group.

These thoughts were churning in my mind when I went to the PARR banquet on the evening of Sunday, November 17. I had no idea if Jerry was aware of the feelings of the coaches present that night. Nor was I going to ask. Why ruin a pleasant dinner? I figured the events would work themselves out however they worked themselves out.

That particular PARR weekend had Dr. Richard McCall as the guest speaker. Dr. McCall had written a very well-received book, *The Way of the Warrior Trader*. McCall is a clinical psychologist, and founder and former director of the Human Performance Institute, one of the nation's most respected performance-enhancement programs. Dr. McCall is also a fifth-degree black belt in Japanese "Bujutsu" and "Kenjutsu"—the original martial arts of the legendary samurai—and he is one of only four American representatives of the famous Takeda samurai lineage, on which the television miniseries *Shogun* was based. A forty-year veteran of these disciplines, Dr. McCall integrates Zen-based philosophies and the martial precepts of the samurai into everything he does, including shooting craps. That's why he's known by the nickname "the Samurai Shooter."

Dr. McCall is the director of the Mastery Group International, a multinational alliance of S&P 500 Futures traders. Referring to the markets as "the world's biggest and most challenging casino," McCall credits much of the design, tactical makeup, and success of his own personal trading method, called the SABAKI Micro-Trading Method, to his over twenty years of craps-playing experience.

Speaking of success, Dr. McCall has documented cumulative winnings of over one million dollars at craps. He believes that his craps winnings are a stark testimonial to the effectiveness of the psychological and philosophical disciplines he practices and teaches. Whenever he is asked just how he was able to take home over one million dollars of the casinos' money, he responds, "The same way you eat an elephant: one small bite at a time!"

Dr. McCall is a charismatic speaker, and his talk that weekend revolved around what is necessary to beat the game of craps. Dr. McCall believes it is possible to achieve incredible success at craps if one follows five basic steps:

1. Do the necessary practice to excel at shooting the dice
2. Study and understand the correct way to time your betting
3. Manage your money effectively during each playing session
4. Come to live by the warrior's "ACTION Plan," which is the core subject of his book

5. Set small, attainable profit objectives and loss limits for
   each playing session, and when that objective/limit is
   hit then stop

McCall's talk finished with a demonstration of focus—he
sliced a cucumber in half with his samurai sword—*on his
son's neck!* The guy was focused! (He jokingly told the audience after this heart-stopping performance that he has a "98
percent success rate" with it.)

Dr. McCall, his son, Ben, and his wife, Lyndee, are avid
craps players. We had played together Saturday night, and
Ben had the big roll of the evening. Essentially, when you are
with controlled shooters or rhythmic rollers, it only takes
one good hand to put you in the black. As Dominator says,
"We pay small dues waiting for the good rolls," and that's
why employing the Captain's *5-Count* is so important. That
night we were paying dues on some of the shooters who
made it past the 5-Count only to seven out on the 6- or 7-
Count. I wasn't particularly hot and hadn't been "on" that
whole day. It had been about four weeks since I'd played
and I hadn't followed my normal practice routine during
that time; I was busy writing and trying to get the mailing
with Jerry off the ground. So, that night, I was one of the
shooters causing my fellow rhythmic rollers to pay dues.

I was at SL1 and Ben was next to me on my left, at SL2.
After I ignominiously sevened out to the general groans of the
"random rollers" (trained rhythmic rollers never groan when
our compatriots seven out, because we all know—sing this in
chorus now—*"It happens!"*). Mr. Finesse was at the end of the
table to my right. He called over: "Frank, come to the dealer
school tomorrow. I see something you're doing wrong."

Now, I've mentioned before that Mr. Finesse has one of
the finest eyes in the game; in fact, I always thought he
should be called "the Owl" because he spots things few

others can. "I'll be there," I said. Then Ben picked up the dice and, twenty-five minutes later, everybody was a happy camper at that table.

On Sunday I went over to the dealer school, where Sharpshooter and the coaches were giving instruction at two craps tables. When there was a break in the action, Mr. Finesse brought me to the table. Some of the other students gathered around to watch my lesson.

"Do your throw," said Mr. Finesse.

So I did.

"Do you know what you're doing wrong?"

"No," I said.

"Do your throw again, but before you actually release the dice I want you to stop, with the dice parallel to the back wall, pause a moment, then loft them. You've been setting the dice but then picking them up and shooting all in one motion. Take that pause and square those dice away."

So I did. Damn! The dice floated down the table, gently bounced, hit the back wall, and died. In the month since I'd played with him in Vegas, I had picked up a bad habit—trying to do the entire throw in one move. It was a totally unconscious change in my normal delivery and it certainly accounted for the rotten rolls I'd been experiencing for the last two days. I did about a dozen perfect rolls in a row. It felt good.

"Thanks, coach," I said to Mr. Finesse.

"Anytime," he laughed.

One of the students came up to me. I didn't catch the man's name. "Hey, Frank, I just want to apologize."

"For what?"

"Well, I've read everything you've written and, frankly, I thought you might be shoveling a lot of shit—the 5-Count, the rhythmic rolling, the Captain. But watching you in the casino and seeing you here practicing, seeing your throw, I want to apologize. You aren't like a lot of the other writers I've met who just talk a good game; you actually do it."

"Thanks," I said. "And when I write about all this," I waved my arm at the room of students diligently practicing their controlled throws, "there will be plenty of people who think I'm making it all up. But thanks again."

It was an interesting observation the man had made, that most of the gambling writers he'd met didn't seem to play the games. My experience with my writer friends was different. Of all the authors I call friend, each and every one is a player. But I do know many authors and authorities whose experience at the tables is limited to the dinner table and whose biggest gamble is which computer program to utilize in tonight's simulated gambling session.

At Sunday's banquet I was seated next to Sharpshooter and Bill Burton. Also at our table were Jerry Patterson, Bucko Bob Fuller, Bagger Vance, and Howard "Rock 'n' Roller" Newman. Howard Newman had a slight problem. That weekend Howard's wife had told him that they needed "new garage doors" and that they were what he was shooting for. In fact, I had kidded him at the craps table by shouting, "Baby needs new garage doors!"

Bagger Vance teaches how to get into "the zone." I've already talked about the "rolling zone," a place in your consciousness where you're just into what you're doing, almost trance-like. Bagger teaches how to find this relaxed focus; he also demonstrates how "thinking" can interrupt the flow of your rhythmic roll. The execution of a good rhythmic roll is every bit as mental as it is physical.

Bucko Bob Fuller, seventy-six years old and going like thirty, was to receive the PARR "player of the year" award for his contributions to the players (for whom he often gets comps at the Taj Mahal) and for his phenomenal roll that took place at the Taj Mahal on August 21, 2002, when he

held the dice for an incredible one hour and forty-five minutes. Bucko told me the story of that day:

"I was supposed to meet my wife at 12 noon. So I went to
the tables, but I was very conscious of the time, because I
didn't want to stand up my wife, so I kept looking at my
watch. At 10:00 sharp I got the dice. I was in a groove. It
felt very good. When I looked at my watch again, it was
11:00. I had rolled for an hour. I thought to myself that I
better tell the floorperson that if I'm still rolling by 11:45,
that he should call my wife in the room and tell her I was
being delayed. So then I rolled for another forty-five minutes
and, don't you know it, I sevened out at exactly 11:45! I
think I put that damn time in my head and unconsciously
sevened out because of it. I should have put 5 P.M. in my
head and rolled for the whole damn day!"

I looked around the room filled with coaches and students, everyone an avid craps player, and I wondered if it
was all going to explode into factions and recriminations—
and if I would be in the middle of it. But the banquet was
fun and Bucko Bob received his award. The wine flowed,
jokes were told, war stories were exchanged, and then it was
time to head for the casino. At the Taj, Sharpshooter took
SL1, Dominator took SR1, I was at SL2, Dr. McCall was
SL3, and Ben was at SL4. Next to Dominator were Mr. Finesse, Bill Burton, Lyndy McCall, and Bucko Bob (I forget
the order they were in, sorry).

Since the entire table was composed of our players, we let
Sharpshooter roll first. He said he was going to "roll from
the Don't." That meant we should all bet Don't Pass. That's
right; the entire table, as one, stuck up Don't Pass bets. The
floorperson stopped in her tracks. The boxman looked
around the table, then said, "Jesus, I have never in my entire
career seen anything like this!" Even several passersby
stopped to gawk.

"Shooting from the Don't," called the stickman.

Sharpshooter set the dice to maximize the possibility of a two or three being rolled or, if it was a number, the four or ten. The ten and the four are the best possible numbers to have as a point when you want the seven to appear, since there are only three ways to make a ten or a four, and six ways to make a seven.

"Ten, point is ten," called the stickman.

Then Sharpshooter set for the seven. He proceeded to roll a four, then a five, then a six, then an eight, then a nine. He hadn't rolled a seven—but, thankfully, he hadn't made the point, either.

"I'm changing my set," he said, "to an anything-but-ten."

He rolled several sixes and eights, then, "Seven! Seven out!" called the stickman. "Take. . . ." He paused, looked around the table, laughed. There weren't any bets to take! "Pay *everybody!*"

The rest of that night I remember as a wash of cheers and chants and high-fives. I know I had several good rolls thanks to Mr. Finesse's coaching, and many of the other shooters had good rolls as well. The table was, to use a tired but quite accurate term, *rocking*. Money was being made; excitement was being felt by all. It was the quintessential craps game.

As the night wound down, I noticed Jerry standing smiling behind the guys at the top of the table, stick left. He was looking at his PARR coaches and some of the new students, all of them having the time of their lives. He saw me and smiled even more broadly. I smiled, too, and thought, *too bad everything good has to come to an end,* and then I thought about Chip and deals with the devil.

15

The Birth of Golden Touch Craps

I WAS on the fence. While I wanted to be a part of a new group that would be a classy alternative to what had come before, that would incorporate better teaching methods and playing strategies, I also wanted to keep things friendly among Jerry, Sharpshooter, and the rest of the guys. In fact, the rest of the guys felt the same way. If we could, we wanted to absorb PARR into our organization, which, thanks to the creativity of Dr. Richard McCall, we finally decided to call Golden Touch Craps.

If I was sitting on the fence concerning Jerry Patterson, Sharpshooter had the fence pickets deeply imbedded in his derriere. While he too wanted to join us, he was fiercely loyal to Jerry. He wanted to "give something" to Jerry for his contributions to the field.

This was fine with me. Jerry had, with Sharpshooter's brilliant assistance, created a course that mirrored the Captain's ideas of how to roll the dice. Where the Captain had coined the phrase "rhythmic roller," Jerry had changed it to "rhythm roller" and created PARR, Patterson Advanced Rhythm Roll. Sharpshooter had then developed a "perfect pitch and delivery system" that was just like the Captain's, without ever having seen the Captain in action.

Dominator, Bill Burton, Mr. Finesse, and I wanted Sharpshooter with us, and we were willing to bend over backward to get the deal signed, sealed, and delivered. After much negotiation, we created a win/win situation for Patterson, Sharpshooter, and Golden Touch. The coaches' differences with Patterson were resolved, and Golden Touch Craps was conceived.

For two months, Dominator and I spearheaded the formation of our new company, Golden Touch Craps International, LLC. Dom did all the legal work; I wrote up the curriculum and the publicity for the new group. Every step of the way, however, the coaches were included in the process, and they offered valuable insights and advice. For example, Bill Burton developed our "Dice Net" device, which helps students maintain the proper arc and angle for their throws and helps insure a landing in the proper area of the table. Mr. Finesse and Billy the Kid offered telling revisions of the curriculum, adding things that I had completely overlooked and removing things that were redundant or unimportant.

We also developed detailed "certification" requirements that all Golden Touch Craps teachers would have to pass. Later I would publish this on our Web site. Here is that Web article:

Controlling the Dice:
The Incompetent Leading the Gullible?

Here is a proposition: If you wanted to have some physical problem checked out, say you've been having severe chest pains, would you go to a "board certified" medical practitioner, specifically a doctor who specializes in chest pains, or would you go to Elmer V. Rodente down the street who says he's the world's greatest chest pain fixer upper? I think most of us would go to a board certified doctor.

Now, let us say you are having severe problems with craps, like you lose a hell of a lot of money at the game but you still love to play it. You've heard that there might be a way to beat the game by something called "dice control." Now, you face a real dilemma. When it comes to learning how to control the dice, to whom do you go? There is no way to tell whose claims are legitimate and whose claims are bogus unless you have the time, money, and patience to go to each and every "expert" proclaiming his or her greatness in this area of casino play. There are no "board certified" dice controllers . . . yet. Everyone is self-certified; that is to say, you have to take them at their word.

A few millennia ago, the same prospect faced people with chest pains and other ailments. There were no board certified physicians, just a lot of men and women who thought they knew what ailed thee. And some of them were somewhat right in their suppositions; and thus their ideas and knowledge were then passed down. Such people as Galen, Hypocrites, Rhazes, and Serapion, among many others, were the founders, fathers, and originators of modern medicine. Over the centuries, as medical knowledge built upon the discoveries and ideas of these men, groups of doctors banded together and formed guilds and societies and came up with criteria for certifying their members. Thus, a doctor studying with them could ultimately become "board certified." It wasn't enough to proclaim, "I am Elmer V. Rodente, the world's greatest chest-pain fixer upper, I should be given a degree from your medical college without having taken the courses and passing the basic tests of knowledge and skill." No, sir, now to be a doctor, you have to go to school for many years and work under the tutelage of working doctors before you yourself can get that degree and be board certified. [. . .]

The Golden Touch Craps board of directors wanted GTC to have the highest standards of excellence in the budding field of dice control. To do this, we set up tough criteria for our instructors and coaches to meet. They had to be skilled shooters and good teachers.

How did we determine what a skilled shooter was?

Since our GTC executive board members carry long-term SRRs [seven-to-rolls ratios] of approximately 1:7 or more, this became our baseline figure. [. . .] All instructors at GTC must demonstrate in extensive practice sessions and then in supervised casino play that they have a SRR at or above that number.

That's the entrance exam, the qualifier. However, to teach requires much greater knowledge than merely being able to go out and do something. Just because someone can hit a baseball doesn't mean he'll make the best batting coach. You want someone who can hit a baseball but also someone who can help *someone else* hit a baseball, too. Therefore, to assure excellence, we set up detailed criteria that our teachers had to master in the following four areas:

I. Knowledge of the 8 Physical Elements of the Controlled Throw
   1. Positioning
      • Table position and how that affects a shooter's performance
      • Body position: how the proper position of one's body can enhance a controlled throw
      • Arm placement: how to place the non-throwing arm to get proper leverage on a throw

   2. Dice Sets
      • Hardway set and how to swiftly make it
      • Reverse of Hardway for all 7s set
      • 3-V set and how to swiftly make it

- Other "V" sets
- The "whirl" set
- The cross "T" set

3. Angling
   - Proper angles for approaching the dice
   - Proper angles for hands in relation to back wall
   - Proper "pick up" angles to maximize grip
   - Proper angles for optimum launches

4. Dice Grabs
   - Over the top grab
   - The sliding grab
   - The anchored grab
   - Utilizing the "squeeze" to keep dice together

5. Dice Grips
   - The three-finger grip
   - The one-finger grip
   - The four-finger grip
   - The "squeeze" grip
   - Understanding thumb placements and their effects on the dice: the bent thumb, the rigid thumb, side thumb, flat thumb.

6. Dice Delivery Methods
   - The perfect pitch delivery
   - The pendulum swing delivery
   - The wrist delivery
   - The "kill shot" delivery (advanced method)
   - The floater (advanced method)
   - Establishing the arc for proper landing

7. Spin Control
   - Assessing optimum spin for launch force and arc of dice
   - Reducing the revolutions to deaden impact
   - Increasing revolutions to create the breaking effect

8. Bounce Control
   • Judging table composition and its affect on bounce
   • How to reduce or increase bounce

II. Mathematical and Scientific Knowledge

1. Understanding the complete mathematical underpinnings of the game
   • How the casino wins more decisions on the pass, don't pass, come, don't come
   • How the casino extracts its "tax" or vig on place bets of all types
   • The probability of each number appearing and the true odds of every bet
   • How the odds bets work
   • How to push the house to give a better bet on "buys" of the 4/10 and 5/9
   • The range of bets that can be made
   • The SRRs needed to overcome the various house edges in different bets

2. Understanding the physics of dice control
   • Why limiting the degrees of freedom in the motions of two dice will create controlled conditions
   • Why spin works to reduce the chances of dice splitting and twisting in the air
   • Why a flat bounce dissipates energy
   • Why the pyramids help create randomness in the game

3. Understanding how each of the 8 Physical Elements can increase influence over the dice

4. Understanding the different types of dice that a casino can use and how each reacts when thrown

5. Understanding how the different tables, designs, layout materials affect the reaction of the dice

6. Understanding how the 5-Count works and the research that proves why it reduces the house's take on

bankroll against random rollers, increases comps, reduces body time and risk time at the table, and "finds" controlled shooters

III. Psychological Knowledge

1. Understanding the "myths" of craps and why people believe in them

2. Understanding how relaxation techniques such as "visualization," meditation, and controlled breathing can affect performance

3. Understanding the risk-aversion and manageable thrills concepts

4. Understanding the A.C.T.I.O.N plan for GTC players

IV. Performance

1. SRR of 1:7 or greater based on long term practice results and supervised play

2. Complete understanding of all areas of the GTC curriculum (assessment: written test)

3. Ability to teach each area of the GTC curriculum (assessment: performance test)

4. Ability to analyze a student's throw in light of all 8 physical elements, make the proper corrections, and improve the student's performance (assessment: supervision and student reports)

5. Ability to set dice swiftly and accurately in practice and casino play

6. Ability to demonstrate all 8 physical elements (assessment: supervision)

7. Ability to teach in a professional manner

8. Ability to articulate the GTC philosophy as reflected in our certification requirements and mission statement.

These criteria have been established to standardize and el-
evate the teaching of dice control by subjecting our teachers
to a rigorous certification process that makes sure they understand, can demonstrate, and can effectively teach all the
essential areas of our curriculum.

So when you take a GTC course, this is what we can af-
firm: Each GTC teacher has demonstrated in long-term play
his controlled shot. Each teacher has worked with several
other teachers in appraising various shooters' styles, grips,
deliveries, etc., and has shown that he can make the proper
adjustments in a student's form when needed. Each teacher
has a complete grasp of the GTC curriculum and the math
and science of the game of craps.

We have now "certified" only a dozen teachers in the GTC
way. We have a half dozen "teachers-in-training" who have
not as yet been fully certified. These "student-teachers" work
under the watchful eyes of our certified teachers to help students but they are not allowed to work alone with students.

We estimate that for a student to become a teacher will
take at least two years of intense training and, of course, they
must be able to pass all the tests. And that will take the
guesswork out of selecting a skilled dice-control practitioner
as opposed to an Elmer V. Rodente.

As for the courses themselves, unlike the PARR class,
which had interminable lectures, Golden Touch would be intensive and hands-on. We would teach a technique, and then
have the students practice it until they understood the mechanics behind the technique, always under the watchful
eyes of a skilled coach. The courses would essentially be divided into three major components:

1. The eight physical elements of dice control: table position, optimum dice sets, pick-up and delivery angles,
   proper dice grabs, optimum dice grips, expert delivery
   systems, spin control, and bounce control

2. Proper betting on oneself and how to select and bet on other shooters
3. How to relax and focus at the table

We would also have sections on getting the most comps for the least action. But the key to everything would be a close appraisal of the students' progress by experienced coaches with years of experience as dice controllers and teachers—the best in the business.

By the time Golden Touch Craps was incorporated in the State of Nevada on Friday, January 17, 2003, Sharpshooter was with us as a major principal, as were a dozen of the best dice controllers in the world. To top it off, we had four students eagerly awaiting our first class. Golden Touch Craps was born like Athena, fully grown and adult, during Sunset Station's spectacular "Beat the House" gaming festival, over the Martin Luther King Day weekend, January 17–19, 2003.

I had been invited to speak about craps at the festival, which attracted over twenty-five hundred players, and over fifty speakers, many of them gambling's luminaries. With the help of Beau and Beth Parker, Dominator, Mr. Finesse, Bill Burton, Larry Edell, his wife, Andrea, and Billy the Kid, we created the largest booth at the festival, at which we not only sold the thirty books/tapes either that I had written or that were in my Get-the-Edge Guide series—but also, more importantly, launched Golden Touch Craps. We had a big banner proclaiming our "dice control" seminars, and glossy, classy flyers outlining our course content and prices. In addition, we had set up a dice practice rig and throwing station, at which we held a No-Sevens contest each day for the players attending the festival, to see who could roll the most times without a seven coming up.

I enjoy speaking at festivals such as the one held at Sunset Station for two reasons, the first of which is simple—I'm a

ham! My motto is "Give me a microphone and point me to
the stage!" My second reason for loving such festivals is the
enormous amount of information that players can get from
recognized authorities at these events. I've done similar ones
at Taj Mahal and Tropicana in Atlantic City, Golden Nugget
and Tropicana in Las Vegas, and Sam's Town in Tunica, and
it's always fun to meet the legions of players who turn up. I
also get to meet my fellow authors and speakers. At this particular festival I saw my old friends Jean and Brad Scott
(Jean is the author of the enormously popular *The Frugal
Gambler*), and Henry and Linda Tamburin; I met Steve
Bourie for the first time—he's the editor of and brains behind *The American Casino Guide;* I talked with Rick Stoff,
publisher of the *New Gambling Times,* and his editor Stan-
ley Sludikoff; I showed Michael Shackleford, "the Wizard of
Odds," the practice rigs for working on controlled throws
(and Dominator gave him a display of his skills, hitting
eighteen numbers in a row before the appearance of that
ugly seven); and then I chatted with poker expert and author
Mason Malmuth, if *chatted* is the right characterization for
the following exchange:

MALMUTH: So *you're* Frank Scoblete?

FRANK: Yes, yes, hello.

MALMUTH: (big pause) *I'm* Mason Malmuth.

FRANK: Ah, yes, nice to meet you.

MALMUTH: I've always wanted to meet you.

FRANK: Ah.

MALMUTH: I don't know why I would want to meet *you.*

FRANK (TRYING TO COME UP WITH A WITTY ANSWER): Uh, ah, uh . . .

· · · ·

MALMUTH (POINTING TO THREE TABLES FULL OF MY BOOKS AND TAPES):
These all *your* books?

FRANK: Yes, either written by me or a part of my Get-the-Edge
Guides.

MALMUTH: How many?

FRANK: Thirty or so.

MALMUTH: Maybe I wanted to meet you out of curiosity. I
don't know.

Just then I was interrupted by Henry Tamburin, who
wanted to introduce me to Charles Lund, the author of a
great book on advantage slot play (yes, there is such a
thing!) titled *Robbing the One-Armed Bandits!* (not to be
confused with my book *Break the One-Armed Bandits*). I
excused myself from Mason Malmuth. I had a discussion
with Lund and his wife, who are, by the way, members of a
rare breed—slot players who have been asked to stop playing slots "because they are too good." And so it went, interesting exchanges with other authors and intense discussions
about controlled shooting with craps aficionados.

I also noticed a curious thing about some casino patrons
at Sunset Station, those who were actually not attending the
seminars, but there to play. They looked with skepticism, if
not downright suspicion, on those of us selling books, as if
to say to us, "Huh, I know you're trying to trick me into
buying something. You can't fool me. I'll take this money
that I would have used buying a book or tape and dump it in
this here machine—so there!" Some of the players who wandered over to our booth—which was on the main casino
floor and in full view of just about anyone who came into
the casino—had that "If you know so much how come you

ain't rich?" look on their faces. (I always answer that with a deadpan tone of bafflement: "I *am* rich.") Others asked point-blank if the casinos were "putting us up to this," because why would the casino want to sell something to players that might help them do better against the casinos? The answer to that is obvious; any astute casino boss knows that very few players will ever develop the savvy necessary to be a threat. Intelligent players might decrease the casino edge over them, that is true, but in the long run these players will probably play more and lose just as much as they did before—albeit over a slightly more extended time period. It's good business for casinos to put on these seminars and have these booths. It creates loyalty in their customers. "Hey, Sunset Station really wants me to be the best player I can be. They want me to have a chance!"

During the festival, Dominator, a natural with the public, gave demonstrations of his controlled throw, explaining the concepts behind the Golden Touch technique. This guy genuinely loves to play and to teach craps.

The Sunset Station "Beat the House" weekend was a great weekend made even greater by a huge surprise.

"How would you like to be on A&E?" asked Beau.

"The cable network?" I said.

"They want to do a story about a professional gambler, something like a 'day in the life' or something, so they called Larry Edell and he recommended me, and they wanted someone to talk to about me—and that's you, if you want."

"Are they going to call me?"

"I think so," he said.

And they did.

16

Golden Touch vs. the Casinos on Television!

I RECEIVED a message from my wife, the beautiful AP, to "call A&E" right away. Actually, it wasn't A&E, per se, but Hybrid Films, which was doing the show that would appear on A&E.

I did so.

I spoke to a young lady named Sherine. Not being the least humble, I told her I was the best-selling gambling writer in the United States, if not the world (I would have added the universe, but there might be some bug-eyed creature on Uranus that has sold more books and tapes on gambling than I), and then I inquired as to the format of the show. Sherine told me it would be a "fly on the wall" examination of a professional gambler. They would follow Beau Parker around and take shots of him playing and such. Then, after thirty hours of shooting, they would stitch together a story.

Since the actual outline of the show was flexible, I immediately offered my idea of what might make an exciting
show (my years as an actor/director/producer usually give
me a dramatic perspective on things and I am *never* hesitant
to offer my opinions). "Why don't we set it up as a challenge
between dice controllers and the casinos? We show several
dice controllers at Beau's home practicing for the big night.
Here we can explain the theory behind what we are doing.
Then we get into a limo and drive to the first casino. Inside
the limo, we talk about the game and our strategies and how
we are feeling about the upcoming contest. The audience is
in on the buildup every step of the way. Then we go right
into the casino, the camera following us all the way, and we
play with real money on the line; win, lose, or draw the audience is caught up in the excitement. Since this is real action
and not scripted, we have no idea how it will turn out. Real
reality, so to speak. What do you think?"

"I like it," said Sherine.

Sherine had the director of the program, Danny Elias, call
me, and I went over the concept with him. He liked it too,
and he added a few excellent touches of his own. I liked
Danny the minute I talked to him, because he could see the
possibilities immediately and he had great enthusiasm. (My
wife tells me that I have a tendency to like anyone who
agrees with me. I say, what's so bad about that?)

I told Danny I would get two of the best dice controllers
in the world, my Golden Touch buddies, to be a part of my
team. I was thinking specifically of Dominator and Sharpshooter. I would have wanted Billy the Kid, Mr. Finesse,
and Bill Burton to be a part of our team as well, but they
had to go home after the "Beat the House" seminars and
couldn't come back for the A&E shoot on Thursday and
Friday. Even though the events depicted were supposed to
be taking place on one night, the actual shooting would

take place over two days. In that time Beau would be filmed in his home helping some other players, with me coming in to assist; then we'd film the dice controllers practicing and strategizing; then we'd film segments at the Gambler's Book Shop and the Gambler's General Store; then we'd play at four casinos: Gold Coast, Treasure Island, Sam's Town, and Sunset Station.

Beau decided to invite Soft Touch, a woman from Texas who had been a PARR student, and a guy named Hardway, who lives in Las Vegas, also a former PARR student, to be a part of his team.

I asked Beau if he wanted to have all six of us play as one team, with a pooled bankroll and a set strategy, but he preferred to have his people play as individuals. "Then we can see which concept worked better, team play or individual play," he said. "I think it would be more interesting for the audience if we all played separately."

When I told Dominator of Beau's decision, he said: "Team play is the way to go for this. The Golden Touch crew should play as a team. I just called Sharpshooter and he's flying out Wednesday evening. I'm going back to Chicago for Tuesday and Wednesday, but I'll come back Wednesday night, too—with tee shirts that say GoldenTouchCraps.com. We'll wear them while we play."

I called a limo company I often use when I'm in Vegas playing anonymously and not being comped, and requested my favorite driver, Tamara, to be our sole driver for the two days of the A&E shooting. Tamara is a beautiful, elegant woman from Poland with a delightful manner and a delicious accent. I figured if she appeared on camera she'd make the rest of us look good.

On Monday, January 20, I moved from Sunset Station to Treasure Island. Since Monday was the second day of our Golden Touch class, I spent the entire day with Billy the Kid,

Bill Burton, and Dominator, instructing the students at a regulation craps table at Beau's house.

As a part of our Gold Chip two-day package, Golden Touch Craps offers a comped meal with the coaches (in this case, me, as the other coaches had all returned home late that afternoon), to be followed by actual play in the casino. That evening we all ate at Francesco's, Treasure Island's gourmet continental restaurant. Beau and Henry and Linda Tamburin joined our first four students—Julius, Todd, Marilyn, and Charles—and me.

The dinner was delightful and Todd, a dealer in Reno, told us interesting stories about dealers and behind-the-scenes action.

"Do dealers ever try to get people to seven out?" asked Marilyn.

"Oh, yeah," said Todd. "If I'm the stickman and a player is obnoxious and not tipping, I can usually get them to seven out. If they are random rollers I return the dice to them with 4:1 or 6:2 on top. That usually does it. My boss knows what I'm doing, because I flip the dice with the stick, and sometimes he tells me to knock it off. But a good dealer can usually get a player to seven out."

After dinner, we all headed to the tables, where each student got to test his or her new technique in live action. As luck would have it (and it probably was luck this early on in their careers), all of them had good rolls and made money. I also had a pretty good roll.

Marilyn said: "Two days ago I looked at craps one way; now I look at it in an entirely different manner. The 5-Count works; so many shooters sevened out so early and I didn't lose any money on them; taking care with your rolls works. I'm really happy I took the course." That made me feel good.

That Tuesday and Wednesday I got back into my normal

Vegas routine. I walked the Strip in the early morning from Treasure Island to Mandalay Bay and back. Then I had a relaxing breakfast, showered, and headed for my first session. I'd play for a couple of hours, then read, perhaps have a light lunch, play an early afternoon session, nap, go to dinner, and then play in the evening.

Between the Sunset Station seminars and teaching our first Golden Touch class, it had been a whirlwind four days.

Dominator was due in around seven o'clock that Wednesday evening, with Sharpshooter set to arrive around 10 P.M. After Dominator got in, he I went to dinner at Treasure Island's Buccaneer Bay.

"I've got the tee-shirts," he said.

"Beau doesn't want to play teams; he prefers individual play," I said.

"But *we'll* play as a team; we even have our uniforms." He smiled. "And we are going to win, Frank. This will be very big for Golden Touch."

Dom has absolute confidence in his—and our—ability to win. He's a positive thinker with a vengeance. I tend to see the dark possibilities, and this time I saw them with regard to three of the four casinos at which we were scheduled to play.

"The casinos have been finalized," I said. "First on Thursday night at eight o'clock is Gold Coast; then Friday morning it is Treasure Island, then Sam's Town, then Sunset Station."

"I've never played at Gold Coast," said Dom.

"Neither have I, but I know Sam's Town has really long tables and so does Sunset Station."

"Not good for us," he said.

"But we have Treasure Island," I said.

"I like their tables," said Dom.

"So we hope Treasure Island bails us out if we get into trouble at Gold Coast."

"We're not getting into trouble," he said.

"Sam's Town does have 20X odds, so we should go the Come bet route there and take advantage of the low vig. Sunset has 10X odds. I don't know what the other has."

When Sharpshooter arrived, Dom and I were playing at a $25 minimum table at Treasure Island—and not achieving anything noteworthy. In fact, we shouldn't have been playing at all; we should have been asleep. But Dom loves to play, and all I need is a little nudge from him and I'm at the tables, even if I'm a little tired and should know better. Sharpshooter decided to try his hand at the table but from the Don't side. So we all put up Don't Pass bets and Sharpshooter immediately rolled a seven, then established a point and hit the point. None of that was good for us, obviously. Then Sharpshooter established a point of four and I loaded up on the odds ($300 to win $150 as I had a $50 Don't Pass bet and Treasure Island allows 3X odds on the four or ten) and prayed that he'd get a seven. I didn't have long to wait. He hit the seven in two rolls. We did another Don't and he won that one as well. Then we called it a night.

We agreed to meet for breakfast at 9 A.M. at the café to go over strategy for the day's filming and the evening's playing.

When I went to bed that night, I had visions of a great victory the next night against the Gold Coast. I recalled what Nancy Patterson had said before my first baccarat tournament. "I am winning. I am winning. I am winning!" I fell into a deep sleep.

At breakfast I took out a list I had made concerning what we should and shouldn't say when the cameras were rolling. I am usually pretty laid back when it comes to most things, but when it comes to a public performance—and our A&E appearance was a public performance—I am, in the words of my wife, a person who "likes to control things." I don't want any "X" factors cropping up to influence what is happening or make our "production" look bad. And in this case our production was everything we said and everything we did while the cameras and microphones were on.

"We have to be very careful about what we say on camera, because this is a cut-and-paste show. We might say something that is innocent and in context makes sense but when cut and spliced makes us look like fools. For example, we can't talk about making high-vig bets, because even though you guys can hit them with consistency, if traditional gambling writers hear us talking about these bets they'll think we don't know what we're doing. Then they'll write about our efforts as if we got lucky—that's *if* we win . . ."

"We *are* winning," said Dom.

"We don't ever want to use the word 'trend' at the table or refer to hot or cold tables. Even though we know that what we mean by 'trend' is how we're shooting, what kind of groove we're in, out of context it will sound like typical gambling mumbo-jumbo. We do not at any time want to look like crazy gamblers. One slip and Golden Touch gets tarnished."

"I agree," said Sharpshooter. "We have our reputations riding on this, not just our money."

"Let's go over how we're going to play," said Dom.

"I think we should have three different betting styles," said Sharpshooter. "When the shooter is shooting he just puts up a Pass Line with odds. Then he only worries about shooting, not betting. Dom and I will do the 6/8 progression [this is a very aggressive progression on the numbers six and eight from $60 to $150 and needs the shooter to hit at least six of these numbers to pull in a substantial win]; Dom will do it when I'm shooting, and I'll do it when Dom and you are shooting. You do the Come betting with max odds and Dom will do the Come betting when you shoot."

"We're talking about only when *we* shoot now, right?" I asked.

"Yes," said Sharpshooter.

"We should seriously consider how we play Beau, Soft Touch, and Hardway," said Dom. "We know we're going to be on . . ."

"I love your confidence," I laughed. "We could get killed, you know. This is the very short run and luck plays a role, a big role in the short run."

"Not with the three of us," he said. "We are the best. One of us is going to get hot, probably all of us." I love Dom. I just wish I had his absolute certainty that we would win the contest against the casinos.

"On the others," I said, "we should half-bet them and use the *5-Count* with Come bets only. So at Sam's Town and Sunset Station, a $5 Come bet with $25 or $30 in odds, maybe even lower, after the 5-Count, until we see if they are hitting numbers or not."

"The public isn't playing with us," said Dom. "It's just the six of us?"

"From what I understand, all the casinos have reserved a table for us," I said.

"Good—we don't have to worry about random rollers," said Sharpshooter.

"Why don't we go to the Orleans and practice for tonight?" I said.

"Good idea," said Dom.

"Yeah, we can learn the tables," said Sharpshooter.

So after breakfast, Tamara drove us to the Orleans to practice. The tables there were long and hard, with strange bounces. We played as a team but only at the $5 level. Still, we wound up losing about $60. Strangely, the pit seemed very uptight when we were playing. One dealer said: "I haven't seen so many suits in this pit in two years. What's going on?" I guessed that the "suits" realized that we were practicing for that night and wanted to watch us in action.

"We got the feel of the tables," said Sharpshooter.

"Practice can't hurt," I said

As Tamara drove us to Beau's house, Dom said, "Did we just go to the Orleans?"

"Yeah, Dom, it's where we are playing tonight," I said.

"It's Gold Coast," said Dom.

"What?"

"We're playing at Gold Coast," said Dom, "not the Orleans."

"Shit," I said. "Are you sure?"

"You said it last night," said Dom. "I just remembered it. And it's right here on the schedule."

"Crap," I said.

"We practiced at the wrong casino?" said Sharpshooter.

"My fault," I said. "Somehow I got the Orleans in my head."

The irony wasn't lost on me. Here I had been lecturing my teammates about being careful throughout the shoot, and I had stupidly taken them to the wrong casino to practice. Orleans, Gold Coast. How could I confuse them? They don't even sound alike. But I had confused them. So our practice was basically a waste of time and money. Talk about "X" factors; factor in my memory.

Beau was in his garage with the A&E crew, filming at his craps table. Danny, the director, had told me to be a part of the "class" Beau was teaching, so I walked into the garage.

Perfect timing! I might have gotten Orleans confused with Gold Coast, but I certainly had made my entrance at just the right time.

"Well, look who's here," said Beau as I walked into the action.

"Hey, Beau," I said.

The camera was rolling, but I ignored it and picked up on what Beau was doing. He had three "students" and for the next hour Beau and I jointly taught them about craps.

When we finished with the "class," around 4 P.M., we took a break. While Danny and his cameraman, Andrew, checked their equipment and made phone calls, Beau and his wife, Beth, along with Soft Touch, Sharpshooter, Dominator, and I, lounged with Beau's "students," Dr. Steve Franzblau of Florida and David and Sharon Andrzejewski of Niagara Falls, New York, beside Beau's pool.

I gave my spiel about controlling what we say during the shoot so as not to look bad and Soft Touch remarked, "All men are control freaks." I then talked about how as a director I didn't like any "X" factors to screw up a production and that I liked to anticipate as much as I could. Those pesky "X" factors would still crop up from time to time, but many headaches could be avoided with just a little planning. We didn't want any "X" factors.

And then the "X" factor arrived.

Hardway.

Or rather, he *blew* in, wearing a racecar shirt that was black with orange-yellow fire shooting out of something (I think it was a car). He immediately grabbed a beer, certainly not his first of the day, and bumper-balled around the room greeting the people he knew and ignoring the rest. Hardway was one of the PARR players that Sharpshooter had taught, but, as Sharpshooter stated after the A&E shoot was over, "He never took much of my advice."

When Hardway had settled down a bit, I introduced myself and shook his hand. He seemed a little unfocused. From what Beau and the others had told me, I knew that Hardway custom-built cars for people and was himself a racecar driver. He was a big player, betting thousands, and his betting philosophy was simple: "When you're losing, just throw more money at it and sooner or later you'll win."

That was certainly different from my philosophy, which was, when you're losing, cut back until you get grooved in.

When it was time to film the players practicing, Hardway took his accustomed spot—at the end of the table, the farthest possible point from the back wall and obviously the most difficult place from which to shoot. I immediately recalled how in the segment filmed previously both Beau and I had emphasized that the best shooting positions were SL1 and SR1, followed by SL2 and SR2. We also emphasized that you had to make the best possible bets to try to wrest the advantage from the casinos.

So the camera started rolling and . . .

Cut to Hardway: "Yep, watch out for me, boys. I'll be setting the 6-T and I throw a lot of craps numbers with that set. I'll be betting up those craps numbers! Ha! Ha!"

Now, the craps numbers—two, three, and twelve, with the 11 sometimes lumped in there—are some of the worst bets to be found at craps, and indeed some of the worst bets to be found in the casino. They have huge house edges and only the very best controlled shooters, like Sharpshooter, Dominator, and Billy the Kid, could overcome those edges. As Hardway roared on about how he would bet all those Crazy Crapper bets (as the Captain calls them), I kept thinking about how traditional gambling writers would view this segment, if it was used, and I cringed. This wouldn't make us look good.

Aside from his betting philosophy and Dean Martin–esque habits, Hardway was a good fellow, a happy good fellow—I mean a really, really happy good fellow. I remembered what AP had told me before the A&E shoot: "You can't control everything."

No, certainly not.

Somewhere in this practice session, as we were verbally strategizing for the camera, Soft Touch said: "I don't know where I'll be shooting from. I'll see how I feel."

I looked at Dom, who was looking at Sharpshooter, who was looking at me. All three of us then looked over at Soft Touch. She was rolling the dice, practicing, and didn't notice our looks. I knew what Dom and Sharpshooter were thinking. Unless you are supremely skilled and versatile (like Sharpshooter and Dominator), it's not good to change your shooting positions too much, especially if you want to perfect your throw. If Soft Touch wasn't concentrating on one position, and focusing all her attention on it, she could jeopardize her performance. It was going to be tough enough to concentrate with the camera on us; it would be tough enough to play those long tables; to have to also think about where you are going to throw from was just an added, unnecessary burden. When I had seen her shoot at Sunset Station the week before, she seemed to have a very nice rhythm from SL1. Dom raised his eyebrows, Sharpshooter gave a small grimace, and then we forgot about Soft Touch and concentrated on our practice session.

During one of the breaks someone broke the news that Treasure Island had pulled out of the show. This was shattering.

"This is going to be a real uphill battle," said Sharpshooter.

Making a television documentary, even the "fly on the wall" variety, requires endless waiting and endless shooting of footage. Danny was going to shoot over thirty hours of film for a twenty-five-minute segment.

"The waiting is killing me," said Sharpshooter at seven o'clock.

"Do you have any peanut butter?" Dom asked Beth. "I need something to eat before we go to Orleans."

"Gold Coast," I corrected.

So we ate some peanut butter out of the jar. Beth also gave us some crackers and cheese.

"I didn't think this would take so long," she said, "or I would have gotten us some hors d'oeuvres."

During the breaks, Sharpshooter practiced at Beau's table. Soft Touch was passing the dice to him so he could shoot endless shots.

"Don't overpractice," I warned him.

"You can't overpractice," he said.

"Yes, you can. You can be like a fighter who leaves his fight in the gym because of too much training."

I'd seen this phenomenon in theater, too. There was such a thing as overrehearsing a show, so that when it came time for opening night you were flat, listless, and dead.

Finally, at about seven forty-five, we started for the limo. I was wired with my own microphone, as were Beau, Soft Touch, and Sharpshooter. Tamara, our driver, had been waiting around the whole time, reading articles I had written in gambling magazines that Beau had in his house, and listening to our conversations about craps. I later found out that her boyfriend was an avid craps player.

Andrew, the cameraman, sat on the floor of the limo so that he could film us as we went into battle for the first time. He'd ask us questions and we'd answer them as we headed for Gold Coast. I looked around that limo and I knew this would be a tough night. We all looked washed out and tired from a day before the cameras. I tried to relax and get my mind focused on the task at hand.

When we arrived at Gold Coast, the place was packed. There was no empty table reserved for us; in fact, the pit boss said the only way we could film would be if we played

with the public at the tables. Thankfully, we were able to get
our positions when, miraculously, several people fled a losing table; on stick left were Sharpshooter, Soft Touch, and
me; on stick right were Dominator and Beau; and on stick
right way at the end was Hardway.

We had previously decided to play "Chinese fire drill,"
which meant that everyone would shoot from his or her preferred position and, when finished, relinquish that position
to the next shooter. Thus, if Sharpshooter finished his roll at
SL1, he'd move out of the way and Soft Touch would take
that position; when she finished, I'd take that position. Being
in position maximized our chances to have winning rolls.

Our Golden Touch team decided that on all the random
rollers we'd use the *5-Count* and bet conservatively with a
couple of Come bets and double odds. If a random roller
had a good roll, we'd make money on him; otherwise the *5-
Count* would eliminate most of them.

As it turned out, we should have used the *5-Count* on all
of us as well, because, except for Hardway's very first roll,
where he hit a bunch of numbers (yes, including the craps
numbers that he was betting heavily on), each and every one
of us stunk up the joint—and that is putting it mildly. It was
"point, seven-out!" all night long.

Now, one of our Golden Touch teachers, Billy the Kid, a
great shooter, has a theory that controlled shooters have
more "point, seven-outs" than random rollers because we
are setting the dice in precise ways, assuming an "on axis"
roll, and if our roll is the least off we are more susceptible to
the seven showing. In short, we are still influencing the dice,
but in a bad way.

Well, that night went a long way toward proving Billy the
Kid's contentions. After Hardway's good roll, we all lost
bundles of money. Hardway, who was betting huge amounts
on each and every shooter, took an incredible beating, and

shortly after we pulled the plug on the shoot he staggered into the neon Vegas night.

What made Gold Coast even more embarrassing was the fact that two of our Golden Touch students, Julius and Todd, were in the casino and came over to play at our table. And what did they witness? Their teachers getting their asses kicked!

Of course, we had valid excuses for our poor performances. We were not rested, having been on the go since the morning; we were hungry, peanut butter and crackers notwithstanding; and we weren't focused.

"I think I did overpractice," said Sharpshooter as we headed for the cage.

"Everything conspired against us tonight," I said. "This whole evening was not conducive to performing well. I'm exhausted."

"Me, too," said Dom.

Standing in front of the cage after cashing in, we assessed the damage. As a team we were down about $1,080, or about $360 each. By the looks of them, both Beau and Soft Touch hadn't fared any better.

"Rough night," said Beau.

"Rough night," I agreed.

Of course, the camera was ever present, but we were so tired and so used to it that we continued our conversation without a second thought to the fact that what we were saying might get on television. Some of it might sound like sour grapes—bitching about the difficult conditions we faced, for example.

"Do you think we were a little too aggressive with the 6/8 progression, especially on Hardway's first roll? I said. "We didn't really take much money from that roll; we just kept building up our bets."

"No," said Dom.

"I don't know," said Sharpshooter.

In the limo, after we had filmed our exit and entrance into the casino a half-dozen times (in television and film things are shot out of sequence and then edited to make them coherent), Dom said, "Where's the rest of them?"

"Oh, Soft Touch decided to go in the Hummer with Danny and Andrew, and Beau joined her," said Sharpshooter.

"Where's Hardway?" I asked.

"Out there somewhere," said Dom, pointing to the city.

The conversation about how to bet continued in the limo, and also when we got back to Treasure Island, and also while we ate. It was one o'clock in the morning. Dom insisted that we should play our game, including the 6/8 progression. I thought we should collect some money before increasing our bets. And Sharpshooter agreed with first one and then the other. We were tired. We were hungry. We were losers. It didn't sit well with any of us.

Then Danny, Soft Touch, Andrew, and Beau came into the café to eat. They had spent some time at the bar having a few drinks. The Golden Touch crew was finished with eating and finished with our evening. I just wanted to crawl into bed.

"Well, you guys have set us up for a great comeback," said Danny.

Comeback? I thought as I wandered off to the elevators. Comeback?

If this were a scripted show, we'd come roaring back the next day and defeat the casinos. But this wasn't scripted; it was real life. We were not guaranteed a win tomorrow (or, rather, later today). We could continue with our losing streak and fall flat on our faces in front of millions of viewers.

Comeback?

Yeah, I thought before sleep covered me, a comeback, *please* God . . .

The phone rang, waking me. It was 8 A.M.

"Hello."

"Hello, my love," said AP.

"Hey, my beauty."

"How'd it go?"

"We got killed," I said.

I explained to her what happened.

"Today's another day," she said. "Don't think too much. You have the ability to win. Just be empty vessels and concentrate. You're rested. You'll win."

"You think?"

"I have confidence in you, Scobe. You always come through," she said.

At breakfast Dom was charged up. He had just spoken to Dr. Richard McCall, the Samurai Shooter. McCall gave Dom great advice, which when boiled down to its essentials was: Be an empty vessel and concentrate. You are prepared; you are ready; do what you've always done; you will prevail. McCall was, of course, right. My beautiful AP was right. We were skilled shooters and in the long run we could get an edge over the casinos.

"We play as we always played," said Dom. "McCall had a vision of an infinity eight," and he made a motion with his hand. "One never-ending eight." He made the infinity sign again.

"The mobius strip," said Sharpshooter.

"Fine," I said. I hated to intrude on Dom's visualization of McCall's vision, seeing as he was so pumped and ready for action, but I felt I had to. "I still think, in the short run, we should take down some wins before beginning the 6/8 progression, and we definitely don't do it on Beau, Soft Touch, or Hardway like we tried last night."

"Forget Hardway. He isn't showing up," said Dom.

"How do you know?" I asked.

"He's gone," said Dom.

"He did take an awful beating last night," said Sharpshooter.

"You can't bet every random shooter and expect to win," said Dom.

"My guess is he isn't going to wake up for a couple of days," said Sharpshooter.

"On Beau and Soft Touch," I doggedly continued, "we use the *5-Count* and just go with Come bets. No 6/8 progressions, no Place bets. Only the lowest-vig bets. Beau is tired; he's been on camera for the whole shoot with no rest. It has to affect his performance. And I noticed a big problem last night with Soft Touch's roll."

"I saw it too," said Sharpshooter.

"She's not pausing just before she shoots to get the sense of the table and the distance to the back wall. She's doing everything in one sweeping motion. It's the same mistake I was making a couple of months ago in Atlantic City until Mr. Finesse pointed it out to me. If she does that today, she isn't going have the touch," I said.

"Except if she gets lucky," said Sharpshooter.

"I don't want to rely on luck," said Dom.

"Why don't we tell her?" asked Sharpshooter.

"I'm not telling her," I said. "I don't think she'd listen to me. She doesn't know me that well and she doesn't know if I'm a good shooter or not."

"Don't bother," said Dom. "She won't listen. She thinks she can shoot from all spots at the table. She's not in the listening mood."

"Let's concentrate on ourselves," said Sharpshooter. "We don't want to get into anything with anyone else."

"No bad feelings," I said. "Maybe she'll come around today and not do one sweeping motion."

"I'll bet she doesn't change," said Dom.

"So we 5-*Count* Beau and Soft Touch, and bet the big money only on ourselves. And don't give unsolicited advice."

"Agreed," said Dom.

"Agreed," said Sharpshooter.

"And on us, no second guessing," I said." Dom, you want to run an aggressive 6/8, you do it. Sharpshooter, you want to take down a few wins before starting the 6/8 progression, you do that. We don't second-guess ourselves. Win, lose, or draw, we are in this together. We trust our teammates."

"We are not losing," said Dom.

"I do feel much better today," said Sharpshooter.

"So do I," I said.

"This is going to be the Golden Touch day," said Dom.

"Goddamn, Dom, I love your positive attitude," I said.

"We're the best," he said. "Why shouldn't I be positive?"

When we arrived at Sam's Town, no one from the shoot was there. Two tables were empty and we went over to them.

"I wonder if they'll let us practice on their tables before the filming?" asked Sharpshooter.

Dom walked over to the floorperson. A couple of moments later, Dom came back.

"Go get your dice," he said to Sharpshooter, "He says we can practice."

As we practiced, eleven o'clock came and went and still no Beau, no Soft Touch, no Danny, and no Andrew. But some of the bosses from Sam's Town showed up and they were concerned. It seems no one had told them it would be a "live game" (meaning real money), and the Sam's Town executives were under the impression that A&E was just going to have one player explain the game to the audience. They hadn't banked on five (or six, if Hardway showed) of us going head-to-head against them.

In fact, one of the executives said he was thinking of asking us to leave. Thankfully, this guy was reasonable and I explained to him that television networks were just like other big enterprises, often inefficient. I apologized for the error and then we started to talk. Turns out we had mutual friends in the casino industry, especially in Tunica, Mississippi. I mentioned Clyde Callicott, who used to be director of marketing at Sam's Town, and Chris Wade, who was currently entertainment director there. He knew both. I told him about the *Goodtimes Show* I did each week with Rudi Schiffer from Memphis. He had listened to it. Whew! Having friends in common and common references makes you less of a suspicious character, and thus this executive was much more willing to come up with a solution to our problem, that problem being, Sam's Town didn't have a full crew for the table, since they only thought one guy would be giving a demonstration.

After a half-hour of talks, Sam's Town came up with an arrangement that would allow us to shoot the A&E episode. By this time, Beau, Andrew, Danny, and Soft Touch had arrived.

"Okay, here's the deal. They're bringing over some blackjack dealers who also deal craps. They are very leery of us playing their 20X odds game so they're giving us true double odds." True double odds means that if you are betting $15 on the Pass and Come, you can back the four and ten with $30 in odds, the five and nine with $40 in odds, and the six and eight with $50 in odds. This was important to the Golden Touch team, since we planned to use Come betting with Beau and Soft Touch. It would have been much better, of course, if we'd been allowed to play the 20X odds.

"We have a $500 maximum bet on the Line with $1,200 on Placing the six or eight," I continued.

"We're not betting that much," said Sharpshooter.

"I think they're worried because they just got burned for over a million dollars by a blackjack team," said Beau.

"We have an hour and a half time limit and the public gets to play at the table as well," I concluded.

"That doesn't give us much time," said Sharpshooter.

"We're going to waste a lot of time with the random rollers," said Dom.

"We just use the *5-Count* on everyone but us. It's possible that a few of the random rollers will have good rolls and we'll be on them," I said.

"I tried to get in touch with Hardway but there was no answer," said Beau.

Dom looked at me with that "I told you so" look. I nodded as if to say, "You were right."

Danny and Andrew started the preparations for the shoot. Soft Touch was wired for sound, as was I. Luckily, David and Sharon Andrzejewski, Beau's two "students" from the previous day, would be at the table. I told them to pass the dice when it was their turn to roll. In fact, David and Sharon did even better than that. They were able to get the whole side of their table to pass the dice!

The Sam's Town shoot started off just the way the Gold Coast shoot ended—with us taking a beating. Beau went point, a couple of numbers, then seven-out. So did Dom, so did Soft Touch, so did Sharpshooter, and so did I. We didn't lose money on Beau and Soft Touch because we were using the *5-Count* with them, but we lost on ourselves. The dice went around the table. A few random rollers shot, all of them sevening out before the *5-Count*. Then it was Beau's turn again. I could see in his face that he didn't have it. Usually Beau is the picture of concentration, but the heavy filming schedule, the late hours, the interruption of his daily routine, and, perhaps, the pressure of doing his first television show seemed to have taken their toll. He went point, seven-out.

Now it was Dom's turn. While others had been shooting Dom had been fishing. That's correct, fishing. Play at a table with Dominator and you'll notice that occasionally he'll mime casting a line into the water and reeling in a big fish. He is harking back to a big salmon he once caught on the Great Lakes. This pleasant memory (pleasant for him, not so pleasant for the salmon) is his way of relaxing and getting into the rolling zone.

This particular roll of his was good, the first good one any of the Golden Touch crew had had thus far. He established his point, made some numbers, hit his point, established another point, and made some more numbers before sevening out. He looked good shooting. He looked confident. After he sevened out, he went back to fishing, all the while keeping one eye cocked to run the 6/8 progression when it was Sharpshooter's turn to shoot and to do the Come betting when it was my turn to shoot.

Sharpshooter had a decent roll, then so did I. The three of us looked at each other and we could see that each of us was beginning to get a feel for the table—we were getting our groove back. Dom nodded and cast his line into the waters.

The Sam's Town session started to go in our direction. Two random rollers had good rolls and because we were on them after the *5-Count* we made money. Dominator and Sharpshooter were consistently making us money with their rolls. I was also hitting enough to keep us in the black for that session. Unfortunately, Beau and Soft Touch just couldn't pull the switch on their rolls. Beau seemed tired and, again, Soft Touch seemed to be rushing her shots.

As the hour and a half time limit neared an end, it was my

turn to shoot. I would close the show. And close the show I did. I was in the rolling zone, and I hit four or five points and a truckload of other numbers to boot. When I finally sevened out, to a thunderous round of applause from the table, I saw that our chip racks were filled. We dumped our chips into one big pile and, as the casino counted them up, I realized that we had made up for last night's loss and were now slightly ahead.

• • • •

THE A&E SHOOTING schedule for the rest of the day would free up Dom and Sharpshooter to get some rest. Beau and I were to be filmed with Howard Schwartz at the Gambler's Book Shop on Eleventh Street and with Wendy Rock at the Gambler's General Store on Main Street. The storyline was that I was coming in from New York to autograph books for Howard and that Beau was meeting me at the shop to set up "tonight's" agenda vs. the casinos. Of course, we had already finished two of our sessions at the casino but, as I said, things are shot out of sequence.

As I write this I have no idea what sequences actually appeared in the A&E special. The focus of the special was, after all, on Beau as a professional craps and blackjack player; it was not on Golden Touch Craps (despite our heroics), or on me personally (despite my good looks and sexy nature). But we shot a hell of a lot of film, and we hoped we could later obtain the raw footage.

By the time we arrived at the Gambler's Book Shop, we were running a couple of hours late; that was due to the delay of play at Sam's Town while we ironed out the playing rules. Once at the bookstore, Danny and Andrew interviewed us concerning what it was like to be a professional gambler. I had to demur a bit since I am not a professional gambler. My definition of a professional is very simple: your profession is what you do to make your living, or at least 90 percent of your living. I make more money from other sources than I do from gambling; I write books and articles, I am a consultant for gaming-related enterprises, I have investments, and I teach craps and blackjack classes. I am not, therefore, a professional gambler, despite the fact that I spend between 60 and 120 days per year in the casinos. So for the show I defined myself as a writer who gambles who writes about gambling. I thought that was a fair description.

The shooting at the Gambler's Book Shop took longer than anticipated, and we had to cancel the Gambler's General Store segment. I was back at Treasure Island by five-thirty. Sharpshooter and Dominator had taken the limo to Sunset Station to scout out the tables and to get in some practice. Although Dom had played there the previous weekend, Sharpshooter had never even been to that casino, so he felt he needed the time to get familiar with Sunset Station's setup. Back at Treasure Island, we all decided to get a half-hour of meditation in before having dinner at Madame Ching's.

It was a smart move. At dinner, the three of us were relaxed and confident. We were not tired or worn out.

"We play the same way tonight as we did today," said Dom.

"It's a good feeling knowing we're ahead going into tonight's game," said Sharpshooter.

"We're only ahead a little, so we do have to be careful," I said.

We arrived at Sunset Station at seven forty-five that evening. The place was crowded but there was one table that was closed. Gary, the pit boss, introduced himself and then asked us what he could do for us.

"Put a reserve sign on the table until the others get here," I said.

"Will you be able to fill up the table?" he asked.

"Just about," I said.

I was figuring that if David and Sharon Andrzejewski came and if we had Tamara, our driver, and her boyfriend, Ron, at the table, it would make nine people—assuming, of course, that Hardway stayed in the land of the missing.

He did.

Also missing were Beau, Andrew, Danny, and Soft Touch.

"Are you sure these people are showing up?" asked Gary.

"Yeah, yeah," I said. "They must have been caught in traffic."

To expedite the filming when the others got there, Sharpshooter, Dominator and I went ahead and bought into the game.

When they finally arrived at eight-thirty, David and Sharon Andrzejewski were not with them. They weren't coming. However, we did have Tamara and her boyfriend ready to take up spots at the table. That would give us seven people and I was praying that Sunset Station wouldn't open the game to the public. If we could have the table to ourselves, I was sure that we could pull off the comeback we had started at Sam's Town, despite the length of the tables and even if Beau and Soft Touch continued to be off.

If you've never been to Sunset Station, you're missing a treat. It's a locals' casino, but it's a cut above the rest. The casino is clean and colorful; the dealers and pit personnel are professional and friendly. It's the perfect getaway from the neon glare of the Strip. Whenever I'm in Vegas for an extended trip, I make it a point to spend a few days at Sunset Station. My host, Bob DeFroda, always sees to it that I get the best they have to offer, and I don't have to gamble an arm and a leg to get the "A" treatment.

And, this night, they made it perfect for us. Gary kept the

"reserved" sign on the table and even asked us what minimum we wanted to play for.

"Five dollars," I said.

"You got it," he said.

"I haven't decided where I'm going to shoot from," said Soft Touch after Danny wired her up. "So I may jump over to your side at any time."

"Fine," I said.

And so the contest began.

Beau was the first to shoot. He looked tired and haggard; they'd been filming at his house while Sharpshooter, Dom, and I had been meditating and eating. Despite that, he had a good roll, his only good roll of the two days, and it got us off to a winning start. Unfortunately, Soft Touch went down quickly. Dom was next up; he hit a few numbers after he established his point and then sevened out. But he looked good. He was doing his fishing thing and his rolls were soft and contained. His seven-out was what we call a "good seven-out" because it was made with one 4 and one 3, which meant that he was "on axis" using the 3-V set. I didn't fare much better than Soft Touch. Now it was Sharpshooter's turn. He went point, seven-out. Now Tamara passed up the dice and then her boyfriend Ron passed them up as well. The dice were back to Beau.

He quickly sevened out.

Soft Touch went down quickly again.

Dom then held the dice for about ten minutes, making several points and a bunch of numbers. He was in a groove and he was fishing away when he wasn't actually shooting. (God knows how many mental salmon he was reeling in but at this rate they would be enough to sink the boat!)

I had a decent roll.

Sharpshooter had a decent roll.

Danny had the camera on me and asked, "How's it going?"

"Good, good," I said. "We're holding our own and it looks like we're getting a feel for this table. You might be about to witness some really good rolls. We're getting in the groove."

Soft Touch said, "I'm moving to your spot."

"Take your chips and move now," I said, "before Beau shoots, so you don't have to shoot from that position again."

She moved into my spot at SL1 and I moved to SL3 to the left of Sharpshooter, who was in SL2. Beau sevened out again, just after the 5-Count, so we lost money on him. Then Dom had another decent roll and we won that money back before he sevened out and went back to fishing. (Aren't salmon an endangered species?)

Soft Touch was now shooting from her new spot for the evening. It didn't help. Although she was setting the dice and picking them up confidently and smoothly, her delivery was all one motion, as it had been for the two days of the A&E special, and this technique seemed to be hurting her performance. If I'd known her better or if I'd known how she would react to advice, I would have told her to take the "pause," as Mr. Finesse calls it, just before she threw. In Golden Touch, when one of our players offers advice, we listen because we know that often another player can see that you're doing something wrong, even though you think you're doing everything right. I don't hesitate to give advice to Sharpshooter or Dom or any Golden Touch shooter, and they don't hesitate to give me advice. But I didn't know Soft Touch well enough to offer unsolicited advice.

Soft Touch sevened out just after the 5-Count. We lost money on her. I believe at this point Soft Touch left the game, although I was not focused on her, and I really don't quite remember. I just don't remember her being at the table—or maybe she was at the end of the table, next to Sharpshooter, and I just couldn't see her. But, for all intents and purposes, she was out of the game.

Too bad, because I could see that the Golden Touch crew was heating up!

Then the magical sequence began. Sharpshooter had a good roll. Then Beau passed up his turn. Then Dom had a good roll. Then I had a good roll. Then Dom. Then me. Then Sharpshooter, then Dom, then me.

And then Sharpshooter closed the show in a spectacular fashion with a display of hitting sixes and eights that was nothing short of miraculous. Dom ran the 6/8 progression on him, several times; I went up on $5 Come bets with $50 in odds when he occasionally hit other numbers, and Sharpshooter rolled and rolled and rolled.

I think he rolled for what seemed like twenty-five to thirty minutes or so, but time wasn't the key to the roll; numbers were. He was setting the 3-V, which is geared to hitting sixes and eights, and those sixes and eights came in abundance.

When he finally sevened out, to hugs and high fives from Dom and me, we had a pile of multicolored chips in our racks.

At this point we called it a night.

"Why did you quit now?" asked Danny with the camera trained.

"We're tired; we just staged a remarkable comeback; Sharpshooter had a tremendous roll. The time is right to quit for the night."

"How much did you guys make?" asked Danny.

"I think we're up about $3,000, after being down over $1,000," said Dom.

As I started to dump the chips on the table, making our

second "chip mountain" of the day, Andrew asked, "How much did you make apiece?"

"Probably between $800 and $1,000 each," I said.

"Do you consider that a lot of money?" asked Andrew.

"We'll leave that for you to decide," I said.

"It's not the money," said Dom. "It's the thrill of victory."

"We came back with the odds against us," said Sharpshooter.

"Sharpshooter earned his name again tonight!" said Dom.

"We all came through," said Sharpshooter.

As the cashier counted out what seemed like interminable hundred-dollar bills, I looked at my teammates. You couldn't find three people more different than the three of us, but we were joined in a way that few people, other than soldiers on the battlefield and athletes on a team, are ever joined. Our fortunes rode on each other's skill and presence of mind. In truth, it wasn't how much we won that mattered, but *how* we won it. Playing long tables, under the gun, the three of us had "come through" as AP had predicted. We had some rocky times, but we played our game, stayed the course, and, to put a dramatic tinge on the event, we prevailed.

In the limo, driving Sharpshooter to the airport to catch his red-eye flight back to Detroit, the three of us were spent.

"I'm glad we caught all of this on tape," said Sharpshooter. "Otherwise it would be hard to believe."

"It was a dream ending," said Dom.

"The best of all possible dreams," I said as I counted out each of our shares. "A happy ending."

····

17

····

It Isn't Always Pretty

NOT EVERYONE finds a happy ending to his or her personal dice-control dreams. For some, delving into the world of dice control to beat the casinos ends up in a nightmare of mounting debts, ruined relationships, and embarrassed about-faces. This book is not being written as a cautionary tale against gambling—there are enough of those sorts of books out there—but since I've shown you the bright side of the issue, some of the great shooters and their great victories over the casinos, I think it only wise to share with you some of the darker stories, as well.

The dark tales of those who have been ruined by dice dreams have a common thread, and it can be summed up in one word: *con.*

No, I'm not talking about the typical "gambling system" con that promises millions but reaps only heartbreak. Nor am I suggesting that those who took courses in dice control such as Golden Touch Craps, or who read the finer books on the subject, were conned into thinking they would set the dice world on fire. Legitimate courses and legitimate books are very careful not to promise the impossible—which means being honest that some people just aren't going to develop enough skill and betting acumen to flip the game in their favor. After all, not everyone who goes to college with the dream of becoming a doctor actually makes that dream come true. Oh, yes, dice control is real; it works and *some* people can do it. Some, not everyone.

Those who have destroyed themselves pursuing the dream of winning millions or making their living from dice control were not conned by others—they conned themselves. Like the performer who just doesn't have the voice or the stage presence, who hasn't learned the rudiments of his profession, but who still thinks he'll be discovered and make it big in Hollywood someday, some would-be dice controllers have conned themselves into thinking they are better than they, in fact, are. Indeed, of those whose lives have hit the wrong notes because of dice control, the ones I know about or have met did not have the ability to alter the game to any significant degree, due to lack of practice or lack of inherent skill (or both), and the few who could actually control the dice were themselves out of control. The Captain has always said that the battle is not between you and the casino but between you and yourself. He's right. Those who destroyed themselves with dice delusions have no one to blame but themselves. They only half-listened to the cautions given by their teachers and instead went full speed ahead into gambling with nary a glance ahead—and they ran right into a brick wall called reality.

The very best dice controllers in the world, including Sharpshooter, Dominator, Mr. Finesse, Billy the Kid, Bill Burton, Howard Newman, and the rest of Golden Touch crew, do not play the game for a living, despite playing for relatively large stakes. Why? Partly because they would not be relaxed, knowing that their livelihood depended on the roll of the dice, and if you can't relax when you are shooting the dice you are not going to be able to perform. You would then be just another random roller looking to gamble away your money on a hope and a fancy.

The Lee brothers are the exceptions that prove the rule. They do make their living playing craps, and a damn good living it is, too. Still, neither Tony nor Larry Lee has a wife or children, they are well financed by Whale, and they have developed the temperament to play full-time and handle the ups and downs that Lady Luck throws them. There are not many dice controllers out there capable of doing what they do.

But there are many who *think* they can be like the Lees. Thus, they con themselves into believing they *are* like the Lees—when, in fact, they aren't anywhere near.

One such player was a woman I'll call "Eve," a dentist who was building a successful practice in Pennsylvania when she decided that she loved playing craps and was going to learn how to control the dice and become a professional. She took a course, practiced a little, even had some successful outings to Atlantic City that gave her the confidence (hubris) to do something very foolish. She closed up her dental office, sold most of her possessions, and headed for Las Vegas. With a $200,000 nest egg, she figured she'd be able to play craps every day and make between $300 and $600 a day. She put a down payment on a condo, bought a car, furnished her new home, and was left with about $125,000.

She wanted to make money fast, so she scaled her betting at $400 or so when others were shooting the dice and $1,100 inside when she was rolling. She thought she could "read tables," so she "charted" what had happened previously at the tables and bet accordingly. She should have known better; when random rollers are shooting, past performance is no indication of future performance, since the game is *random*. Streaks do happen in random games but they happen only in the past; they cannot be predicted with accuracy in the future. If the game is not random, because a controlled shooter is changing the nature of the probabilities, then what happened in the past—i.e., a player having a signature number or numbers—will probably continue to happen in the future, at least statistically.

This distinction is crucial, because too many players think the actual *tables* have trends when, in reality, only certain *shooters* can be said to have such trends. If you are a recreational player betting "entertainment money," then whatever superstitions you enjoy can be safely enjoyed, because losing your entertainment dollar is no big deal—*that* money is, after all, there to be lost. But if you are trying to actually beat the game of craps or, harder still, make a living playing craps, then superstitions can be dangerous to the health of your bankroll and the health of your head.

So it was with our dentist; she got drilled. Her first three months in Vegas saw her playing every day and losing just about 80 percent of her sessions. By the end of this time, she had no money in the bank. But she was able to sell her condo for a slight profit; she moved in with another craps player who also fancied himself a professional gambler, and—they both proceeded to lose continually. No wonder. Neither one of them could control the dice or themselves.

Then our dentist became frantic. She had the edge, or so she thought, so why wasn't she winning? She started to borrow money, first from gullible relatives, then from close friends, and then from anyone who would be foolish enough to listen to her spin her dreams of "advantage play," promising to pay the money back from her "winnings" and then some. Because few of her old acquaintances knew that she was falling deeper and deeper into the big, black hole of gambling debt (she would always brag about how well she was doing), when she asked them for "investments" so she could win "even more," they gave her the money. She had conned them into thinking she was a winner; what's worse, she had conned herself as well. But there were no real winnings. The few sessions she won, she won because she was lucky. And in Las Vegas, a town built not on luck but on math and the indifferent designs of probability, our dentist found herself in grave trouble.

But she hadn't hit bottom. That came later. After six months in Vegas, she was broke and in debt, so she started to "live" with a series of men, mostly reprobates, who helped her fuel her dice delusions.

Finally, she asked someone who was successfully employing dice control in his casino adventures to lend her money that she would pay back with her "winnings." He knew she wasn't going to win anything, so he rented a truck, moved her stuff from her "boyfriend's" apartment, and paid for her plane fare to go home to Pennsylvania.

Her story does have a satisfactory ending, of sorts. She's back to drilling instead of being drilled, for one, but I have been told that, strangely enough, she is now an inveterate poster on craps message boards on the Web, where she attempts to debunk the idea that dice control is real. She accounts for her massive losses by portraying herself as a victim of a scam perpetrated by others, either purposely or because they had blind faith in a method that just doesn't work. It is she, unfortunately, who is blind to the truth, that truth being she was the architect of her own dice demise. She doesn't seem to understand that just because she wasn't able to do it doesn't mean that it can't be done. After all, I couldn't hit a baseball five hundred feet in my baseball career, but Barry Bonds could. Still, she isn't playing anymore, and that is a good thing.

"Adam"'s story has a different ending, if we can consider

it ended. He, too, took up dice control. But instead of practicing at home and taking it easy in the casinos when he first tried to apply the technique, Adam went wild. "I thought because I knew about the topic from my reading that was the same thing as being able to do it. It wasn't. I was and am a gambler at heart and I would bet it up when I'd roll. But I actually had no control over the dice. All I was doing was setting them and then delivering them softly, but they still bounced all over the place. I just pretended in my mind that I was a controlled shooter. I wasn't. I don't even own a pair of dice, so I never practiced at home.

"I guess I should have just placed table-minimum bets and worked on the various elements of controlled throwing, but when I'd get to a table my adrenaline would flow and I'd want to get in the action. If I lost money on my own rolls, I'd try to make it up with even bigger bets on other shooters. I had no discipline. I still have no discipline. The only difference between me now and me two years ago when I was pretending to be a controlled shooter is that now I'm broke. I can't afford to play at the Strip casinos anymore, so I play at the 25 cent and dollar games. I still play like a wild man but now I don't even try to exercise any control over the dice. I don't have control over myself, so how can I control anything else? Maybe someday I'll wake up and either quit gambling or really learn how to play craps. For now, it's just the rush that I'm in it for, nothing else."

As of this writing, Adam is indeed playing in those 25 cent and dollar games, and still playing in an undisciplined fashion. His is another example of the self-con, but at least when he woke up to what was happening he blamed the right person, himself, for his problems.

"Seth" is the quintessential example of someone who buys everything and buys *into* everything as well. "I have bought every craps system on the market, looking for the one that would make me rich. Instead I've helped to make the casinos richer. I bought your book [meaning *my* book *Beat the Craps Out of the Casinos*] but that *5-Count* stuff was just too boring. There would be times the dice would go around the whole table and I hadn't gotten into the action because everyone sevened out just like that. Then it was really frustrating when I'd get past the 5-Count, get into the action, and the shooter would seven out on the sixth or seventh roll. I played it for a couple of sessions and I didn't like it.

"Some of the systems I bought worked for awhile and I'd accumulate a lot of little wins and then I'd get hammered with a huge loss. I tried to win by playing only low-house-edge bets like the Pass Line and the Come. I played the Don't Pass; I'd chart tables, make graphs. Nothing worked. Then I read about controlled shooting and I had a few private lessons with a guy who claimed he was this big-shot professional gambler. After I spent about $2,000 on private lessons with this guy from upstate, I realized that the guy was a phony—he couldn't control the dice any better than I could. But I figured that dice control was a real skill, just that this guy was a scammer. I read a couple of books on the subject, including *Forever Craps* by you, but you always caution about discipline and that's not the kind of player I am. I crave the action, even though I am looking to win. But I did start using the 3-V set and I tried to have a nice soft touch.

"Believe it or not, I think I now tend to win money on my rolls. But I always give it all back and then some on the other shooters. I just can't seem to help myself. I think controlled shooting is a real skill, but another real skill is not being out of control yourself. I guess I should use the *5-Count* or qualify other shooters in some way, just to reduce my risk, but that reduction in risk also reduces my action and less action means more boring, if you catch my drift."

Seth is the reason why casinos probably don't have too much to fear from all the players now looking into learning dice control. Like Seth, most craps players "crave the action," and this craving is what prevents many of them from honing their skills and self-discipline. A baseball analogy will fit here: A good dice controller without self-control when others are shooting is like a batter with a beautiful swing who goes after bad pitches; he'll strike out. There are plenty of strikeouts in the world of dice control.

18

Mississippi Dreaming

WHEN THE GTC team completed the A&E shooting in January 2003, we knew that the biggest challenge for us was not what we had just finished, but the very first full-blown Golden Touch class, which we would be holding in Tunica, Mississippi, in March of that year.

This was going to be a spectacular weekend—or a spectacular bomb. We'd planned a four-day event: on Friday, we would hold a one-day Sharpshooter Craps Festival, which consisted of talks and hands-on demonstrations and craps contests; Saturday and Sunday would be our regular two-day seminar; and on Monday we would offer Dynamic Dimensions, a new course Sharpshooter was developing that would teach advanced techniques to skilled players, techniques such as Tony Lee's "trick shot," which we now referred to as a "kill shot."

But first we had to find a place to hold the event. I suggested one of Tunica's casino hotels. Some of the GTC members thought this might be inviting unwanted scrutiny from the casinos. I thought differently. Any savvy casino boss would want an influx of novice would-be dice controllers to his property, for two reasons:

1. Because dice control takes time and a lot of practice to achieve, most new dice controllers are not yet playing with an advantage. Where would you want these neophytes to practice their techniques—at your casino or someone else's?

2. Most craps players who could afford our course would probably bring spouses or friends with them to the casino, spouses and friends who played the machines or other table games. For example, Mr. Finesse's wife, Miriam, and some of the other wives are avid $1 and $5 slot players. Slot players' losses, in the long run, will more than make up for any craps winnings a controlled shooter enjoys.

Even so, approaching a casino and saying, "Look, we want to hold a dice-control seminar on your property in which we teach people a viable technique for beating you," is easier said than, well, *said*. Many casino executives run scared when confronted with anything new, so I knew I would have to ask someone who had vision and courage. So I asked my friend Chris Wade, the director of entertainment for Sam's Town in Tunica. I knew that, if anyone would see the great possibilities of such a weekend, Chris would. He's a clear and daring thinker. Several years before, he had invited John Robison, Walter Thomason, and me to give lectures at Sam's Town. These events had gone over well.

Chris didn't hesitate when I made my pitch. He booked the dates, reserved a block of rooms for the attendees, and said: "This could be something really good for Sam's Town and Tunica. An event geared to gambling."

Now, we just had a very "simple" thing left to do—get the craps players to come!

. . . .

IF YOU'VE never been to Tunica, Mississippi, you are missing one of the great visual treats of casino gambling: *Viva Las Vegas* meets *Gone with the Wind*. The very first time I went to Tunica, in 2000, I was struck by the dichotomy—beautiful modern casinos set in the midst of sprawling, horizon-to-horizon cotton fields, rice paddies, and soybean fields. Broken-down tractors, crumbling shanties, patched-up cars—with sleek limousines cruising past them, taking gamblers to and from the Memphis airport.

It's quittin' time at Tara.

Here's how I described my first trip to Tunica in 2000 for *Chance Magazine.*

Tunica, Mississippi

Let's start at the end, shall we? After three nights and two days in Tunica, Mississippi, it was time for my wife, the beautiful AP, and me to get in the Sam's Town car and head for the Memphis airport.

I had come to Tunica to do seminars on gambling with slot expert John Robison and Walter Thomason, author of the best-selling book *Twenty-first Century Blackjack.*

This was a first really, as Sam's Town was paying for these talks and rarely do casinos bring in gambling experts to teach their patrons the real ins and outs, the real odds and ends of casino gambling. But Chris Wade, the talented, visionary Entertainment Director of Sam's Town, is not the typical casino executive. So here we were in Mississippi.

Now it was Monday, almost 7 A.M., and the car and driver were supposed to be there promptly at seven. But I had learned something in my two days in the land of Dixie—time doesn't press on the Southerner the way it does on us

Yankees. As the "devil" time was approaching (in craps the
seven is often called the devil), I was getting nervous. What if
the car doesn't show up? What if the driver is off in one of
the endless cotton or soybean fields smoking his corncob
pipe or snoring away on a break? What if I don't make it
back to New York and all the deadlines and all the corre-
spondence and all the . . .

Chris Wade, Entertainment Director, Sam's Town:
Players are going to find the gaming in Tunica to be just
like Vegas, maybe even better, but they're going to find
the pace maddening if they expect to experience the
Vegas and Atlantic City energy. Everything is slower
here. Everything. This is the land of laid back.

I'm used to having my driver in New York show up about
15 minutes early and, well, wait for me. I'm used to knowing
everything will be done without a hitch—before it's really
time to do it. New Yorkers are constructed that way. *On*
time means early!

The driver was on time. Seven came and there he was. It
was like that all weekend. When things had to be finished,
they were finished, just. A half hour before my first seminar
on Saturday, I walked into the room and it hadn't been set
up. The worker arrived several minutes later: "When's yow
talk [towk]?" he asked. I told him. "Oh, plenty a time." And
he left. I almost had a heart attack.

"Relax," said another Sam's Town employee, "ya'll in the
South, sugah, it'll git done."

It was. The seminars went off without a hitch. By the way,
the women all call you "sugar" and "honey" and their ac-
cents sound just so sexy. Of course, they liked my accent,
too. "Yew sound sweet, sugah, real cute when yew talk." Actually, I was 19 when I stopped saying "youse" as the plural
for you—so youse readas can get an idear of how a New
Yawka sounds. But if the Southern belles thought I sounded
cute, hey, I ain't arg-you-in wit dem.

Then I saw the driver get out of the car, one huge muscle at a time. The guy was a mountain in uniform. He looked like the standard Southern sheriff from Hollywood casting. Big. Beefy. Dangerous. I flirted with the idea that he was not going to drive us to the airport but, rather, take us into the swamps and skin us for being, well, from up you-know-where. I had seen many rebel flags on many a pickup and flagpole. In fact, the Mississippi flag sports the stars and bars. If I had known at that moment that his former job was as a bounty hunter, I think I would have walked to the airport.

Of course, I completely misjudged him.

David Whitten was indeed a mountain of muscle but a soft spoken, polite, intelligent and highly knowledgeable mountain. He was the quintessential driver, one of the best I ever rode with and I've ridden with many. He should be hired as the official tour guide for new visitors to Tunica because of his knowledge and delivery. He made the ride to the airport a delight as he told us about Tunica county, Memphis, Elvis, cotton, soybeans, drive in "the-aters" and, of all things, Africans.

David Whitten, driver: Yes, sir, we got real Africans workin' hyere. Most don't know English yet but they come hyere ta work hard and make a livin'. Ya'll find them in the food services gen-rally. And if you look at the builders, ya'll see many Spanish, workin' the construction jobs. Tunica was the poorest county in the country before the casinos. We was number one as the poorest. Now people who want ta work are workin'.

"Tunica was the poorest county in the country, now we're one of the most prosperous." Time and again I heard variations of that mantra repeated by PR people, who are paid to repeat it; by politicians who get elected when they repeat it; but also from sales clerks, cage personnel, waiters and waitresses, dealers and players and other sundry folk who repeat it because it's true. Everyone, from average citizen to casino executive, marvels at the profound economic good the casinos have done for Tunica County. Everyone, that is, except for this guy on television that I saw Sunday morning.

Television Preacher: *Ah say ta yew that the whirled is filled with abominations. Gamblin'! They call it "gamin'!" Ha! It is a say-in against Gowd. Read Ex-oh-dus! Thou shalt not covet! Covetousness is gamblin' and it's the devil's work! If yew gamble yew are goin' to hell!*

Well, Beelzebub is going to have a lot of playmates because on the weekend I was there, every casino I visited was packed. But from the comments of many dealers and other workers, so were the churches. Interestingly enough, many of the big name entertainers do their one-night shows on Friday nights, not Saturday nights.

"Saturday night many people prepare for church on Sunday," Ronda Cloud, the Public Relations Director for Sam's Town, told me. "This is the Bible belt and church is a serious business. We respect that."

But the casinos are an even bigger business. It is estimated that in 2000, Tunica's 10 casinos grossed close to 1.2 billion dollars. Tunica is currently the third largest casino destination in the United States, behind Las Vegas and Atlantic City, but ahead of all the others. Tunica attracted close to 10 million visitors in the year 2000. No wonder. Its 10 casinos range from gorgeous (Gold Strike) to gargantuan (the Grand) to Western class (Sam's Town) to tinsel-town tack (Hollywood) to pre-theme-park Vegas chic (Horseshoe). In fact, there is a casino to fit the taste and wealth of gamblers from nickel slot players to purple-chip high rollers and everything in between. When Chris Wade said that inside Tunica's casinos you would find games that might equal or surpass Vegas, he was not hyperbolizing—he was speaking plainly.

Walter Thomason, gaming author: Tunica has the best craps games in the country, better than Vegas. You have 20X odds but you can also buy the 4 and 10, 5 and 9 and pay commissions only on the wins. The blackjack games range from single-decks all the way to eight decks and you can find whatever game suits your fancy and your bankroll. The rules are generally quite liberal as well.

John Robison, slot expert: You won't find much in the way of video poker compared to Vegas but the paybacks on the slots certainly compare favorably with Vegas and far surpass those of Atlantic City.

Inside the casino it is Las Vegas, the feel, the games, the smell—that rich mixture of adrenaline and smoke, of hopes fulfilled and dreams dashed. But outside, it is a whole different world. The casinos sit literally in the middle of the South's original claim to economic fame, cotton, because, as far as the eye can see, there are cotton fields, and soybean fields, and even rice paddies. Interspersed—one here, one there—are houses that range from delightful to decrepit. This is farming country, growing country. There are even signs on the highway to watch out for farm machinery crossing!

The Mississippi air often hangs on you like an extra skin and there are bugs and snakes and other creepy-crawly things that the imagination gives rise to in the wee hours of the morning when you stray too far from the glare of the neon night that surrounds the immediate proximity of the casino clusters. Outside that glare is nature.

Chris Wade, Entertainment Director, Sam's Town: Once I was riding along on a lawnmower going to Isle of Capri [now an adjunct property to Sam's Town] to check on a fireworks display that we were going to have that evening and I almost hit a huge water moccasin crawling along the grass. I thought to myself, "If I hit that thing, I'll turn over and it'll get me." Another time I had to physically remove a family of possums who had decided to get involved with the show at the River Palace Arena. Those things got mean and spit!

Ronda Cloud, PR Director, Sam's Town: There are giant bugs outside. They cross the roads and you think to yourself, "Should I stop?" We also have a herd of deer that grazes nearby and sometimes they come right up to the hotel.

Here's another thing. The casinos are not all bunched together as they are on the Strip in Vegas or on the Boardwalk in Atlantic City. They are in separate clusters. There are the "casino strip resorts," which consist of Sam's Town, Isle of Capri, Harrah's and Hollywood. These are within walking distance, if you don't mind crossing a sometimes-busy highway on foot. Otherwise there are shuttle buses that run regularly between them. There's "casino center," where the Horseshoe, Sheraton and the magnificent Gold Strike congregate. These casinos are so close you can actually walk to each. Just north of the casino center are Bally's Saloon and Gambling Hall, and the Grand, the largest casino in the county.

Alene Paone (the beautiful AP), writer and publisher: The Gold Strike is very impressive and when I was in it I felt as if I were in Vegas. It's the Mirage on the outside and the Golden Nugget on the inside. It's a beautiful place.

The law in Mississippi stipulates that gambling can only take place "on a navigable waterway." My first thought was that these casinos were actually on the mighty Mississippi River. They aren't, although they are near it. Instead, water was brought to the building area via a large trench dug for that purpose. The barges that would become the casino portion of the properties were then floated down this trench, set in place in pools of water, the trench was closed, and voila! you have a "riverboat."

Each casino has a method for making sure that its "gambling barge" sits atop enough water to obey the rules of the gaming commission. Some actually pipe the water in and it's pure Mississippi River—because it's muddy as all get out ("get out"—that's a Southern term), a greenish-brown that makes the East River in New York look almost pristine by comparison.

Clyde Callicott, Co-host of the Goodtimes Radio Show on audiovegas.com: Tunica is becoming the place to see great action fights and terrific entertainment. In fact, Mississippi has more professional prizefights than Las Vegas. Also, some of the finest entertainers in the world perform here. We might not be Vegas but we're growing and we offer everything a gaming enthusiast could want. And our comps are even looser than our slots! But if friendliness counts, then we're first in the nation in that department.

Madeliene Bizub, gaming writer: I've lived in Vegas and in Mississippi. Mississippi is called "the Hospitality State"—and the name is well deserved. They offer reasonable rules, and generous paybacks on many slots. There's a relaxed attitude about winning, for the most part, that I just don't see at other gaming resorts. I've even seen dealers who didn't take their break in turn when they were on stick and a good dice roll was going, because they didn't want to interrupt the player's "rhythm." Now that's classy.

When I went to activate my credit line at Sam's Town, the young lady—an African American—took my driver's license.

"I want to activate my credit line," I said.

"Whachew mean by dat, act-tub-ate?" she glared at me.

"Uh, ah, activate . . . so I can take out a marker."

"Whasa marka? Yew gowinta scrawl on our walls?"

"No, no that, uh . . ."

Then she laughed. "Ah'm jus foolin ya, honey. Ah sees yew was from New York and Ah thought yew might think we was a little slow down here."

"You had me going," I said.

"All the paperwork is done, honey. Yew got your credit. Don't play foolish, now."

Then her supervisor came over.

"Yew from New York?" she asked.

"Yes," I said.

"Hillary is going to win," she said. [This took place just before the senate race when Hillary Rodham Clinton moved from Arkansas to New York and captured the Senate seat.]

"Now that Guiliani is out, yes, I guess maybe so."

"I didn't know you followed New York politics down here," said AP.

"Oh, yes, we do. It's in the papers and we follow it," she said.

"That's more than some people in New York," I said.

"Ah like Bill Clinton 'cause he's cute," said the supervisor. "He jus' picked the wrong woman. Never pick a woman who loves and then loves ta talk, know what Ah mean? He has a weakness that's all. Some men got that weakness."

"If I had that weakness, my wife would kill me," I said.

"I sure would," said AP.

"Yew pick the right woman and nobody needs to know a thang."

Is the charismatic radio personality Clyde Callicott right when he says Tunica is friendly? The answer is yes. Does this make it a different kind of casino experience? Yes again. It also takes some getting adjusted to if, like me, you're used to Las Vegas and Atlantic City, where the business end of

casinos is usually, well, handled like business. But in Mississippi, while folks have a job to perform,—they activate your
credit, give you change, cash your chips, wait on you in the
restaurants—they are also always willing and eager to chat.
It's as if a part of every job description is socializing with the
guests.

It's not just the dealers whose tips often ride on their ability to be pleasant and friendly, it's everyone. Everyone is
"gladtaseeya"—everyone kids you as if they've known you
for years. At the Billy Bob Steakhouse [now Twain's] at
Sam's Town, the hostess referred to me as "the handsome
Frank" because frankly she and everyone else seemed to have
trouble pronouncing Scoblete.

---

*David Whitten, driver: Ah saw Elvis twice when Ah
was growin' up. You wouldn't want to be him [heem]
because when he wanted to go eat, he had to rent the
restaurant after hours or when he wanted to go to the
moo-vees, he'd have to rent the whole the-ater.*

Elvis looms over this part of the country like the Oversoul
and his Graceland Mansion is the Mecca for pop music pil-
grims. The "King" is at the head of a pantheon of local
deities that includes John Grisham and a host of blues musi-
cians. And while country-western music is popular, Tunica
isn't "cowboy" country, it's "R" country as in . . .

REDNECK. There, I said it.

Now, I have only seen one Jeff Foxworthy routine (he was
coming into Tunica as I was leaving) and it was very funny. I
long ago forgot the jokes because the butts of those jokes—
the "R" people—are not a part of my Eastern landscape.
Then I hit the South. It is no joke that the "R" word is freely
spoken, and universally satirized, by many Mississippians
and Oklahomans and Arkansasians (is that how you say it?)
and by folks who came to Tunica from parts north, south,
east and west (and from Africa) to work. Jokes like:

Caller: "*Ah wandta make a reservation foe me and ma wife and sister for dinner tonight.*"

Maitre'd: "*Fine, sir, so that's a table for two.*"

Or:

"*You are invited to the wedding of Mable and Maurice. Tie mandatory. Teeth optional.*"

If there is a PC code in the South, it doesn't cover the "R" word. And the "R" folks do actually exist. In fact, at times the "whoops" and "Yee-has!" that came from the casino slot areas were noticeably different from the "whoops" and "Oh yeahs!" I'm used to.

"Those yelps you hear," said Rudi Schiffer, the host of the popular *Goodtimes Show*, a local radio show that highlights Tunica's casinos, "those are from the rednecks. And they drive pickups and they wear eclectic clothes and they aren't like any people you meet in the North. They are a Southern artifact and they are real."

Another thing I found of significant interest in this part of the country was the fact that most of the workers I saw in the casinos were African-American. From waiters and waitresses, to dealers, floor personnel, cashiers, bellhops, front desk personnel and credit checkers, the African-American presence in the work force is overwhelming. I talked with one young lady, a former resident of Winona, Mississippi, who was now employed by one of the casinos. She had grown up in an "extended family" of 17 brothers, sisters, "onts" and uncles virtually none of whom had ever held a job before the casinos arrived.

E.S., worker from Winona: Ah'm the first in ma famlee to work and that is because of the casinos. Ah was a tough kid and Ah be always gettin' in people's faces. In school I'd always be sayin': "Ah want chew foe six!" Now Ah don't fight no more. Ah'm happy workin'!

"I want you for six" or "give me six" is how many disputes are settled between teenagers in the surrounding parts.

That means that the two antagonists will fight with their fists for six minutes. No wrestling, no hugging, no rolling on the ground, no friends allowed to jump in and help. Just one-on-one punch-it-out for six or fewer minutes and then it's over. All things considered that's rather a refined way to handle disputes considering the New York, Los Angeles and other big-city mode is to gang up on the enemy or, worse, shoot him down in a drive by. The young lady's words rang in my ears: "Ah'm happy workin'!"

Television Preacher: Gamblin' and drinkin' and fornicatin' is all ya'll see with these casinos! And when Gowd judges yew, He'll put his foot on yo neck and crush the life outta yew for the abominations yew have allowed! There can be no place in Gowd's whirled for bettin' and no good can come from it ever!

As David Whitten dropped us off at the Memphis Airport, I knew that I would definitely come back to Tunica. For me, a two-and-a-half-hour plane trip from New York is well worth it. After all, it takes me over three hours to drive to Atlantic City where the games are not as player-friendly and almost six hours to get to Las Vegas. Tunica is a perfect place to visit for East Coasters such as myself on those extended three- and four-day weekends. So ah'm comin' back to Tunica real soon, ya hear?

Yes, in Tunica people are just so laid back, except for the occasional minister. And friendly, except for the few who want to see you wind up burning in hell. I informed some of my GTC comrades, who had never been to Tunica, that old Southern stereotypes are alive and well and can be found in the living flesh and blood of the local people who work and play in the casinos. So be prepared.

When you are used to the high-energy attitudes of Vegas and Atlantic City dealers, floorpeople, and players, and when you come from New York as I do, where people rush when they are *resting,* Tunica is like going on a religious retreat, except this retreat has casino games that are far better than any you'll find in your local church's Las Vegas night— or in Las Vegas, for that matter. In craps, I discovered, you can now buy the four, five, nine, and ten for $30, paying the $1 commission on winning bets only. This knocks the house edge on these bets to about 1 percent. Incredible.

As God is my witness, I'll never be hungry again.

But would we be able to attract an audience to Tunica, the way we could in Vegas and Atlantic City? We started our advertising campaign and, after a month, we had only five people signed up for the one-day festival and one person signed up for the two-day class, and he wasn't sure he could make it. I was worried. Tunica is a huge slot market; fully 90 percent of the players are slot machine buffs. Would we be able to fill the 25 spots we needed to break even for our two-day seminar? Would we be able to get 50 people for our one-day festival as we hoped? Would *anyone* show up for the Dynamic Dimensions course for advanced shooters?

Chris Wade had booked us into the Delta Room, which is composed of four banquet rooms, right across from the big Arena. It was almost six thousand square feet of space. Five people and a few coaches would rattle around in that room. Six weeks before we were to hold the seminars things looked decidedly gloomy.

Maybe we had overestimated how many people would be willing to part with their hard-earned money to take a course in dice control, even if the world's best shooters gave it, especially in a little-known place like Tunica. Many casino gamblers just don't care to go any further in learning a game than buying in and betting. They don't want to really explore the games they are playing. Maybe we overrated the appeal of dice control. Maybe Golden Touch was going to be stillborn. Damn.

As we confronted an impending disaster, Dom and I reflected on how very hard we had worked and on how carefully all the members of GTC had planned how the seminars would be taught. We knew we wanted to take dice-control instruction to a new level, away from the idiosyncratic opinions of self-proclaimed dice controllers and craps experts, to a more scientifically oriented, teachable method. Of course, Sharpshooter's engineering background would allow us to teach the technique in a very methodical, step-by-step fashion. We wanted everything we did to be grounded in good math and good science. Just before the seminar we got a lucky break when Dr. Don Catlin, professor emeritus of mathematics at the University of Massachusetts, finished an exhaustive study of the *5-Count* that proved beyond a shadow of a doubt that everything the Captain had said about it was right on the money. This report is in my updated, expanded edition of *Beat the Craps Out of the Casinos* and can also be found in the article section at *www.goldentouchcraps.com.*

Dom, Bill Burton, Mr. Finesse, and I had also discussed how we wanted the room to look when students were taking our seminars. We designed what we considered to be the most effective "learning environment" for dice-control teaching. We planned on having a regulation-sized craps table in the center of the fourth room, surrounded by practice boxes and throwing stations. This would allow everyone to get intense hands-on individual instruction from his or her instructors and also to practice on a regular table throughout the two days.

We were raring to go.

But what if you threw a party and no one showed up? In that case, you'd eat all the pizza you could and freeze the rest. But what if you gave a dice-control class and no one came to it? You'd have egg on your face.

Frankly, my dear, I don't give a damn.

The beautiful AP told me not to worry. Our publicity—in newspapers, magazines, on the radio, and by direct mail— would bring out the people, she told me confidently.

I hoped so. I prayed so.

And she was right.

Slowly, then steadily, we started to sign up people in the last month. By the time the weekend arrived, we had 118 people signed up for one, two, or all three events.

As we were setting up the instructional area, Billy the Kid, Jake from Pitt, Randy "Tenor" Rowsey, Dom, Mr. Finesse, and I saw the GTC dream coming alive. When we put the regulation craps table in the room and set up our practice stations, when we set up the stage area where the speakers would make their presentations, we each looked at the others and nodded. We knew now—we had done it! Golden Touch Craps was a reality.

Now, we just had to teach the course to forty-seven people in the two-day seminar, entertain the 118 people signed up to come to the Sharpshooter one-day festival, and wow the seventeen advanced students in Monday's Dynamic Dimensions course.

Piece of cake!

I knew we had the goods as far as speakers and teachers were concerned. At the last minute, Dr. Richard McCall had notified us that he would be coming and I quickly inserted him into our speaker schedule for Friday and our instructional schedule for Saturday and Sunday. Rudi Schiffer, the host of the *Goodtimes Show*, was our opening speaker. Rudi is a funny guy and his topic was simply "Why Tunica Is a Good Bet." Dominator was to speak about "How to Be a General at the Table." Sharpshooter would then explain

"The Physics of Dice Control." Then we'd have a No-Sevens contest like the one we'd held at Sunset Station's "Beat the House" festival. Then I'd speak.

We had divided the festival into talks and demonstrations, which also allowed the attendees to get some hands-on practice with the Golden Touch instructors between talks.

It went off without a hitch.

The festival was fun; the two-day seminar, on the other hand, was fantastic.

We had brought in just about all of our top instructors: Dominator, Sharpshooter, Billy the Kid, Dr. Richard McCall, Bill Burton, Mr. Finesse, Street Dog, Jerry "Stickman" Stich, Randy "Tenor" Rowsey, Howard "Rock 'n' Roller" Newman, Daryl "No Field Five" Henley, and Jake from Pitt. Each instructor had responsibility for five students. When Sharpshooter, Dominator, or I gave a lecture about a certain aspect of controlled shooting or betting, when that lecture finished, the instructors reinforced it by giving hands-on practice to the students in the areas just discussed. At the end of the two days, several students "complained" that their arms were about to fall off from so much practice and every student queried said they had never taken such an intense and enjoyable seminar, be it on gambling or anything else.

We also saw what our new method of teaching could accomplish. We had students who had never attempted a controlled throw before who, after two days, were handling the dice as if they had been practicing for months.

I got around and met most of the forty-seven students who attended. My job, in addition to introducing the speakers and segments, and lecturing on the 5-Count and comps, was to help students with small improvements in their form. One thing about most people who are serious about learning dice control: they are an intelligent, eclectic, fun bunch and they are eager students, the kind any teacher would love to teach.

At the end of the two days, we gave out awards to the most improved students—those who had come the furthest in their skill levels.

There was Debbie Gray from Massachusetts, a vivacious, lively young woman. At first, she couldn't get the dice down to the end of the table without them flying off this way and that. By day two, after intensive practice at the seminar and in her room, she had a lovely throw with a good backspin. In fact, she even had a good roll in the casino right after the seminar ended.

There was Lynn Tryon, who by day two had improved so much that he went into the casino at lunchtime and had a one-hour roll (we scolded him for coming in late for class!). There were Mr. and Mrs. Carl Compton, who were so determined to become expert shooters that they bought practice tables, several sleeves of dice, layouts, tee-shirts, and every book they could get their hands on in an effort to become the best they could possibly be. Did they show improvement? Absolutely!

And there was a local businessman who "was completely skeptical" about dice control, signed up for the course at the last minute, and then won $22,000 in two sessions after taking the course. "I never rolled so many sixes and eights!" he exclaimed. We had doctors, airline pilots, stewardesses, businessmen and -women, the young and the old. Some of the forty-seven people were former PARR students whom Jerry Patterson had signed up for the GTC course. Every one of them told us that the course far exceeded their expectations and was better than anything they had taken in the past. That was high praise coming as it did from such experienced shooters as "Chip and Dip," a lovely couple from the Humboldt, Tennessee, and from Darrell and Mary Dowd,

Barbara Keib, Steve Fixler, and Tommy Lohrke, among others. As one attendee, whose pseudonym is Mykey, said, "The GTC organization is doing gamblers a great service." Another one said: "Don't change anything. You guys are doing everything perfectly!"

A young man, Don Wheeler, who goes by the handle of Word Slayer when he posts on various Web sites, especially impressed me. Not only did this young man have a beautiful throw, which he practices daily; he also has a story that is at once heart wrenching and inspirational. Here's his story, in his own words:

> I was born in Geneva, New York, in 1962; we lived in upstate New York between the towns of Hall and Gorham till 1972. In 1972 we moved to Houston, Texas, and in a couple of years we moved to Duncanville, Texas, just outside of Dallas.
>
> In Dallas I took up bodybuilding and at sixteen I was five-foot-nine weighing 180. I had the nickname Mini Hulk. At seventeen I had an accident in a gym and had to have my first back surgery. In 1984, at age eighteen, I married and my wife and I bought ten acres of land and moved to East Texas. My parents bought seventeen acres right next to ours.
>
> I eventually got a job in East Texas and took up hunting and training dogs as hobbies. I did this for several years and was fairly well known in our area. In 1990 I had an accident at work and had to have four more back surgeries. After the surgeries I was told I was 100 percent disabled and that I had to be careful or I could be paralyzed for life. During this time my marriage started to go downhill and, although we are still very good friends, my first wife and I decided to divorce. We had been married for fourteen years.
>
> During this time I met Jeane [pronounced Jeannie], who became my second wife. She was and is a godsend for me. After we met I started having more problems with my back and neck and after much investigation I found I had a rare

condition called *ankylosing spondylitis*. It is a condition that they really do not know much about. It causes the spine to fuse and the tendons to stay rock-hard tight all the time. It is an extremely painful condition and is life-threatening due to its progressive nature and how it attacks the body.

I didn't like the fact that the doctors couldn't tell me about my condition and only wanted to give me stuff to kill the pain. I took a different route. I studied and became a certified iridologist and holistic health practitioner. I have worked on my condition and brought it under control and made it bearable. Jeane and I now run a Web page and help others with this condition and other health issues.

We settled in Springfield, Missouri. We bought a house over time from a man whom we discovered, after couple of years of "lot clearing" and making a home, that the IRS was chasing for back taxes. We also discovered that he hadn't been paying the bank on the house we had been paying him on—and spending every extra penny of ours on. Needless to say Jeane and I were devastated. I contacted several attorneys and they all said the same thing: cut your losses and get out of there. It would be too expensive for us to try to recoup what we had paid him in mortgage payments and what we had invested in the house.

We had to find a new home. Six months later I made a trip down to Texas and talked to my ex-wife and my mother. My father had passed away by then. I had decided to just start all over, find some land and buy a mobile home and do it so that no one could take our home away again.

After a few days I had a few prospects and my mother offered us a small part of her land that she wasn't using. The next day I was in Tyler looking at mobile homes and found one that I thought Jeane would love. It was used but they were completely remodeling it. In one month we were in our new home in Quitman, Texas. I had to put up a fence for our dogs and underpin the trailer and get the electricity and water hooked up, plus put in a septic tank. I did this in short order. I had set the mobile home payments up so that in three years it would be paid for and we could relax.

Jeane and I had been trying to find something we could do together and enjoy. My health was slowly getting worse and my neck was bothering me again. In iridology I help people but do not charge anything because most of these people cannot afford to pay.

My brother started talking to me about gambling and roulette. Again I started doing research. After a while I saw the game of craps as possibly the best way to go. I found Web sites and started learning and practicing. Jeane and I were both getting excited about the possibility of getting the edge at the game. I felt like I wanted to take this to a higher level so I joined PARR and in a few months I was learning and understanding the game even more. Many of the PARR members started sending me books on craps and this is where I first heard about your books. John Patrick sent me one of his books on craps. I bought a few books off eBay and now have a library of about twenty craps books.

I noticed that many of the authors seemed to be writing for the casinos and not for the players. Most of their thoughts and ideas were not for conservative players and long-term players who were actually looking to beat the game. Those writers were writing for people who looked at craps from an entertainment viewpoint. I discarded those books.

Jerry Patterson offered me a deal on helping him with the archives on DICE [Jerry's Internet listserv] and I accepted. We had thought about going to a Vegas PARR seminar and Jerry generously offered to even help us with the airfare. I was blown away. I declined because I knew we couldn't afford the hotel rooms. Since I also needed a scooter to get around, it would make traveling to Vegas difficult.

It was a few months later that GTC was formed and then Jeane and I heard about Tunica and knew we could do that.

I still look at my gambling endeavor in the long term. I

expect it will take maybe two years before we really can make any decent money at this but I am patient and look at it like paying our dues. Jeane and I practice every day and I am always looking for ways to improve our practice so that we can always get better.

Don's disability prevents him from seeing the back wall when he stands SL1 and SL2 or SR1 and SR2. His head is in a permanent "down" position. Yet his endless hours of practice have paid off. He is remarkable. He can throw the dice with either hand with equal aplomb and most times his throw hits the precise area of the layout it needs to in order to bounce once, gently hit the back wall, and die. Jeane is also no slouch in the dice-control department and has an excellent throw. Starting with a bankroll of $500, they made their first trips to the casinos several months before the GTC Tunica seminar, and by the time of the seminar they had tripled it to $1,500. They are extremely conservative bettors, as they must be to survive in this game on such a short bankroll. Our Golden Touch Craps instructors were so impressed by Don "Word Slayer" Wheeler that we gave him a special award, as the most inspirational craps player.

We even had an award for one of our coaches, Howard "Rock 'n' Roller" Newman, who had won the longest roll contest at Fitzgerald's with a roll of forty-six numbers before sevening out.

When Tunica was finished, the instructors had a postmortem and a party! We knew we had pulled off the greatest dice-control seminar ever given. Now, it was time for us to play.

And play we did.

Although we had played on the evenings of the seminar, it was time to relax and do what we love to do—challenge the casinos for real.

Bill McCulley, the casino host at Sheraton, made us an offer we couldn't refuse. Bill, an inveterate craps player (and great guy), had attended our Friday festival and said to us, "Any time you guys want to come to the Sheraton just tell me and we'll give you a table and a dinner at the Steak House."

So we told him.

Bill comped fifteen of us to dinner at the Steak House Sunday night and then had the casino reserve a table for us to play on when we finished dinner. Now, you would think that with Sharpshooter, Dominator, Mr. Finesse, Billy the Kid, Bill Burton, Randy "Tenor" Rowsey, Jerry "Stickman" Stich, Street Dog, and Jake from Pitt at one table, the casino would lose a fortune. But that didn't happen; instead, something really strange did.

Since the Sheraton had handed us an incredible gift, we decided to capitalize on it as best we could, and that meant playing only four spots and rotating shooters. It went like this:

Billy the Kid was to take SR2, Dominator was at SR1, Sharpshooter was at SL1, and I was on SL2. These would be the only four shooting positions. In fact, Billy and I would really shoot from the "1" position when it was our turn, as both Dominator and Sharpshooter would move back to let us in. You couldn't ask for anything better than that. If, after two rounds, a shooter didn't make us money, that shooter would relinquish his spot to another GTC team member and we'd just keep rotating. That was the theory.

This was the reality. Sharpshooter was first up. He set the dice, aimed, and established his point, a six. I loaded up on the six and eight. Sharpshooter can usually make those sixes and eights in his sleep. He sevened out immediately. I did the same thing—point, seven-out. Billy the Kid and Dominator fared a little better but not by much. Back on our side of the table, Sharpshooter and I again went point, seven-out.

Sharpshooter was looking confused. "Something's wrong," he said. Now, usually when a GTC player sevens out he looks to his own form to see if he's doing something wrong. Not Sharpshooter. He has such confidence in his throw that when he says "something's wrong," he doesn't mean something's wrong with him.

"Maybe it's that shadow at the end of the table," I said. "It might be confusing our sight lines."

Since I had sevened out fast twice, I relinquished my spot to Mr. Finesse. For the next half-hour, those of us on SL went point, seven-out or close to it on every opportunity. Our compatriots on SR were doing slightly better, but they were not hammering the casino either. Then Billy the Kid did something we all should have done the second we hit the table. He moved his hand along the "shadow" at the right end of the table, where those of us on SL landed the dice, to see what that shadow was.

"Hey, guys!" he yelled. "There's a damn bubble going across the landing area over here."

I walked down to the end of the table. I felt the felt. There it was. The layout had bunched up. What looked like a shadow going across the entire section of the layout on the SR wall was actually a wrinkle, a bubble, an unintentional speed bump that was causing all our throws from SL to be off. But that half-hour had cost me and other GTC players a lot of money. Only Mr. Finesse and Bill Burton, who had used the *5-Count* on everyone, were close to even. The rest of us were down significantly, because we had bet on every shooter figuring one of us would get hot, as almost always happens. Well one of us *didn't* get hot. At best, one or two of the SR people got lukewarm, which wasn't enough.

For the next hour and a half, we only shot from stick

right. We slowly came back but it was a losing evening. A golden opportunity for all of us to play at one table had become a losing evening, due in large part, not to the speed bump, but to our carelessness in not examining the table, and in our betting on our comrades without using the *5-Count*. Bill Burton and Mr. Finesse combined lost less than a hundred dollars because they used the *5-Count*. The rest of us lost thousands.

Sometimes you have to learn the same lessons over and over. I learned that, once again, until I know a GTC shooter is "on" I must use the *5-Count* on him just as I would on any random roller. I did it with Beau and Soft Touch during the A&E shooting and it helped immensely. I usually do it on everyone, at least the first few times they shoot, but I paid for not doing it at the Sheraton that night in spades.

Dominator, Jake from Pitt, Randy "Tenor" Rowsey, and I stayed in Tunica for several days after the seminars to play craps. We moved over to the Horseshoe casino, to which I had never been before. Now, the Horseshoe is run by Jack Binion, of the legendary Binion family, whose father Benny Binion was a gambling visionary. Jack used to run the Horseshoe in Vegas until he lost a family dispute of some kind and sold the place to his sister. The two Horseshoes are different experiences, like night and day. The Vegas Horseshoe is, to be polite, a dank, damp, moldy dump that was once the best gambling joint in Vegas despite its ambience but is now just a dank, damp, moldy dump with mediocre games and a disgruntled staff. The Horseshoe in Tunica is a Las Vegas Strip casino with the old downtown Vegas gambling attitude, which is to say, it is a table-game player's Valhalla. It is also the number-one property in Tunica, as its philosophy is not to bean count but in the words of pit boss, Sam Dexter, to "look at the total gambling experience. We know that per square foot of floor space our poker room might not make as much as the same space of slot machines but we know that a poker player who has become tired of the game goes over to blackjack and will bet big. We know that blackjack and craps players have spouses that play the machines. So we know that you have to look to the total gambling experience and not just floor-space-to-profit ratios in any one game. And we are very generous with comps. We feel if you gamble with us we're going to take good care of you."

That philosophy seems to be working. While other Tunica casino table-game areas are nearly deserted on the weekday mornings and afternoons, the Horseshoe's tables are hopping.

I made a comeback from my disastrous Sheraton experience over the next few days, and between playing craps and blackjack at the Horseshoe and several other casinos, I was able to get away with a small profit, infinitesimally small. Oh, one last thing: I almost won the Gold Strike contest, too. If you can establish and make all the point numbers during one hand; that is, if you can make 4, 5, 6, 8, 9, and 10, you win an extra $4,000. I established five of the points, but I just couldn't turn the trick.

Still, Tunica launched Golden Touch for real. We were now on the map and ready to move into the future.

19

Gladly Will I Play
. . . and Gladly Teach

SOME OF you reading this may recognize the paraphrase that forms the title of this chapter; it comes from Chaucer's *Canterbury Tales*. When introducing the Oxford Clerk in the General Prologue, Chaucer writes that the man is a true lover of learning, and that he enjoys not only learning but also teaching what he has learned to others: "And gladly would he learn and gladly teach."

I've been asked by countless players why I discuss controlled throwing so publicly and why I am a part of a "school," Golden Touch Craps, that teaches these techniques to others. Cynics will usually imply that charging for lessons in these techniques is a rip-off or that, as one skeptic stated, "if these techniques worked, you'd keep them secret and just use them yourselves to make millions. The fact that you teach these things means they don't work. You're making money from the gullible. Yeah, controlled shooting works, all right, for those who are teaching the classes."

I can understand why the cynics are cynical and why the skeptics are skeptical. In the world of gambling, plenty of scammers promise huge wins if you just buy this or that system. In books and articles, I've exposed plenty of these scams for what they are—*betting schemes* that can't really overcome the house edge in the long run.

Controlled shooting is different. It is no scam. It's the real deal, and the men and women who are a part of Golden Touch Craps can indeed beat the game of craps in the long run using this physical skill. As I've stated elsewhere in this book, I don't think everyone can do it, just as I don't think everyone can hit a baseball five hundred feet the way Barry Bonds, Mickey Mantle, and other major leaguers have. Often critics will look at a skill and leap to a logical fallacy that runs: "I can't do that. And if I can't do that, nobody can do that. Therefore that can't be done."

The evidence for controlled shooting is as valid as the evidence that Babe Ruth could hit home runs at a rate greater than any player of his generation—because he *did* it, people *saw* him do it, and *statistics* were kept of his at-bats and home runs. Well, I and others have *seen* the Captain, the Arm, Dominator, Mr. Finesse, Billy the Kid, Sharpshooter, Howard Newman, Bill Burton, and others *do* it, and *statistics* have been kept of their SRRs and of their winnings. We even have videos of such shooters, including the A&E special I wrote about in chapter 16. If skeptics are still skeptical even after such evidence is presented to them, there's no reason to disabuse them of their skepticism or even to engage them in dialogue. After all, there are still members of the Flat Earth Society around, and no one feels the need to prove to them that the earth is not flat but round. And the casinos do need plenty of losers to make it possible for the few winners to continue their winning ways without alarming the bosses, after all.

Okay, let us grant, then, that the techniques we are talking about are real and are learnable by the dedicated and the disciplined. Why are my fellow Golden Touchers and I teaching others to do this? Is it to make millions of dollars from their tuitions for our classes? No.

While I like making money, as do the rest of my colleagues, the money doesn't primarily drive us. We charge for our time and our expertise. This is not unlike any course you would take at a university—you are paying tuition for the salary of the professor and for the upkeep of the property on which the professor teaches. In the Golden Touch case, students pay for our overhead and for our instructors' salaries. I don't believe in asking skilled people to work for nothing as they teach their skill. That can cause resentment, the same kind of resentment that was evident in PARR.

Speaking of nothing, I have found that people usually don't take "freebies" seriously. Having to pay tuition separates the dilettantes and time-wasters from the serious-minded. Just compare the sleepy-eyed, listless, bored public high school kids who get a "free education" to the energetic college students who have to pay for their own tuition either by working or by taking loans. The old saying "You get what you pay for" may not always be true, but it's true often enough to have become an old saying. As King Lear said to his youngest daughter, who could say nothing flattering to her father as he was about to give her a third of his kingdom, "Nothing comes from nothing."

But there's another, even more important reason why we teach these methods: because we love to play craps. The Golden Touch classes exist not just so we can teach others to play but also so we can fine-tune our own abilities. Nothing allows you to learn a topic inside and out like having to teach it to another. We all become better shooters when we teach our curriculum to others, because we must refresh ourselves step by step in our techniques. We all go back to school when we teach. Thus, Chaucer's description of the Oxford Clerk is apt for all of us. We teach; we learn; we play. Gladly.

Win, lose, or draw, there is a soul-shaking thrill involved in attempting to actually beat the casinos at craps by utilizing a skill. While other casino games such as blackjack and video poker are open to advantage-play as well, the thrill of the contest at these games is not that great. At blackjack and video poker, you make your decisions by rote. You win based on statistics; if you play the hand correctly, over time you'll have the edge. Yet, the dealer always deals in blackjack, and the machine's random-number generator always picks what's coming next in video poker. You're just playing the percentages. Winning is always fun, of course, even at blackjack and video poker, but nothing can compete with the following *delicious* moment in craps: the dice are pushed to you by the stickman; you pick them up, set, grip, and deliver them down the felt where they come to a dead stop at the back wall and *winnah! winnah! winnah!* Dice control is the attempt to catch lightning in a bottle; it's taking your fate into your own hands; it's putting yourself on the line.

Putting yourself on the line, that's the key for me, I think. . . .

Let me tell you a little story.

When I was in eighth grade at Our Lady of Angels elementary school in Bay Ridge, Brooklyn, our basketball team went undefeated, winning fifty-five straight games, starting with exhibition games in September (some against freshmen and junior varsity high school teams) and concluding with a big win in an invitational tournament that pitted teams from all over the East against one another. In between, we won

• • • •

our borough, then county championships, and along the way several citywide invitational tournaments featuring some of the best of the best teams.

At the beginning of the season, although everyone knew we'd be *one of* the best in the city, no one realized just how great our team would be (the *New York Daily News* would later call us "the powerhouse team that has mowed down all opposition"). In fact, several other teams were rated more highly than we were in the preseason polls (yes, even in eighth grade, city teams were *closely* watched), for example, the incredible St. Cecilia's of the Bronx, which had a win streak of thirty games before we played them, and St. Jude, whose imposing center was a young man standing 6′10″ tall named Lew Alcindor—who became Kareem Abdul Jabbar.

Our starting team was composed of kids I had played ball with in schoolyards ever since I was a little kid. We were all friends and schoolmates (though fierce rivals in those school-yard basketball wars), and teammates at Our Lady of Angels. I can remember them now as if it were yesterday—and as I write this it was over four decades ago!—the real dream team: hard-nosed Stevie Gardell, silky smooth Billy Bell, dogged Douglas Bernhardt, and the awesome 6′8″ Patrick Heelan. Our sixth man was leaping Ken Pederson, a 6′3″ bundle of energy. Our coach was the brilliant Brother Barnabas, of the Franciscan order. He worked us in practice until our tongues hung out. We worked on pressing the other team, going to the sides for the fast break when Pat Heelan grabbed a rebound, mixing up the defense and offense so we were never predictable.

I was the team leader. It was my job to shut down the best scorer on the other team, a job I relished. Not one hot-shot high-scoring opponent ever scored more than 8 points against me when I covered them, because I stuck like crazy glue to them from one end of the court to the other. I was also our second leading scorer, behind the awesome Heelan. And my game "rose to the occasion" when the chips were down.

When we met the undefeated St. Cecilia's in the finals of the St. Francis Prep tournament, they were favored to beat us, and their players sneered at us whenever they looked our way. Well, why not? Although at the time we were 17 and 0, they were *30* and 0. St. Cecilia's had three guys who could dunk, their backcourt guys were *shaving,* and one of their forwards had a mustache! In their red-silk uniforms, they looked and acted imposing.

In the first three minutes of the game against St. Cecilia's, I stole the ball from their big-shot backcourt six times—in a row! They couldn't even get it past the half-court line. We were up 16 to 0 halfway through the first quarter and beat them by 42 points in the game. We had blown out the number-two-rated team in the city. The only team considered better than us now was St. Jude.

A month later we faced St. Jude in Manhattan at the LaSalle Tournament. We were now the number-two team, but the Lew Alcindor–led St. Jude was still number one, and they were also undefeated. They were the biggest team we ever faced, with Alcindor at 6'10" and two forwards who were both 6'3". Even their backcourt was big—coming in at 5'10" and 5'9". (Remember, we were all only in eighth grade!)

This match-up between the two best teams in the city drew a standing-room-only crowd to the LaSalle gym. All the newspapers in the city wrote about the battle of the schoolboy giants, Alcindor versus Heelan, and basketball aficionados came from all five boroughs to see the game.

In the very first quarter Heelan got three fouls and had to sit out the rest of the half. At the time he sat out, the score was tied. When he came back in the third quarter we had a

10-point lead. We got that lead by clawing and fighting and pressing St. Jude until *their* tongues hung out. Three of us surrounded Alcindor. We swarmed their backcourt. Ken Pederson even blocked one of Alcindor's shots! I stole the ball out of Alcindor's hand under our basket while he was holding the ball up over his head (it almost touched the rim!). I leaped up, snatched it, and in one motion put it into the basket. We won the game by 15 points, our closest contest of the year. From that point on there was no question as to who was the number-one team in New York City—Our Lady of Angels from Bay Ridge, Brooklyn!

At the end of the season, after our fifty-fifth win, I knew, even though I was only an eighth grader, that I had been a part of something special that September through June. We would all go to different high schools and to other teams and on to life. But no team I ever played with since that season was quite the same. To be the very best at what you do, to be far and away the best, is a very, very special feeling, no matter at what age it comes—and when I think of Stevie Gardell, Ken Pederson, Billy Bell, Doug Bernhardt, and Pat Heelan I think of them as a picture painted in sacred colors and tinged with gold. We shared something profound that season. We faced challenges together and came through them all. We put ourselves on the line and always put out a full effort. We never beat ourselves, even when going up against intimidating opponents. We faced each team and went at them with all the energy and drive that Brother Barnabas had hammered into us. And we prevailed because we were connected. It was like we were one gestalt organism on that court, even though we were six distinct personalities off it.

Sadly, I've lost complete track of all of my fellow teammates. I have no idea how life treated them or how they played the game of life up to this point. I moved out of the neighborhood to go to college in 1965 and I never went back.

But I know that for me that one season has colored my entire life. I think in some very real way I have tried to re-capture in my adult life some of the sense I had about things during that one year. To that end, I acted on stage for ten years, and produced and directed plays as well. While acting had some of the excitement of that championship season, it was not the same. And, while writing is fun, there is no adrenaline rush of victory to it. You work hard on an article or book and then . . . poof, it's out there and, though you occasionally get some feedback, there's no equivalent in writing to facing one of St. Cecilia's players in a contest of skill and will.

The nearest I have come to recapturing the essence of that one year so long ago is when I step into a casino—and see my fellow Golden Touchers at a craps table. When I see Dominator "go fishing" prior to the stickman sending the dice to him; when I see Sharpshooter tapping the felt to get a tactile sense of what kind of bounce he's going to get when the dice get to the end of the table; when I see Mr. Fi-nesse pause, sip his water, take a deep breath, and then step up to the table; when Billy the Kid tells us just how many of thus and such a number has been hit; when Bill Burton sets his "whirl" alignment—and bangs out three Crazy Crapper numbers in a row; and when I set my 3-V and I hear my Golden Touch mates say, "Come on, Frank, you can do it!"—in short, when I see my teammates and friends in Golden Touch Craps begin their contests with the casino, and I have my money on the line because I trust their skills and determination, I get a feeling very much like the one I had when I saw Lew Alcindor's St. Jude step onto the court and I knew that Stevie, Billy, Doug, Kenny, Pat, and I *had* to beat them. Well, the casino is an even bigger adversary than Alcindor's St. Jude.

I don't think random rollers have the same feeling about craps that controlled shooters do. A random roller's fate is in the hands of the gods of chance, and those gods are fickle and unforgiving. They'll win your loyalty with small rewards and destroy you with devastating losses. I don't trust anyone with my fate, deity or human, *except* my teammates.

And that's why I play craps as I do.

And that's why I teach it. Because I want to share a feeling that is wonderful, but that feeling can only exist with hard work and dedication. If Brother Barnabas had been a craps player, he'd be coaching in Golden Touch.

The casinos may be Goliath, but we Golden Touchers are little Davids armed with laser-guided stones that rarely miss their marks. It's great to be, once again, a part of something that is the best!

. . . .

20

. . . .

Frank Scoblete's Las Vegas Diary

THE FOLLOWING *diary was originally written for the members-only pages of the Craps Club, which can be found at* www.goldentouchcraps.com. *It's the before, during, and after of a two-week trip to Vegas.*

• Day 1: Wednesday, April 16, 2003 •

NO MATTER how often I've been to Vegas, I still get excited about the idea of going there. I was just in Tunica a few weeks ago, and a few weeks before that I was in Atlantic City. I mean, I get plenty of casino action, about 60 to 120 days per year. But Vegas is special. I guess it's the difference between going to church at the local wood-framed house of worship or going to St. Peter's Basilica. It has something to do with scale.

And energy.

And adrenaline.

And money.

For my wife, the beautiful AP, and me, Las Vegas has been our savior. From 1990 until 2002, we never lost on a trip to Vegas. That's not bragging, because when I finally did lose in April of 2002, it was a staggering loss and put my growing gambling ego and me in perspective. That whole trip, my first losing one to Vegas in over a dozen years, was a disaster from the get-go.

Here's an article I wrote for *Midwest Gaming and Travel* about the trip:

My Vegas Vacation

I don't have a therapist who gets paid to listen to my whines, moans and complaints. For that, I have you, my indulgent readers. So, please indulge me, because this column is all about me. This is a column I knew someday I would have to write: I was just hoping that someday was somewhere over the rainbow.

Here goes: I finally lost on a "trip" to Las Vegas. That's right, in more than 12 years of going to Sin City, in trips as short as four days and as long as two months, I have always come back ahead, sometimes a lot, sometimes a little, but always with more. My wife, the beautiful A.P., and I referred to this as "the record" or "the streak." I never wrote about it (that would be bragging), and only a few of my closest friends, such as John Robison and Walter Thomason, even knew about it. I can't say the same for any other casino venue that I have visited. I've had plenty of losing "trips," but not Vegas.

My friend, Fred Renzey [author of *77 Ways to Get the Edge at Casino Poker* and *Blackjack Bluebook*] would think me foolish for even considering the concept of a "trip" as anything more than some moments in a continual session. He'd say, and rightly, that the cards and dice have no idea when my "trips" begin or end; it's all one game. So you are either ahead of the game at any given time or behind at any given time. I wish I could really feel that were true, but my emotions won't buy it. Like a baseball team, I divide my play into winning and losing games (trips), as well as total runs scored for or against (the overall bottom line of my gambling to that point).

The trip from hell began with omens and ended with an oh-man.

At Kennedy Airport in New York, wending our way through the metal detectors, the alarms started sounding. I figured it was some idiot who hadn't taken off his jewelry. No. It was I.

I was pulled over and had to be given the full wand treatment and frisking, with all the other travelers looking at me as if I were some kind of deviant. What set off the alarms were a key, a roll of peppermints, and, of course, my $11.50 watch. I was spun, wanded, frisked; spun, wanded and frisked some more. Omen.

We were traveling first class using our upgrade miles and expected to get a good meal on the plane. Then, just before we boarded, an announcement was made that no food would be served on the flight. Imagine five-and-a-half hours to Vegas and no food. Omen.

So we bought some sandwiches to bring on board. Arrived at Las Vegas and the car that was supposed to pick us up was not there. Omen.

Finally, the car arrives, takes us to our hotel, and the room isn't ready. Omen.

I wasn't going to play until I had showered and napped, so we hung around for a couple of hours and talked about "the streak."

"You don't think all these little snafus are omens, do you?" I asked A.P.

"What would Fred Renzey say to that?" she countered.

"Right," I said.

That first night of play I lost more money than I had ever lost in any trip to any gambling venue in the country. That's how bad it was. For four days I slowly dug myself out of the hole and was ahead a few bucks before the second-to-last day (I never play on my very last day in Vegas, for discipline). Then the roof fell in. I had a last playing day that was even worse than the first. That night I slept in the fetal position. I would have sucked my thumb, only my $11.50 watch glows in the dark and it would have been right in my eyes.

That morning, the very first thing I said was, "I can't believe the streak is over."

"No big deal," said A.P., "it had to end sometime."

"Did it?"

"We'll have a nice breakfast, get some sandwiches for the plane, and you'll live to fight another day."

"We've taken a beating. I should have known this was going to happen from all those omens," I bemoaned.

"Don't be superstitious," she said.

So we went to the airport that afternoon to catch our plane. I made it through the metal detectors, no problem, as I had taken my watch, my belt, my roll of peppermints, my key, my *empty* wallet, and dumped them all in the tray.

"At least I wasn't given the wand treatment," I said to A.P.

When they called for the first class passengers, A.P. and I stepped forward. I handed my tickets to the attendant and then I heard: "Sir, step aside, please." A security guard.

"But I'm first class. I'm not jumping the line."

"Come with me, sir," he said. "Bring your bags." A.P. came with me. "Not you ma'am, you get on the plane," said the security agent.

"But he's my husband."

"Get on the plane, ma'am."

Then in full view of all the other passengers, Mr. First Class, Mr. Big Shot, Mr. Big Gambling Writer, Mr. ME, got the damn wand again. Had my belt removed. Was frisked. And then had to open my carry-on bag (dirty underwear and socks on top for all the world to see).

I was finally allowed on the plane when the security agent discovered nothing more dangerous in my bag than a book I had written about how to beat the casinos at their own games. The irony was not lost on me.

Seated next to A.P., at last, I just looked at her: "Do I fit some kind of profile?"

"Look at the way you dress," she said.

"Yeah, well that guy over there dresses worse than me," I said.

"That's a woman," she said.

"Oh, oh yeah, right. Do I look like a terrorist?"

"No, it's just been one of those trips."

"Yeah," I said.

"It started with all those omens, after all," she said.

"Oh, man," I said and promptly fell asleep.

Until that time, Las Vegas had been our own personal paradise. God, I was so smug by April 2002 that I honestly thought that I couldn't lose. Oh, I could, and did, lose on trips to Atlantic City and elsewhere, but Vegas, Vegas *belonged* to me.

I made the transition from being a red-chip blackjack player to a black-chip player in one summer at the Maxim's famous single-deck game. Check out these rules: you could resplit Aces, you could split any first two cards, resplit up to three times, double on any first two cards and on all splits, dealer stood on soft seventeen, surrender was allowed, and, if you got a blackjack with $5 or more wagered, you were given a coupon worth one dollar that could be used as cash at any Maxim outlet or restaurant. I averaged about $50 a day just in coupons. How? I played two hands for eight hours a day and the beautiful AP also played two hands for eight hours a day. When we arrived at the Maxim, we were $5 players, spreading from $5 in neutral and low counts to $25 in high counts on each of two hands. By week eight, we were playing for five times those amounts. *And no heat whatsoever from the pit, who knew we were counting cards!*

When we were getting ready to leave in late August to return to New York, AP had to sew the money we had won into the lining of my sports coat because I was paranoid about having so much cash on me. In those days I was skinny but all that money made me one fat—and contented—cat on the plane.

Not every trip required such extraordinary measures. One trip I only won $16, after expenses, but a win is a win.

I never wrote about the true nature of my Las Vegas gambling successes in any of my books, because nobody likes a braggart. And I could just hear the critics: "Not only has he invented this godlike creature he calls the Captain, but Scoblete claims he has never lost on a trip to Vegas! Who could possibly believe such baloney?"

Of course, I am no longer quite so confident in my ownership of Sin City. Having taken that first hammering in Vegas and knowing that I am not invincible, I look with joy, anticipation, and trepidation to this upcoming trip.

Not the least of my reasons for fearing this trip has to do with the fact that I'm writing this diary. I don't want to fall flat on my face in front of my readers and have to write: "Well, even though I lost [fill in the amount here], I still had a good time." A few weeks ago, I squeezed out of Tunica with a small win, after a disastrous couple of evenings at Sam's Town and one horrendous night at Sheraton. I had no one to blame but myself for those awful beatings—had I used the *5-Count* on my fellow GTCers, I would have been at least even on those nights and then I would have won a substantial amount by the time I left Tunica.

AP and I are looking forward to this trip for other reasons, social reasons. AP will be meeting one of her best friends, Penny, and the two of them intend to hit the museums and points of interests that have nothing to do with gambling (yes, I know that is weird, but AP actually goes to the public library when she's in Vegas), and then AP plans to write about "the cultural Las Vegas." Women!

AP and I don't *need* to win at gambling anymore. My two sons are grown up, one's married and just bought a house, and the other has a great job.

Of course, I'm excited for other reasons as well. It's a chance to play with Dominator for two straight weeks! And then Howard "Rock 'n' Roller" Newman comes in for about five days; during the time we're giving our special GTC class at the dealer school. For me, then, it's not all about the money anymore; it's camaraderie and then cash. It used to be only about the cash.

· · · ·

EVERYONE PREPARES for a trip in his own way. For me, I fantasize about the perfect roll. I see the dice in the center of the table. I watch the stickman push them to me. I select two; set my 3-V, take a breath; grab, grip, aim, and deliver the dice softly and with just enough backspin to land them with a breaking element so that they die at the base of the back wall. In my mind's eye I see roll after roll, and I see them step by step, element by element, and they are perfect.

Of course, there are the mundane things to do. Packing the bags, making sure we have all our pills and paraphernalia. AP always worries about what she'll wear and she worries about the fact that I *don't* worry about what I'll wear.

"You have to start dressing like an adult," AP says to me.

"I want to be comfortable."

"You look like a bum," says AP.

"God, you're beautiful, you know that?"

"Don't change the subject."

"No, no, really. You are just so beautiful."

"Stop. Stick to the point," says AP.

"That is the point. How a beautiful woman like you could love a guy like me," I say.

"It's the way you dress."

"I'm comfortable," I say.

"You're not going to wear those same cargo pants every day, are you?"

"I have a couple of pairs of them," I say.

"Two pairs of pants for fourteen days?"

"I'm comfortable in them."

"And when Dom meets us for dinner on Easter Sunday at the Eiffel Tower restaurant, what will you be wearing?" she asks.

"My 'Fuck France' button."

"I am going to ask Dom to outfit you," she threatens.

"Fine, just as long as I'm comfortable . . . and you are *too* beautiful."

I don't know what it is about clothes and me. I've never liked to dress up. My regular outfits are sweatpants and T-shirts, preferably old and about to disintegrate. That's what I wear when I write and I write every day. To me wearing cargo pants *is* dressing up. I would have been comfortable in a toga in ancient Rome. I once had a beautiful dinner with AP at Windows on the World at the World Trade Center wearing sweatpants and a suit jacket. So I can fit two weeks' worth of clothes in an overnight bag.

• • • •

WE ALSO have to take care of our bird, Augustus. Now, AP really loves me. I am her favorite human. But the big love of her life is this damn little bird. Augustus is a Quaker parrot, sometimes called a monk parrot. Religious connotations aside, this "Quaker-monk" can be hell. He's bright, like a two-year-old, and, like a two-year old, he wants what he wants when he wants it—and, if he doesn't get it, *squaaaawwwwwcccckkkk!!!!*

He can also be an endearing little thing. He can say the following:

"Love King Scobe." (He tries to snow me with that one.)

"I'm a good little bird." (Usually after he's pooped on your shoulder, hand, or head.)

"Eat." (Yes, when he wants to eat.)

"Drink." (Yes, when he wants to drink.)

"Eat and drink." (Yep.)

"Want a bath." (When he wants a bath.)

"I love you." (After he's done something really irritating.)

"Kiss, kiss." (Then he makes a clucking noise and does his version of a kiss.)

"Go to sleep." (When he wants to be covered for the night.)

And he also competes with any sound he hears. So, if another bird is outside trilling away, old Augustus squawks his beak off trying to out-trill the outdoor bird.

But, for the seven days AP will be with me in Vegas, Augustus will make his home with my in-laws, who live about a mile and a half from us. My mother-in-law likes to talk (a lot), but Augustus is a good listener so they get along.

I have to pack now. I'm ready. I'll post this. The next post will be on Friday, and it will be all about Thursday, as long as I can figure out how to use my new laptop and get on the Internet from afar.

• • • •

ADDENDUM: So much for the new laptop! It arrived and Dell got the entire order wrong. Instead of a laptop with a seventeen-inch screen, I got a laptop with a twelve-inch screen and a separate monitor with a seventeen-inch screen. I basically jumped up and down, called Dell every name I could think of that my mother told me never to say, and packed everything up and it's now sitting outside my house waiting for the UPS guy to pick it up and cart it away. So I have no idea if I'm going to be able to pull off this diary as I planned it, day by day as it happens.

That is just my luck with electronic equipment of any kind. I never get the right thing on the first try. The computer I bought just before the one I am now using had a virus in it. I took it back and the guy at the store said, "Gee, never saw that before." I bought a thirty-seven-inch television and when I hooked it up the picture wouldn't come on. I had to take it back. Same with my VCR, my DVD player, and new phones I've bought. The first cellular phone I ever bought, when they were those big models, *melted*. Some kind of "freak electrical happening," said the dealer.

Now you can see why I am hesitant about buying a plane. I don't want to be up in the air when some "freak electrical happening" happens.

Wish me luck on this diary. Dom is going to take me to a store when we get to Vegas tomorrow and we're going to buy a laptop there. Maybe I should buy two, so that when the first one explodes the second one will work.

Again, wish me luck!

• Day 2: Thursday, April 17, 2003 •

THE CAR came to pick up AP and me at 6:15 in the morning for our 7:50 America West flight, a nonstop to Las Vegas. I like America West because it is one of the few airlines that has nonstop service to Vegas from Kennedy. Even nonstop, the trip to Sin City is an agonizing five and a half hours; when you take flights with layovers, you can take upwards of ten hours to get to Vegas.

So nonstop is the way to go.

AP and I travel first class. We put all of our expenses, however large or small, on an America West credit card. We then buy the cheapest possible fare and upgrade using our mileage. Five and a half hours on a plane is not quite as awful in first class as it is in coach.

You never know what you're going to get when you get to Kennedy. It's a big, crowded, confusing airport. Thankfully, our driver, John Smith (I kid you not, that is his name), knows the airport and most of New York like I know the odds on certain craps bets. John owns his own limousine service called Reliable Limo. And he is reliable.

We zipped right through the passenger line (the privileges of first class!) and, having learned my lesson on that big losing trip to Vegas (no metals, no belt, no watch, no coins, no shoes), we zipped right through security. By six forty-five, we had time to kill with some 125 other passengers waiting to go to Las Vegas.

I'd forgotten that this was spring break for most New York schools. The waiting area for the flight was loaded with kids, kids of all ages: crying kids, lying kids, running kids, whining kids, sleeping kids, kids drinking from bottles, kids sucking on their thumbs, kids sitting on the floor, tiny kids looking confused, teenagers looking pathetically cool, and one kid, a *big,* pasty-faced, lumbering girl of maybe sixteen who, as I glanced over at her, gave her father, himself another *big,* lumbering, pasty-but-pig-faced monstrosity, a slam with her elbow that almost upended him. Not to be outdone, Dad came roaring back with a forearm smash that would have made Bruno Sammartino proud, a smash right to his darling daughter's upper chest that saw her slam against the concrete pillar that evidently helps to hold up the roof of the waiting area. Daughter Dearest sprang from the wall and pushed her father so hard that he bumped into his wife, a brutish low-browed woman who snarled, "I hate you two."

I turned to AP, who had also witnessed this family fun and said, "Should we tell anyone?"

AP shrugged. "The kid holds her own. This is how they relate to each other."

"Like apes," I said.

"Well, we're in first class," she said, "We won't have to deal with that type."

"No, we won't."

• • • •

YES, WE will.

God has a great sense of humor, doesn't He? Of course, the Family from Hell wound up in first class, Dad and Mom in the two seats in front of us, behind us Daughter and a shriveled, hideously wrinkled, face-lifted creature that I think was the grandmother next to her, and in the aisle across from us a puffed and bloated "little brother" and some other "thing," also related in some way to these cave dwellers. I refused to look at it.

I tried to keep my eyes closed for most of the trip but, unfortunately, my ears were always open. All the Family from Hell did was eat and argue, argue and eat. The daughter got up frequently to annoy her parents; the parents made it a point to tell her their feelings. "You suck!" said the father. "You're disgusting," said the mother. "I hate you both," said the daughter. "Any more food up there?" said the bloated brother. "Do you think it's good tanning weather?" asked the wrinkled one behind me.

When the flight was finished AP and I let the Family from Hell exit first and, as I saw them heading off into the jingle-jangle of the airport slot machines and the rushing crowds, I was glad to be rid of them.

Except we ran into them at the baggage area . . . literally. There they were, puffy, bloated, lumbering, and arguing. Dad and Daughter were engaged in their perpetual shoving match, and as AP leaned over to get her luggage on the conveyer Daughter staggered back (perhaps from another forearm smash) and bumped AP, and my beautiful wife found herself dangling precariously half on, half off the conveyer belt that was going around and around with people's luggage. I was able to grab her shirt and start dragging her to safety. Once rescued and clutching her luggage in her arms, she said, "Who pushed me?"

Then she heard Dad and Daughter exchanging pleasantries. "You are so ugly," said Dad. "You blow," said Daughter.

"Figures," said AP.

• • • •

SINCE WE were doing the A&A approach to Vegas (alone and anonymous) instead of having a limo pick us up at the airport, we waited on the longest taxi line in history. It was almost to New York. But it moved fast, and as we made it to the front of the line I could feel my adrenaline surge. Vegas. Las Vegas. *My Vegas.* Two straight weeks of the ultimate challenge—beating the casinos!

AP would meet her friend Penny and they would go to all the places that Penny wished to see. AP would be a kind of tour guide.

The first six days of the trip would see us staying at Bally's. Now, for those of you who have long memories, Bally's, once called MGM in another incarnation, had one of the most devastating hotel fires in history in 1980. Almost ninety people died. The rumors circulated that some people were injured because they refused to leave the casino. I have no idea if those stories are true, but I was at the Maxim once when the fire alarms went off and the sprinklers started spraying and no one, I mean *no one*, left the casino! A soaked blackjack player was scratching for a hit as the dealer put the plastic box over the chips and locked them up before leaving. "Hey, hey, I'm playing here!" he screamed as the dealer walked away.

We upgraded our room to a suite for an extra $20 a day and we were in. AP and I immediately took a nap. It was about noon.

At 2 P.M., Penny arrived. We arranged to have Penny's room on the same floor several doors down from ours. Then we all went down to lunch. After lunch Penny and AP went off for a walk and I went over to Bellagio to play craps.

I'm in good shooting shape and I've been playing quite a bit lately. But I still felt that I had to go slow in the beginning and get the feel for the tables. I've had too many trips in which I had to dig myself out of a big hole—a hole I dug for myself by betting too aggressively, especially on myself, early on.

Bellagio is one of the seven wonders of Las Vegas, along with Venetian, Mandalay Bay, Caesars Palace, Mirage, MGM Grand, and whichever casino is your own personal favorite. The craps tables at Bellagio are very much like the craps tables at Treasure Island—just about perfect for a controlled thrower. With some exceptions, the crews are generally very professional and friendly.

This afternoon the crew was good and I was great. When I started to roll, the stickman asked me if I had taken a course with the *Crapsguy,* "that dice teacher who [solicits] students at the tables." I knew to whom he was referring. I told him no.

I had four twenty-minute rolls in a row at a half-filled table. The other players were cheering me, the dealers were happy as they were making a lot in tips, and a good and profitable time was being had by all . . . all, that is, except for Mr. Mumbles, the mustachioed boxman. He seemed to take it personally that I was hot. He couldn't yell at me for missing the back wall because I never once in eighty minutes of rolling missed the back wall. But this didn't sit well with Mr. Mumbles, who kept muttering under his breath that I would never be able to get away with such a "soft roll" at any other casino. When I'm on, my dice just die as they hit the wall; they barely move. That was how they were behaving this afternoon.

I thought Mr. Mumbles, whose face kept changing colors from brown to red to browner and redder as I rolled and rolled, was going to have his head explode. I have never understood why casino personnel take it personally when a *careful shooter* has a good roll. It wasn't Mr. Mumbles' money we were winning. Besides, all those cheering players would hang around until they lost their money (and then some)—or, because of a desire to re-experience the incredible adrenaline rush that comes from a hot roll, they would come back time and again until they did lose their money (and then some). That's how most craps players are. They might win big one night, but there is no way they will keep the money. The casino personnel should realize that (some do), and they should welcome the hot shooter who gets those players' juices flowing.

Mr. Mumbles didn't understand that. He just kept mumbling. After my third roll, Mr. Mumbles was given a break and another boxman took over. He seemed unconcerned that the players were having a good time of it. In fact, when they cheered he would smile as if he was happy they were winning. He was, in short, a real pro.

When Mr. Mumbles came back I was into my fourth incredible roll of the afternoon. The break had done nothing to calm Mr. Mumbles' choler. When I finally sevened out I colored up and left the table. The cashier's cage at Bellagio is right near the craps tables, and when I was cashing in I half expected to hear a big *boom!* and see brain matter sailing through the casino.

Back in my room at Bally's I tried to get on the Internet using the hotel's television set. Nothing worked. The screen was frozen. I called maintenance. When the maintenance man finally came, he couldn't figure out what was wrong with the set either. "Never saw *this* before." I'll make a long story really short: I decided to say to hell with attempting to get on the Internet while I was in Vegas to post this diary and, instead, I decided I'd write it in longhand and rewrite it when I got home. Computers and me, we just don't get along.

That night, Penny, AP, and I ate at Chang's, the Chinese restaurant at Bally's. After dinner, AP and I played some double-deck blackjack at Bally's while Penny went for a walk.

Boom! No, not Mr. Mumbles' head, but my money exploded. In fifteen minutes of head-to-head blackjack play at the automatic-shuffling double-deck game at Bally's, AP and I won almost as much as I had won during eighty minutes of torrid craps-rolling. I didn't lose a hand for thirteen minutes! When I finally lost three hands in a row, AP and I quit for the night. We went outside, watched the fountains at Bellagio across the street, and then went upstairs to our suite.

DAY 2 RESULTS: +128 units
TOTAL FOR TRIP: +128 units

• Day 3: Friday, April 18, 2003 •

WENT FOR a long walk this morning with AP and Penny. We went all the way north on the Strip to Treasure Island, then headed south to Mandalay Bay. We went to the end of the property where the Four Seasons is, said hello to a little flower bed (I actually said, "Hello, flowers") and then headed back to Bally's.

After breakfast, I wrote my notes in my journal and then Dom called. We decided to hook up at Bellagio that afternoon.

At Bellagio Dom had a good roll to start the day and so did I. The *5-Count* saved me a fortune on other shooters; the dice made their way around the table without me placing a bet. Dom had another good roll. I didn't. Then two other players appeared at the table; one of them was the freelance dice-control teacher, the *Crapsguy*, whom yesterday's box-man had asked me about. We played for about forty-five minutes together, but no money was to be made. I had several really bad rolls in succession and I finally left the table when other shooters started getting past the 5-Count only to seven out on the 6-Count or 7-Count, not a good thing at all. I lost about 15 units.

Dom had also cooled off at the first table, so he joined me at a new one. He was the first to roll and he went for a good fifteen minutes. Then I got the dice, just as the boxman was relieved. And who should be the new boxman? Why my old friend, Mr. Mumbles! As soon as he saw me he started mumbling. Then he called over the floorperson, an elderly gent who looked a lot like Clarence the angel who wants to get his wings in *It's a Wonderful Life*. Mr. Mumbles whispered in Clarence's hairy ear and nodded in my direction. On my second roll, lo and behold, one die missed the back wall. You would think I had just murdered the Pope! Mr. Mumbles started screaming, "Listen, you, you better hit that back wall hard!" Then Clarence the wingless angel flew in, and, leaning all the way over the table to get into my face, said, "If you're setting the dice, you better hit the back wall."

I figured repentance was the better part of valor, so I said,

"I'm sorry. I didn't do that on purpose." Mr. Mumbles har-
rumphed and Clarence nodded and walked away.

I then had a terrific roll to the general grumbles of Mr.
Mumbles, whose head seemed to swell with every number I
hit. After my roll, the table got crowded, so Dom and I went
to an empty table. Dominator had another good roll. So did
I. The boxman at this table was friendly and professional.
The dealers were great—just what you would expect from a
place like Bellagio.

At night, Dominator, AP, Penny, and I had dinner at Il
Fornaio at New York, New York. We talked about what it's
like to have people attacking you in print and on the Internet, which has been happening quite a bit since we started
GTC. Dom is not used to people taking cheap shots at him
on these craps Web sites. It was getting to him a little, especially the hysterical attacks on GTC and the vicious attacks
on his character by some posters.

AP and I explained to Dom that, when you are in the public eye, all manner of insults would come out of the people
who live in the floorboards and crevices of life. The mission
of the crevice creatures is to try to cut you down to their
size. Dom just had to develop a thicker skin. The best way to
do that was to not go to any Web site where you know
you're being attacked, to ignore the attacks made on you
when you do find out about them, and to focus on the good
things being said about you. It also helped to focus on the
work at hand, in this case making GTC the ultimate dice-
control experience in the world.

It took me several years before I could develop the thick
hide I have now. I don't visit any Web sites but GTC's and a
few private sites. Occasionally someone will e-mail me what
somebody else said about me either in print or on another Web
site; when that happens I tend to rate what is being said on a
scale of cleverness. Two of my favorites are the prominent

blackjack authority who said that, if he ever woke up and found out he was Frank Scoblete, he'd kill himself, and the poster to an Internet site who called me a "blood clot."

We then went to see Rita Rudner. Dinner was great and so was Rita. Laughter is the best remedy for just about anything that wears on you.

Despite my initial downturn at Bellagio, I still wound up winning another 20 units today. Not bad.

DAY 3 RESULTS: +20 units

TOTAL FOR TRIP: +148 units

• Day 4: Saturday, April 19, 2003 •

WE TOOK our usual walk this morning. Said hello to the flowers of Mandalay Bay. In the afternoon, AP and Penny went to the Elvis Museum and I headed over to Green Valley Ranch in Henderson.

I'd never been to Green Valley Ranch but Dom loves the place. As I entered I could see why. It is the old Desert Inn reborn, only more stately and luxurious than the Desert Inn. I had arrived about a half-hour early, so instead of calling Dom I went over to the craps tables and played. (Dom had spent most of the morning sunning himself at the pool and I didn't want to disturb him.) As soon as I set the dice and rolled, the stickwoman asked me if I was the *Crapsguy*'s student. I said no. I had a half-hour roll and one of the players, a dealer at Sunset Station who likes to play at Green Valley, complimented me on my style. I gave him one of our Craps Club Black Chips with our phone number, and whispered to him if he was interested in learning how to roll like that give us a call.

You know, I shouldn't have whispered that, because when Dom arrived I had several terrible rolls, as did he, and this dealer *scooted* from the table. In fact, Dom and I left the table and headed over to blackjack to give ourselves time to lick our wounds. It was no better. In the space of a half-hour, between craps and blackjack, I lost 40 units. I was also treated to a lecture about the "F" word when one of the obviously inebriated blackjack players started saying "F this" and "F that" as he lost hand after heartbreaking hand, and the dealer got understandably upset.

Dom and I weren't faring any better.

"I hate the 'F' word," said the dealer.

"I agree," I said and lost a hand.

"It has replaced good vocabulary words," said the dealer.

"I agree," I said and lost another hand.

"In public, you shouldn't use such language," said the dealer.

"I agree," I said and lost a split with a double down on both ends of it.

"I don't think people have been brought up properly," said the dealer.

"Yes, I agree," I said as the dealer hit to a twenty-one, beating my twenty.

"I hate that word," said the dealer as she turned over a blackjack.

"Yeah, me, too," I said as I turned to Dom and whispered in his ear, "Let's get the fuck out of here!"

We colored up what few chips we had remaining and ended our afternoon of playing at Green Valley.

I lost another 15 units.

Dom got me the Green Valley limo to go back to Bally's. I had lost 55 units that afternoon, a big loss. I was still ahead some 93 units, but I was down emotionally. I just hate to lose.

• • • •

THAT NIGHT Penny, AP, and I again ate at Chang's (I love Chinese food), and AP and I played that double-deck black-jack game at Bally's again. And lightning struck again! In fifteen minutes we won 18 units!

Went to bed high on my win.

DAY 4 RESULTS: -37 units

TOTAL FOR TRIP: +111 units

• Day 5: Sunday, April 20, 2003 •

THIS IS Easter Sunday.

I think I have spent the last ten Easters in Las Vegas. Usually the weather is perfect, mid-seventies in the day, mid-fifties at night. Perfect. So far this trip, the weather has been unusually cold. Some days barely got above the fifty-degree mark. The walks in the morning require a jacket, which is fine by me since I get to wear the GoldenTouchCraps.com windbreaker Dom designed. The jacket is quality, since Dom knows his clothes and fashion (I, on the other hand, am a troglodyte), and across the back is our Golden Touch Craps URL for the entire world to see. You can't ask for better publicity than walking up and down the Strip with your company's URL on your back.

After breakfast, I played that double-deck game at Bally's again, and again I had a great run for about a half-hour. I did lose *some* hands, but overall I am having some of the greatest streaks of my life at this game. It's a typical double-deck Strip game: dealer hits soft seventeen; you can split, re-split, and double on any first two cards. The automatic shuffler keeps the game moving, first the red decks, then the blue decks, then the red decks, then the blue decks. I won 10 units.

Penny had brought money from some of her friends to play. She wanted me to bet it "so I can tell my friends that the world's greatest gambling authority was the one I had gamble with their money."

"Not too much pressure," I said.

"Oh, they know they can lose," said Penny.

No they don't. They *think* they know they can lose, but in their heart of hearts they feel that someone like me, Mr. Big-Shot Gambler, must win all the time, and they expect to see a profit from the money they give over. They intellectually know, and they'll even utter the words to this effect, that even the best gamblers lose and lose often, but emotionally they feel they have a lock. When I first started coming to Vegas, I would take other people's money and try to win for them. On a given night, I'd say, "The first two hands in this high count I'll bet Jim's money." And what would happen if I lost Jim's money? Why, then I'd say, "Well, that didn't count; that was my money." By the end of the trip I tried to give everybody double whatever they had given me to gamble with, figuring this would make them happy. (Most of these folks just gave me between $50 and $100 to bet.) Double your money back didn't always satisfy them. One man, upon receiving a $75 return on a $75 investment, said: "Is that all? I thought you'd win much more!" It would have taken him a dozen years to double his money in a bank; I had done it in a couple of weeks. I didn't think Penny's friends would be any different, but Penny would never allow me to just give them a win—I actually had to play the money in front of her. Damn! That's pressure.

Bally's craps tables are great—except for one thing. They are way too high. My stomach, which should be above the rail, gets squished below the rail, and it is very uncomfortable for me to shoot there. But Penny was going home in a few hours and I had to try to win those friends some money.

"Give me the money and I'll bet it," I said.

"I'd like to bet it," said Penny. "When you roll just tell me what to do."

We cashed in at an empty table. I positioned myself at SL1.

"I'll tell you when to bet," I said as the stickman passed me the dice. I put a Pass Line bet down and set my 3-V. I stood up on my tiptoes and rolled. I established my point on the first roll; it was a six. I put the full odds behind the six and placed the eight. I then told Penny to place $12 on the six and eight.

"Put a $25 chip down and say, 'Twelve dollar six and eight,'" I said.

"Twelve dollar six and eight," said Penny, dropping a green chip on the table.

The dealer took her bet and returned a $1 chip.

"Pick that chip up," I said. She did. "Now, you are rooting for me to hit a six or an eight. Here goes."

I took a deep breath, set the 3-V and focused on the end of the table. I got all the way up on my tiptoes and . . . "Eight, the easy way, eight!" said the stickman, who gathered the dice and pushed them toward me.

"Collect your money," I said to Penny.

"Boy, we won so soon?" she said.

I set, stood on my toes, and . . . "Six! Winner! Six. Pay the Line, take the Don'ts."

"We won again?"

"Yep," I said.

"Shooter on the come out," said the stickman as a couple of people cashed in at the other end of the table.

"Put a bet on the Pass Line in front of you," I said to Penny, "Just the way I'm doing, see?"

Penny put up a $5 Pass Line bet.

"Now, you're rooting for a seven or eleven."

I took a deep breath; the stickman pushed the dice toward me. "Dice are out."

I set the All Sevens set, stood up, and . . . "Seven! Winner seven!"

"Pick up your win," I said to Penny.

The dealer passed the dice to me again.

"Seven and eleven," I said to Penny.

"Seven and eleven," said Penny.

"Seven! Winner seven!" said the stickman.

"Hey, this is easy," said Penny, collecting another bet.

"Oh, yeah," said the stickman, pushing the dice toward me. "This is a real easy game when you've got a good shooter."

I stood, set, delivered. "Yo-eeeleveeen! Winner!"

"Good shooting," shouted one of the guys at the end of the table. Then someone cashed in next to Penny.

"How's the table going?" asked this new player.

"We're winning," said Penny.

"Good, good."

I established a point on my next roll, a four.

"Put $15 behind your Pass Line bet, like this," I said as I put odds behind my Pass Line bet. "I hit this four and you're going to get paid $30 for that $15."

"Come on, four!" shouted Penny.

"Dice are out," said the stickman.

"You want the four, six, and eight," I said.

"Come on four, six, and eight!" shouted Penny.

I took a deep breath. In every game there is a moment when you turn a corner or hit the wall. Penny had $44 at risk now. She had won $39 on my previous rolls. If I could hit a few sixes and eights and maybe turn that point, she would be able to bring home a profit for her friends. If I sevened out now, she would bring them home less than they had given her and my reputation as a big-shot gambler would be ruined.

I stood, set and delivered. "Six, winner, six."

And then in rapid succession, "Six! Winner six. . . . Eight, winner eight. . . . Eight, winner eight! . . . Eight, the haaar-rrd way. . . . Six. The haaard way!"

"Way to go, shooter!" yelled the man at the other end of the table.

Several people came over and cashed in. The table was now almost full.

Penny chanted: "Four, six, eight! Four, six, eight!"

"Dice are out."

In *s-l-o-w* motion, I stood, set, delivered . . . the dice went down the table, gently, softy, then a chip came flying in from somewhere, hit the dice in the midair and they split and landed, not touching the wall, hitting other chips . . . "Seven out! No bet on that thrown chip!"

"What happened?" asked Penny.

"We just lost," I said.

"It happens," the boxman. "You were having a good run there until that chip hit you."

Penny was able to go home with some extra money for her friends, enough to maintain my reputation as Mr. Big Shot. I won another 6 units on that roll of mine. I was now up 16 units for the day.

· · · ·

THAT NIGHT, Dom, AP, and I would eat at the Eiffel Tower restaurant at the Paris Hotel-Casino. This is one of the premier restaurants in Vegas, with one of its most spectacular views, not only of the Strip but also of Bellagio's fountains. However, before dinner, I decided to go over to Aladdin and play there for a little while.

I had never been in Aladdin before—the *new* Aladdin, that is. I used to frequent the old Aladdin in the mid-1990s, when they had the best two-deck game in Vegas.

I knew the Aladdin was having trouble meeting its debts. I also knew that Planet Hollywood was interested in buying the place and converting it to a Hollywood-themed hotel. Now, I want you to ponder some questions:

One, if you had a hotel named Aladdin that went bankrupt and you tore it down and started all over from scratch, would you name your new hotel Aladdin as well, even after the old one of that name had failed? Would anybody name a new ship today *Titanic*? You're asking for trouble. Would you have a giant mural on the main casino floor of Arabs looking warlike? Maybe in the 1950s, when Arabs were considered exotic; not in the twenty-first century, when the phrase "warlike Arabs" brings to mind the terrorists who have been blowing up our buildings, embassies, ships, and servicemen and -women.

And, do we *really* need *another* Hollywood themed hotel-casino? There was a time when that would've seemed exotic, too, but these days many of their stars lack luster. I just can't see myself happily eating in the Susan Sarandon gourmet room, amongst the pictures of Hollywood stars kissing Fidel Castro's cigar, sipping a Barbara Streisand (that's a martini made of two-thirds vodka from the old Soviet Union and one-third French whine), ordering a Tim Robbins, an appetizer made from the finest communist Chinese chickens, eaten raw, and having as my main course a Danny Glover, a red crab marinated in malarkey. It would be enough to make you throw up your Michael Moore, which is a dessert made from whole cloth.

At the Aladdin, I cashed in at a table that had only three people playing. My SL1 spot was open and I settled in. An Asian woman was shooting the dice at the top of the table on my side, and a Hawaiian kid at the opposite end of the table on stick right was betting heavily on the Don'ts. This kid (he couldn't have been more than twenty-five years old) was betting a stack of black chips on three different numbers, plus the Don't Pass Line. And he was loudly rooting for the seven. Usually Don't players are quiet. Not this kid. Wearing a flamboyant, multicolored Hawaiian flower-print shirt, opened halfway down his hairless chest, and sporting all manner of jewelry around his neck, Don Ho Two shouted, "Come on, seven! Whoop! Whoop!"

I looked at his chip rack. It was filled with black and purple chips. "I'm from Hawaeeeee!!!" he shouted as the lady tossed the dice. Then he banged his fist on the rail. *Thump! Thump!*

"Seven! Seven-out," said the stickwoman. "Sir, please don't bang on the table."

"I'm having fun. What's the matter?" said Don Ho Two.

The Asian woman sniffed at him, the way you would if a smelly dog had just entered the room, and she walked away from the table. The next to shoot was the man right next to Don Ho Two. "Another loser," said Don Ho Two as he placed a $300 Don't Pass bet.

The man rolled three craps numbers in a row, a two and two threes. "Big loser! Big loser!" shouted Don Ho Two, collecting his money.

Finally, the man established a point, a five, and Don Ho Two put up a Don't Come bet and laid the full odds on his Don't Pass bet. The man hit a couple of different numbers and Don Ho Two laid the odds on each.

"Loser! Big loser! Come on, seven! Ha! Ha! Seven!"

I looked over at my dealer, a pretty young woman. Our eyes caught. She gave a little shudder and rolled her eyes ever so slightly as if to say, "What a jerk." I rolled my eyes as well as if to say, "I agree."

And . . . "Seven out! Take the Line, pay the Don'ts!"

"Wha-ha! Wha-ha!" shouted Don Ho Two. "Next loser!" he said—looking straight at me.

"Do you want to shoot, sir?" asked the stickwoman of Don Ho Two.

"Pass it to the loser," he said.

The dice were passed to me as I put down a Pass Line bet.

"Good luck, sir," said the dealer on my side of the table as I set the dice in the All Sevens set. Don Ho Two put up a $300 Don't Pass bet.

"Two or three, baby, two or three," said Don Ho Two.

I took careful aim and rolled.

"Two craps, two. Pay the Don't, take the Line," said the stickwoman.

I looked over at my dealer, who said again, "Good luck, sir."

"Come on, old man, let's see another crap, wha-ha!" shouted Don Ho Two.

Old man? Old man? That hairless little creep!

"Dice are out," said the stickwoman.

I took a deep breath, prayed a split second for justice for anyone over fifty (*old man,* indeed), set the All Sevens again, and this time I nailed an eleven.

"Not good shooter, not good," said Don Ho Two, replacing his Don't Pass bet.

Then I hit another eleven.

Then another eleven.

Don Ho Two stopped making Don't Pass bets. He waited.

I set the 3-V and established a nine as my point. I placed the six and eight, put full odds behind the nine. Don Ho Two put out a $300 Don't Come bet. I put a Come bet down. I rolled a four. He loaded up the odds on the Don't, so did I on the Do. He put another Don't Come down; I put another Come bet down. This was war. I hit the four right back. He loaded up again. I hit the four again! He loaded again. I hit a six. He loaded up the odds on his $300. I then hit a ten. He loaded up the odds.

I better start really focusing, I thought to myself, because those outside fours and tens, while nice to hit, mean my throw is not quite perfect. And I wanted it to be perfect, just perfect, for Mr. Don Ho Two.

He started dangling his hands over the table just above where my dice were hitting. I really focused and put all my *self* into hitting my spot on the table in just the right way. And I made the point of nine on the next roll.

He was dangling his hand over the rail and this time he had a $500 Don't Pass bet. "Let's see your crap!" he said disdainfully. "Come on shooter, crap!"

I didn't set the Any Sevens because I didn't want to lose my Come bets.

"Dice are out," said the stickman, who had replaced the stickwoman, who was now my dealer.

"Good luck, sir," said my former dealer from the other side of the table.

"What's the matter, no one wishes me luck?" said Don Ho Two.

"We are all wishing you luck," said the dealer.

Yeah, bad luck.

He was dangling his hands over the table again. Then I did what I was free to do on the Come Out roll. I set the 3-V and deliberately aimed at his hands! On the Come Out, except for the loss of the Come Bets, you are free to do certain maneuvers. Usually if someone has his Pass Line bet up around the spot I want to hit, I'll aim for his chips and, if my dice hit them, I'll groan and say, "Damn chips." Often a good stickperson will ask the offender to move his chips to the side. By doing it that way, I don't draw attention to myself the way I would if I requested that the player move his chips to give me a landing zone.

The same held true for Don Ho Two of the dangling hands. I whipped the dice down the table in a line drive and hit the back of one of his hands. He went, "Ow!" and moved both his hands back. "Point is six," said the stickman. "Sir," said the boxman with a twinkle in his eye, "Please don't put your hands over the side while the shooter is shooting."

The boxman looked deadpan at me; I looked at him. Don Ho Two was rubbing his hand and glaring at me. Don Ho Two laid the full odds on his Don't Pass 6. I took the full odds on my Pass Line 6.

Oh, the war was on, all right. He knew it. I knew it. The dealers knew it, the boxman knew it, the suits that were standing behind the boxman (I hadn't even seen them come over) knew it, and the small crowd that was starting to watch the game knew it, too.

I proceeded to pick off all his Don't Come bets. I nailed the point as well. He kept putting out the bets. I kept knocking them off. My rack was filling up; his rack was diminishing rapidly.

Finally, I landed the knockout blow. He was down to his last hundred dollars. He put it on the Don't Pass just after I made another point.

This time I set for the seven, because by now I had placed all the numbers and a seven couldn't hurt me.

"Any Seven for the dealers," I said loudly and threw out two red chips.

"Thank you, sir," said my new dealer, the young man who had been the stick for the past twenty minutes. "Good luck, sir," he then said as the stickwoman passed me the dice.

I set the dice, looked at my spot, and let the dice go. I was willing a seven; I was demanding of God and the universe that the dice land on the seven. The dice bounced, hit the wall gently, and died.

"Yo-eleven! Winner! Yo-eleven."

Okay, so it wasn't a seven. But it accomplished the same thing. It blew Don Ho Two all the way back to Hawaii. He stormed from the table with an expletive.

I then established a point and sevened out just like that.

"Whew!" I said. "Glad that came now and not before."

"We are too, sir," said one of the dealers.

"He was very aggressive before with other shooters," said another dealer.

"I understand what you mean. He lost money. You and I made money—actually, Aladdin made the most money!" I said, and colored up to go to Easter dinner with AP and Dom.

I had won 50 units. I was now up 66 units for the day.

As I was leaving the table, I then noticed the small crowd that had been watching the game was dispersing, except for one young Asian man. He was looking at me and smiling broadly. Damn! It was Tony Lee! He wasn't supposed to be in Vegas this month.

"That was some display for the man," said Tony.

"Did you watch the whole thing?" I asked.

"Yep. I saw you at the table and was coming over to speak to you, but you had the dice. So I stood where you couldn't see me and I watched you blow that obnoxious bastard away."

"You out here with the team?" I asked. "I thought you guys were supposed to be in Reno."

"Larry had to go home for some family business, and the others decided to take a few weeks off to relax. We've been on the road a couple of years straight."

"Listen, I'm having dinner with Dominator. I've told him about you. He'd love to meet you. What do you say?"

"No, no," said Tony, reiterating my agreement with him: "No one is to know what we look like or who we are. I can't screw up what we have going for us. It's like with the Captain."

"Yeah," I said.

"Don't even tell him you met me," said Tony.

"No," I said. "He'd be looking around every time he played hoping to see you. You'd love Dominator; he's a great shooter."

"No," said Tony.

When Tony says "no" he means "no." So I told Dominator that a young guy who seemed to recognize me had watched the game as I destroyed Don Ho Two. I never did tell him it was Tony Lee, although he'll find out when he reads this.

. . . .

THE EIFFEL Tower restaurant has its own private security guard outside the elevator. You are not allowed up unless you have a confirmed reservation. When I dined there when it first opened, the waiters seemed to be affecting a French accent. This evening none did. AP and I are boycotting any French products (AP now refers to French toast and French onion soup as freedom toast and freedom onion soup) but Americans own this restaurant—I hope. As I mentioned, it has a panoramic view of the Strip and Bellagio's dancing fountains. The food is expensive but well prepared; the waiters are at the top of their profession. The Eiffel Tower restaurant is a good example of the old axiom that you get what you pay for.

. . . .

AFTER DINNER, Dom and I went over to Bellagio to play and AP went back to our room to sleep. During this trip

AP suffered from an allergy attack brought on by stress. What was she stressed over? Meeting Dominator! She wanted to make a good impression. AP suffers from what I call Anticipatory Stress Syndrome (ASS for short), which means that before any event she is anticipating, be it a good event or a bad event, if she gets stressed out, she gets a severe "allergy flare-up"—or, in the worst cases, her ulcerative colitis flares up. AP worrying about making a good impression is similar to Babe Ruth during his heyday worrying about hitting a home run. Ruth's home runs came and the beautiful AP invariably makes a good impression, because what's not to like?

At Bellagio, we headed for the craps tables. We found one, a half-empty table, with our positions open, Dom SR1, me SL1, and we cashed in. The table quickly filled up. Next to me a really elderly gent cashed in. And then his wife cashed in.

Everyone knows what rubbernecking is; something awful, or interesting, or awfully interesting happens and you just can't tear your eyes away from it. That was this guy's wife. She was ancient but she had had a facelift that made her look as if she were twenty years old. Except for her mouth, which was so stretched that her lower lip had folded over and protruded, much like those natives you see with plates in their lower lips in *National Geographic* specials. It looked as if someone had pumped air into her lower lip. Also, she drooled; she had to keep wiping spit off her lower lip. She had also had a "hand-lift," so what you saw were these desiccated old arms with these young hands at the end of them. I couldn't stop turning my head to look at her. She also had this very old voice coming out of that young face. And she must have had breast implants too, because there were these bosomy things swelling out of her blouse with all this

wrinkly skin above them. She was fascinating, like Franken-
stein's monster, all body parts that didn't add up.

I blame her for the fact that I didn't have any noteworthy
rolls that night at Bellagio! (Hey, you have to blame someone.) I couldn't take my eyes off her.

Neither Dom nor I could get it going that night at Bellagio, so we went over to Aladdin to give it a try there. I
looked around to see if Tony Lee were still around. He
wasn't.

Aladdin wasn't much better than Bellagio. Dom and I finally realized it wasn't happening and we called it a night. I
went back to Bally's. Dom went back to Green Valley
Ranch.

I had lost 11 units in my sessions at Bellagio and Aladdin.
I was still up 55 units for the day.

That night, while I slept, Dom played craps at Green Valley Ranch. He had a thirty-minute roll followed by a forty-
five-minute monster! And *that's* why he's the *Dominator!*

DAY 5 RESULTS: +55 units
TOTAL FOR TRIP: +166 units

• Day 6: Monday, April 21, 2003 •

AP AND I went for our walk in the morning. It never ceases
to amaze me how some people can be drinking beer or
booze at 6 A.M. It also amazes me to see the young girls out
so early, or rather up so late, walking barefoot on the litter-
strewn sidewalks of the Strip in an attempt to look cool. The
sidewalks of Vegas in the early morning hours are often lit-
tered with broken glass, bodily fluids, and porno pictures;
definitely not the place to be walking barefoot.

I am so glad that I am now at an age at which I don't have
to be cool. If cool means you have to have pieces of metal

hammered through your tongue, nipples, and genitals, or uninspired, drab tattoos scratched into your skin, count me out. Of course, I was *never* cool. In my teenage years, there was the "in" crowd, the "out" crowd, and Scobe's crowd. And everyone in my crowd was different from everyone else in my crowd.

Speaking of "cool," on this walk I saw another ancient lady; this one had blood-red lips and was dressed in fashionable combat camouflage gear with her midriff exposed—and she had sparkles on her belly and a facelift that stretched her red mouth from ear to ear. She was painfully thin and painfully trying to be young and painfully trying to be, here is that word again, *cool.*

• • • •

AFTER BREAKFAST, I spent most of the morning writing up yesterday's adventures. I realized that if I kept trying to capture everything that happened in a day, I'd spend one day living and one day writing about it—which, I guess, is not that much different from what I do in my real life anyway.

In the afternoon AP and I went over to the Tropicana to see the "exotic bird show." AP has become a lover of birds; she calls them "little schweeties." I keep telling her that not all birds are "little schweeties"—for example, vicious eagles that can rip up and eat a young child. But she comes back with, "I love those little schweeties." Yeah, well, just wait until you meet up with an eagle, baby.

The bird show was fun, and free, and then we went across the street to see the lions at the MGM Grand. The lions were asleep on a glass overhang that allowed you to walk under them and see them plastered against the glass, sleeping, oblivious to the humans taking pictures of them while they dreamed their lions' dreams (eating "little schweeties," perhaps?).

AP whispered to me, "Don't look, but over there is someone with depths." The word "depths" is our code word for someone who looks as if they have depths of derangement. That a lot is going on beneath the surface, mostly dark, weird things; scratch that surface and get a tsunami of emotional complexity you didn't really want to have to deal with.

Of course, I immediately looked. It was that old woman in camouflage with the sparkles on her belly. And she was arm in arm with someone who could have been her grandson—or great-grandson! They were smoochy-woochying, so it obviously wasn't her great-grandson—or, if it was, she had depths to her depths!

After watching the show at MGM Grand (not the lions, the old lady and the boy), we headed out to Green Valley Ranch to meet Dom. AP decided to go to a movie, and Dom and I went to the craps tables.

I had several good rolls and made 23 units when all was said and done.

Dom was annoyed by several of the dealers and suits at Green Valley. In the past few months Dom had noticed a distinct cooling-off of the friendliness of the staff, not only toward him but also toward anyone who tried to take care with their rolls. Just like at Bellagio, while I was shooting one of the dealers asked me if I had taken a course with *Crapsguy,* "that guy" who teaches the dice courses. Unlike the dealer at Bellagio, however, the Green Valley dealer's tone dripped with scorn. Then, after Dom and I had back-to-back fifteen-minute rolls, the boxman asked if Dom and I were brothers. Again, he said this scornfully. The best way to handle scorn is to pretend you don't hear the tone and answer the question in a way that deflates the questioner. So when the boxman asked scornfully, "Hey, are you two guys brothers?" I said innocently, "Yes."

"Uh, well, what I meant, was, uh, you guys shoot alike," he said.

"We're brothers," I said simply.

He knew our last names were different, and Dom and I look nothing alike. But I wasn't going to say anything more on the subject and that was that.

We had dinner at Bullshrimp. After dinner, we played again and had some good rolls.

My throw is definitely on now. Maybe this will be the diary in which I kick ass and look like a real big shot!

DAY 6 RESULTS: + 35 units

TOTAL FOR TRIP: +201 units

• Day 7: Tuesday, April 22, 2003 •

DOM FLEW back to Chicago today. He will be coming back out on Friday, when we'll be joined by Howard "Rock 'n' Roller" Newman.

After our walk, AP went to see the paintings at Venetian and I went to Casino Royale to play their 100X Odds game. Even though it was only ten o'clock in the morning, the two craps tables were packed. So I went over to the "tub," which was empty, and cashed in.

A "tub" is just a small craps table, about 1½ times the size of a blackjack table. It's sunken, like a tub, and is manned by only one dealer, and you must sit down to play it. The back wall is only a few feet away.

Now, based on dice-control theory, the closer you are to the back wall, the better it is. That is true, but when you are sitting you must use a completely different body movement for your throw. It took me a while before I could really figure out the best delivery system for the tub.

I was down 20 units in the first hour of my play at the

tub. Then I played another two hours, slowly got the feel for the table, and came back to win 20 units. I was tired by this time, and I figured my "win" was the ability to come back from defeat and break even.

AP and I had dinner at Bally's Steakhouse. We had the most delicious French, excuse me, *freedom* onion soup, followed by a great filet mignon.

Life is great, except I lost 21 units at the Bally's blackjack game. The only reason I even stayed at the game long enough to lose 21 units, when I was tired, was the fact that the really nice floorperson used to live in the town where we have our post office box, Lynbrook, and she had also lived in the area where my wife now works. So AP and this floorperson, Gloria, talked about what had happened to the area of Long Island known as the Five Towns—a very depressing conversation.

We talked and we lost.

DAY 7 RESULTS: -21 units
TOTAL FOR TRIP: +180 units

• Day 8: Wednesday, April 23, 2003 •

TOOK AP to the airport this morning. She has to go back to work next week and she wants to get some time at home to relax. The hardest thing in the world is saying goodbye to the person you love. Even though I know I'll see her in a week, I still feel that wrenching feeling inside my stomach when I kiss her goodbye at the airport.

Before AP got her first attack of ulcerative colitis, we were never apart. Since that first flare-up, I've made many trips without her. I'm hoping that, if her current remission lasts long enough, she'll be able to make all or at least most of the trips with me. My GTC schedule and my speaking and seminar schedules call for frequent trips to the casino towns of America. And I want AP with me because, one, I love her, and, two, people want to meet her since she is a kind of celebrity due to my books. People will ask me, "Where's the beautiful AP? I wanted to meet her." Maybe in the future.

I checked out of Bally's and moved over to the Rio. A part of this trip is for me to go to casinos and judge their craps games for *Casino Player Magazine*'s "Best of Vegas" issue. The GTC instructors and other craps-playing associates have helped me with these ratings, because among them they have played just about every craps game in Vegas in the last few months. So I will be able to give the best possible rundown of the Top Seven Craps Games. I'm also to write a piece giving my opinion as to the best overall hotel-casinos at which to stay and play. Again, I am getting plenty of help from others on this, since I haven't stayed and played at every casino-hotel in Vegas.

The "new" Rio has come in for accolades from people who stayed there, so I decided I'd give this place a whirl for a couple of days before heading to my personal favorite, Treasure Island. I'd been to Rio, but that was long before it became such an "in" place.

This casino-hotel is all suites, although the newer tower suites are really not suites, not the way, say, the suites at the Venetian are suites. But the rooms are nice and many have spectacular views of the Strip and downtown.

Once checked in at the Rio, I went to the craps tables. All but one were long fourteen-footers (and that one was open only once during my two-day stay), and the lighting at every table left a lot to be desired. In fact, what was left to be desired was, actually, *lighting*. The tables were in shadows and it was hard to see the layout or back wall clearly through the shadowy patterns. I had a horrendous afternoon. I couldn't shoot worth a damn and I lost 40 units in a little more than an hour. The *5-Count* failed me here as well since the other players would make it past the 5-Count only to go down in flames on the 6-Count.

I had dinner at Antonio's with Barney and Debbie Vinson. Many of you reading this know who Barney Vinson is—a terrific writer who used to work at the Dunes and then at Caesars Palace as a "suit." I've called him the Will Rogers of casino gaming writers for his sharp humor and great insights. His books are *Las Vegas Behind the Tables, Casino Secrets, Chip-Wrecked in Las Vegas, Ask Barney,* and *The Vegas Kid.* Barney had been involved in a long court case with a former publisher who hadn't paid him royalties for six or seven years and then tried to stop Barney from going to another publisher. Barney won the case, but it cost him both emotionally and financially.

After dinner, I noticed that the twelve-foot table was open and empty. So I went there and had a nice roll, winning back 19 of the 40 units I had lost that afternoon.

When I got back to my room a message was waiting from AP: "Got home safely. Everything was fine. But the Family from Hell was on the flight, but thankfully this time they were in coach. There was some big commotion with them and a stewardess but I fell asleep and never found out what it was." My guess is that they were fighting over a banana.

DAY 8 RESULTS: -21 units
TOTAL FOR TRIP: +159 units

• Day 9: Thursday, April 24, 2003 •

I TOOK a two-hour walk today. I had a fitful night's sleep. Listening to Barney Vinson's travails with his former publisher had gotten to me. When you make a substantial part of your living from writing, you realize how fragile your relationships are with publishers and editors. You realize how easy it would be for them to just not pay you. I have heard horror stories that are similar to Barney's from other writer friends of mine, specifically Walter Thomason and John May, who really got screwed when Carol Publishing, the number one nonfiction publisher in the world at the time, went bankrupt, still owing the writers tens of thousands in unpaid royalties that they have never been able to collect.

In the afternoon I headed over to Casino Royal again. Again I couldn't get onto the 100X Odds table, so I sat down at the tub. This time I had my "tub-throw" down pat, and in a couple of hours I had won 27 units.

That night I had dinner at Fiore at Rio. After dinner, I looked to see if the twelve-foot table was open but it wasn't. Instead, I went to my room and finished my article on the best casinos to play craps in—naming Treasure Island as number one:

> 1. *Treasure Island: Second year in a row, TI is #1. Why? Because they have savvy, friendly, professional crews on every shift who focus on the game, not on private conversations; good rules on buy bets, decent odds bets (3X, 4X, 5X), great tables (12 footers with true bounce), and good players.*

I also rated TI as the number-one place to stay:

> 1. *Treasure Island: A small (by Strip standards) casino, good double- and six-deck blackjack games, best craps game in the city, and dealers who should be giving lessons on how to be a dealer. Excellent rooms, clean, always renovated, good views and terrific restaurants. To top it off, it has the best show in town, Mystere. Good comps.*

Tomorrow I would check into Treasure Island. I love Treasure Island. The dealers and pit crews at Treasure Island have it together. It's a pleasure to play there and it's a great place to stay, too.

DAY 9 RESULTS: +27 units

TOTAL FOR TRIP: +186 units

• Day 10: Friday, April 25, 2003 •

LET ME *eat my words* and let me never write anything in advance ever again!

Howard "Rock 'n' Roller" Newman picked me up at the Rio around noon. We went to the dealer school on Sahara Avenue, where we would be holding our GTC class that weekend, to check a few things out. Then we went to Treasure Island. Howard had gotten in very late the night before.

He was supposed to have four free nights, but when he checked in he discovered that the casino had given a different Howard Newman the four free nights and *this* Howard Newman didn't have a room. Howard went to a host to explain that he knew the other Howard Newman (which is true, as the *other* Howard Newman is a chiropractor in *this* Howard Newman's hometown in Florida), and that the *other* Howard Newman wasn't even coming to Treasure Island this weekend. The host who had made *this* Howard Newman's reservation (also my host) was away on vacation, and the other host, instead of performing the great "gesture," as Cyrano de Bergerac once said, gave the typical corporate response when she said, "Sir, I can give you tonight but the rest of the nights you'll have to pay."

Howard tried to explain to her that he was staying at Treasure Island because he had been promised four free nights. He had free nights downtown that he could use.

The host couldn't (wouldn't) help him, so Howard was hoping I could help with the problem, as I was an RFB player at Treasure Island and I'd given them a lot of play and a lot of good publicity over the years.

I tried to help, but it seems that my host had given *this* Howard Newman the room because he thought he was the *other* Howard Newman, who was a bigger player. We even spoke to another host, who looked up Howard's past play on her computer—and told us there was nothing she could do.

At least Howard would be charged the discounted casino rate for his room, and I was pretty sure that, if he played enough, he'd get the room for free. Howard's average bet should be enough for a room comp, anywhere.

This comping thing is *comp*licated. I enjoyed the first half of my trip because I was under no obligation to give any casino any level of action for any given amount of time. I could play where I wanted for whatever stakes I wanted and comps be damned. But at Treasure Island I was doing the high-roller routine. I'd give them four hours of play a day at an average bet that was enough to get me RFB. I didn't like having to do that but, if you want to get the comps, you've got to give them action and time.

After I checked into Treasure Island, Howard and I went down to play craps. This would be one of the few times I've played craps at Treasure Island during the afternoon (day shift); in the past I've usually played in the morning (graveyard shift) or in the evening (night shift). My epic seven-hour tag-team roll that opened this book took place with both the night and the graveyard crew, because it started around 11 P.M. and ended around 6 A.M. From what I understand, the dealers who witnessed our play that evening/morning still talk about it.

Howard cashed in, I took out a marker, and we started to play. When it was my turn to roll, there was a stickman, Sasquatch, who kept saying stuff under his breath like, "Oh, another of *Crapsguy*'s students." Sasquatch also made it a point to put his rather large, muscular body over the table so that I had to get way out over the layout in order to throw. He would then put his stick in the fishing position in an attempt to interfere with my sightlines. I had never seen this guy at Treasure Island before, but, then again, I hadn't played all that often on the afternoon shift.

When next I got the dice and Sasquatch was on stick, he turned to me and said, "Move about a foot down the table." I was on SL1 and I wasn't cramping him, but he still insisted I move. I made a faux move and set the dice. Then he went fishing again. He had the stick so low that I hit it with my arm. Since he didn't seem the least inclined to change the position of his stick, I had to change my throw. And I had a tip out for the dealers, too—I always have tips out for the dealers. A good, professional stickperson, when he sees that you are taking care with your roll, will move back to give you the clearest sightlines possible—especially if he sees that you tip generously. Not Sasquatch.

I tipped this crew when I rolled, and Howard tipped, and I had some good rolls that afternoon, and so did Howard, but only one dealer ever thanked me for the tips and no one thanked Howard. Sasquatch actually sneered whenever he was the dealer who got to take down the tips. He never once said "Thanks."

I went back to my suite to take a nap, and I wondered if Treasure Island was going to become just like many of the other casinos in Vegas—you had some good craps dealers and some bad craps dealers. I didn't want that. I wanted to have one casino where every craps dealer was outstanding. It had been Treasure Island, but Sasquatch's sarcasm and attitude had really thrown me. Then again, maybe he was the exception. I hoped so.

• • • •

DOMINATOR WAS coming back in from Chicago around 5:30 P.M. I arranged to have the Treasure Island limousine pick him up at the airport. I told them to write DOMINATOR on the sign. He'd like seeing that sign when he came out of the baggage handling area.

Dom, Howard, and I ate at Buccaneer Bay, the second-floor restaurant from which you can see the pirate battles in the Treasure Island lagoon as you dine, but it was too windy for the pirate show. We discussed how we would handle the class the next day; we also talked about the afternoon crew, especially Sasquatch's surly attitude.

It had become evident to us that some of the best casinos for craps in Vegas, casinos that had had good crews and pit personnel, had seemingly overnight become cool, cold, or downright hostile to dice setters and careful shooters. Some GTC members had a theory that the *Crapsguy,* the freelance dice-control instructor, had been too public, aggressive, and up-front at the tables about what he was doing, so much so that many of the crews associated any careful shooter with him. Some had even asked me (and Dom and Howard and other careful shooters) if I (we) had taken a course with him. In all respects, this teacher of dice control is a very nice and a personable guy, but he is a hard-driving, let-it-all-hang-out businessman, and maybe he had polluted the craps river and burned many of the dice bridges behind him, bridges we were now crossing with difficulty. (By contrast, even when GTC did our course at Sam's Town in Tunica we were laid back at the tables and never talked about dice control or handed our business cards across the table to drum up new business as the *Crapsguy* is wont to do.)

That night Howard, Dominator, and I had a series of good rolls—with Dom and Howard really knocking the lights out. I noticed several people at our table who had attended the Las

Vegas Craps Festival in September 2002. Most of them passed the dice when it was their turn to roll, so Dom, Howard, and I, who were in our positions, got in some extra turns.

DAY 10 RESULTS: + 69 units

TOTAL FOR TRIP: +255 units

• Day 11: Saturday, April 26, 2003 •

I WASN'T able to go for my walk this morning because I had to do the *Goodtimes Radio Show* at 7:30 A.M. My segment on the show this morning focused on two things: the sale of Aladdin, and my disappointment that all but the high-roller-room blackjack games at Treasure Island were now being dealt from continuous-shuffle machines. This change increased the number of hands players would play in an hour by 20 percent—which meant more in losses over time for the players. The continuous-shuffle machines do something else as well: they focus the attention of the dealer and the player on the machine. Just as a television set that is on will immediately focus the attention of a group of people at a bar or party (at least at first), the continuous-shuffle machines do the same thing at the tables. The dealer is always putting cards in and taking cards out of the machine. While she does so, the players watch the cards go in and come out. The personal interaction between player and dealer, one of the enjoyable aspects of the traditional blackjack game for many players, is diminished significantly by these machines.

I found that my experiences on Friday had left me a little saddened. Yes, I had rolled just fine most of the day, and, yes, it was a winning day. But something was lost when Sasquatch ruined my illusion that Treasure Island had universally good dealers. And those shuffle machines made me long for a return of Mirage founder Steve Wynn and the ousting of the corporate MGM-Mirage suits who seemed to be ruining my favorite property. I was also disappointed that Howard hadn't been given a free room when, after all, it was Treasure Island's mistake in telling him he had four free nights, not Howard's mistake.

The GTC class was being held in the dealer school on Sahara Avenue. We were limiting the enrollment (we had ten students) so that we could work at two craps tables. Doing this would give us the opportunity to really get a lot of hands-on work with the students.

And we did.

Many of the students wanted to know where we would be playing that night. This is a common situation. Most of the students GTC has taught want to play with the instructors. First, they want to see us in action, to see if we are as good at the tables as we seem to be in practice, and, second, they want to make money on our rolls. The instructors are in a different situation. When you teach for seven or eight hours, you find that you are exhausted by the end of the day. Most of us just want to go back to the hotel and take a nap. Playing the first night of a class can be dangerous, to our reputations and our bankrolls. In Tunica, I took a beating the first night of the seminar. My throw wasn't on and I was really tired. So, knowing this, why did we still plan on playing that night?

We're *players!*

And that night, after a delicious dinner at Francesco's at Treasure Island, both Dom and Howard were again hot as Hades. I wasn't. Still, thanks to Dom and Howard, the evening was a success for me. And a success for those same half-dozen people who seemed to appear at our table whenever we rolled. And the crew and pit were just fine, too.

DAY 11 RESULTS: +8 units

TOTAL FOR TRIP: +263 units

• • • •

• Day 12: Sunday, April 27, 2003 •

I WOKE up at 6 A.M. and I had a choice. I could go out for my walk or I could shower, eat a little breakfast and go down and get a session in. Normally I would choose to go for the walk, but I was disappointed in my performance the night before, so I decided to play now that I was rested and refreshed.

I got down to the table at seven forty-five. I'd have a half-hour to play before I had to get to the dealer school for the second day of the seminar.

There were two people at the table and my position was open. I cashed in and started the *5-Count* on the guy who had just been passed the dice. He made it past the 5-Count, then I put up my bets, and he sevened out.

It was the other guy's turn; he was at SR2. He also got past the 5-Count and, with all my bets at risk again, seven-out he went!

I was then passed the dice.

Three of the people who always seemed to be at the table when the GTC crew rolled cashed in to the left of me. I recognized their faces from the two days before, but I didn't know their names. They weren't the ones I had met at the Craps Festival.

The morning Treasure Island crew was friendly and professional, and when I set the dice and aimed the stickman made a point of taking a half-step back to give me room and good sightlines. I established a point of four. I placed the six and eight for twice what I normally would bet on a chicken-feeder, and then I went six and eight *crazy*. I estimate that I hit the six about sixteen times and the eight about nine times. I also hit other numbers, but nowhere near as many of them as of the six and eight. I made only one point, my four, or maybe two points, as I vaguely recall I might have hit a nine for a point. The next point was a ten but I never hit it. I hit those sixes and eights. I started to press my bets slowly as I won. Dominator is an aggressive presser; I'm not. But I had doubled the bets by the time I sevened out. And I sevened out when one of my dice hit a chip.

"Let him shoot again," said one of the three people who always appeared when GTC crew came to the tables.

"Yeah," said the second; I think she was his wife.

"Pass the dice," said the third; maybe *she* was his wife.

"I've got to go." I looked at my watch. It was 8:25.

"When are you playing again?" asked the man.

"Tonight," I said.

"Will the other two be with you?" asked the first woman.

"Yes," I said.

As I colored up, one of the dealers said, "Nice roll, Mr. S."

I felt a hell of a lot better now. I had won some money, 58 units, *and* I had been treated in the old Treasure Island way. Just that one dealer saying "Nice roll, Mr. S." had made my morning.

And the class was great too.

Part of learning a controlled throw has to do with the ability to handle the stress of an actual game. There are some shooters who are just dynamite in practice, with SRRs that are staggering, but in a real game, with real money on the line and real pressure to perform, they just can't pull the trigger. So, to test our students under game conditions with money on the line and pressure on them to perform, we hold No-Sevens contests. The winner of the contest gets $50, the second-place finisher gets $20, and the third-place finisher gets a GTC T-shirt. Each student gets to roll the dice twice—with all the instructors and other students watching. They have to perform under pressure and show a desire to win, the two ingredients needed for successful controlled shooting.

Walt Cherry, a poker dealer from Laughlin, Nevada, won the contest with twenty-nine rolls, and TNT, a young man from Washington, came in second with nineteen rolls.

That Sunday, the "Three Musketeers," as Howard started to call us, ate at Madame Ching's at Treasure Island and then headed for the tables. We found one that had two people at it and we cashed in. Then the crowd arrived, nine people total. By now I had learned some of the names: there was George, Arman, Bob Swanson, Angela Sparks, Gary, and the three from this morning, plus one more whose name I didn't know at the time. We now had fourteen people at the table. Howard was the first to shoot. He shot the lights out for maybe twenty minutes. Then Dominator put on a show like only he can. He had an eight point, forty-plus-number hand that lasted easily a half-hour. When Dom sevened out, I rolled for about fifteen minutes, and made five points and a bunch of numbers.

Here's how one poster on Jerry Patterson's DICE listserv described what it was like to play with GTC's Three Musketeers those few days:

> I had several sessions at the craps tables with Frank and some of the other G.T.C. crew, Dom and Howard. Needless to say they walked the talk and made a believer out of me. Each one putting on spectacular hands; sometimes all three in a row, like a three cylinder machine, one after another. There were several other PARR players at the tables and we just passed the dice around, letting the G.T.C. crew do all the work.
>
> Of course, we collected many units due to our lack of participation. Most of us were nowhere near our normal shooting spots. After the first night when these guys hit the craps pit it was like someone set off an alarm and the table would fill up before they finished buying in. In the four sessions I witnessed, only one time did one of them not have a nice hand or two.

This was the first time I witnessed heat at the T.I. It seemed to come from certain suits and dealers but not all. Some stick personal leaned out over the table, tapped the stick, waved it around and made noise when the shooter started to throw. Others leaned back out of the way, helped with the dice sets, etc. . . . In my opinion the T.I. is still a nice place to play but expect some heat. . . . Also you may want to practice getting out over the middle of the table when you shoot to avoid the stick man. That's it for now!

Good Rolling

Jim Hatfield from Cincinnati

We had several more good rolls after that as well but, finally, the "three musketeers" succumbed to fatigue and we went to our rooms, delighted in the knowledge that we had indeed put on a show worth remembering.

DAY 12 RESULTS: +150 units

TOTAL FOR TRIP: +413 units

• Day 13: Monday, April 28, 2003 •

TODAY WAS a replay of yesterday. The Three Musketeers played in the late morning at an empty table; that is, it was empty until we started to cash in and then, *whoosh!* seven people came over, including Bob, Angela, George, Jim Hatfield, and three of the others from the night before. They must have been camping out at the casino to catch us playing.

We had a good session at Treasure Island, and then Howard had to check out and move downtown where he had a free night at Main Street Station. Dom went with him. I went back to my suite to work on this diary.

We were going to meet around 2 P.M. at the Venetian because Dom wanted to establish himself as a player there. I went over to the Venetian at about one-thirty and played some double-deck blackjack (won 1 unit!) and then a little craps. The Venetian has good tables but their dice are smaller than usual and therefore they tend to bounce much more than the larger dice. You have to land the dice about six inches further from the back wall than you are used to or the bounce is just too powerful to overcome randomness. (I won another 1 unit.)

Around 2 P.M., in walked the *Crapsguy* with some students. One of the dealers said scornfully, "Guess who's *baaaack?*" and nodded over at the *Crapsguy*. I colored up and walked out. I called Dom on his cell phone and told him that the Venetian might not be so hospitable if they saw us with "him," as this crew didn't seem at all enamored of him. So we decided to play an afternoon session at Treasure Island.

When Dom and Howard arrived we headed for the tables, and so did a half-dozen other people who had been waiting for us.

This afternoon was much like all the other sessions we'd had. We made money on our rolls, most of the others at the table passed the dice, and so it went. The dealers were neither friendly nor grumpy; as sticks they didn't make any effort to give us clear sightlines, but neither did they lean too far over the table.

We had dinner at the Steak House and then headed to the tables around 8:30 for an evening shoot. So did our entourage! Again we instantly filled up an almost empty table. The boxman was a young man I'll call Dour because of the permanent pout on his face; he made a point of chronicling what was going on at the table—to no one in particular but to the world at large. "Look at this. What is this? No one shoots? They all pass the dice?"

But shoot GTC's Three Musketeers did. It was another

· · · ·

great performance. Mr. Dour was extremely agitated that we were winning, just as Mr. Mumbles had been at Bellagio, and he called over the floorperson on more than one occasion and scowled and pointed at us. The floorperson, with a sly grin, kept saying to Mr. Dour, "It's the power of the pen! The *power* of the pen!"

I heard him saying this but I didn't relate it to me. Dom thought that the floorperson was saying that I was a writer or some such. Naturally, casino aficionados know what the expression "the power of the pen" means. It refers to the individuals who can rate the players and/or give out comps.

At a certain point we decided to switch tables. The previous floorperson, Mr. Power of the Pen, whose real name I didn't catch, came over to talk to the floorperson at our new table. Again, I didn't associate that with me.

Our boxman was a guy named Joe. He was pleasant and friendly and we had some good rolls at his table, too. Joe did, however, mention that he hadn't seen the *Crapsguy* lately, and that he, Joe, had "probably run him out of the place." Joe then asked me, "You were with him last time I saw you here. You friends with him?"

"No, no," I said, "I barely know him."

"Okay, then you guys are welcome to play here any time you want," said Joe.

By 11 P.M., we were ready to call it a night. We had played for two and a half hours, a long, long time considering the long day we'd had and the fact that we were doing most of the shooting for the table.

DAY 13 RESULTS: +97 units

TOTAL FOR TRIP: +510 units

• Day 14: Tuesday, April 29, 2003 •

DOM AND I had breakfast together and then went over to the host's area by the cashier's cage. Dom wanted to find out what his rating had been to see if he could get his room and food fully comped before he left this morning. Last night he had asked Mr. Power of the Pen to tell him what he had been rated. Instead of doing so, the guy acted annoyed. "I've got a lot to do," he said, but finally, after Dom waited patiently, Mr. POP turned to him and . . . played Twenty Questions! He asked Dom what *he* thought he should be rated. Dom told him. Then Dom again asked what his rating was. Mr. POP told him—it was $30 less than Dom had figured.

Interestingly enough, when the hostess on duty checked Dom's play for his stay, she found that Dom had played approximately 14½ hours in four days and his average bet was indeed $30 more than Mr. POP had rated him. Considering that Mr. POP's rating was part of the overall rating, that meant the other Treasure Island raters had actually given Dom a higher rating than Dom had given himself.

I decided to ask for my rating and I was somewhat surprised to discover that between yesterday morning and this morning, my average-bet rating had gone down $40! It was still enough to get RFB but somehow overnight my rating had sunk drastically.

Strangely enough, while Dom was given a free room for his play, a mere $82 of food charges to his room were not picked up. Yet Dom's average bet was well over $82! Why wouldn't Treasure Island pick up such a paltry room charge?

Dom left for the airport a little while later and Howard and I played a session at Treasure Island. It was disastrous. We both stunk up the joint! And, of course, we did have some of our usual witnesses watching two of the Three Musketeers shooting themselves in the feet!

I lost 40 units before I turned to Howard and said, "That's it. Let's take a break. We're getting killed."

Since I was leaving tomorrow, I went back to my suite and packed most of my bags. I also took a nap to clear my head.

I met Howard at 2 P.M. at the Treasure Island craps tables. Bob Swanson, Angela Sparks, and Gary appeared as we cashed in. It so happens that Sasquatch was at this table, but he was on SR at the moment and wouldn't be interacting with me. The stickwoman, a washed-out blonde whose skin had weathered many tans, and whose name I never got, passed Howard the dice. Howard was back in form and had a good roll. Then I started to have a good roll, when one of my two dice skimmed the back wall, landing flat against it, making the point of five. Shades of Mr. Mumbles and Clarence! The boxman, a sallow, well-coiffed blonde young man (I didn't get his name either), leaped at me: "You have to hit the back wall every time!" Usually the first time you miss the back wall with one or both dice, a boxman might say, "Don't forget to hit the back wall." The nasty tone of voice is usually reserved for those players who continually miss the back wall. But the coiffed-blonde boxman had acted as if this were my fiftieth time missing the back wall, not my first. (And for the record, I *didn't* miss the back wall. My dice hit it and died.)

Even the floorperson, a man I've known for several years and one of the people I think of when I use the word "professional" in the context of writing about casino staff, looked over at the stickman. This floorperson then winked at me as if to say, "I know the boxman overreacted. Ignore it."

Since my dice had indeed touched the back wall, I nodded my head, and said, "Gee, you know, I thought they *did* hit the back wall."

That was the stickwoman's cue to jump in. "Sir, the rules are the rules!" she shouted. Since I was standing right next to her, I didn't understand why she was shouting. My ear rang. "You have to bounce them *hard* off the back wall! They just can't *touch* it; they have to hit hard! Those are the rules of the game! They have to bounce back! You understand that, sir?"

I looked over at the floorperson and our eyes caught. I made a slight gesture as if to say, "What's with this stickwoman?"

The stickwoman must have caught my expression and she launched again: "You don't think you have to follow the rules, sir? You have to bounce those dice off the back wall. Bounce them! Everybody has to follow the rules!"

I thought to myself that in a moment or two this stickwoman was going to start foaming at the mouth—God help me if she was to bite me!

"I'm not arguing with you," I said calmly. "I know the rules."

"These are the rules!" she spit and shouted, but finally passed me the dice. She then planted her stick right on the Horn area of the layout. It looked like a flag pole that I had to shoot around.

"I'm not *arguing*," I said again.

I set my 3-V, lofted them, and the dice hit the back wall all right—on the fly! They came ricocheting back almost halfway across the table. "Six. Point is six."

"Make sure you keep hitting the back wall," snorted the coiffed-blonde boxman.

I nodded.

"Those are the rules," said the stickwoman. "Do you understand that?" *(And do you understand that you should be flying on that stick during Halloween?)*

I set the dice and lofted them. This time, they hit the back wall softly and died. The boxman was about to say something but . . .

"Seven out!" shouted the stickwoman and then she rubbed it in loudly: *"SEVEN OUT! SHOOTER SEVENED OUT!"* She seemed so happy that I had gone down in flames, even though that meant the three bets I had up for the dealers were burned as well.

I turned to Howard. "Let's get out of here."

I invited Bob, Angela, and Gary to come with Howard and me to Bellagio. I called Treasure Island's VIP services and asked for the limo. It would be twenty minutes.

I told the others that I wanted to go back to my room to make a few calls, which I did. I called *Casino Player* magazine and changed the ratings of the top places to play craps in Las Vegas. How could I possibly rate Treasure Island as the number-one place to play craps when I was literally *fleeing* an angry, surly, unpleasant stickwoman and boxman? I felt bad about this, because most of the dealers and most of the pit crews at Treasure Island, as I've said, are still first-rate. But to be number one, everyone has to be good. Sadly, this just wasn't the case at Treasure Island anymore.

At Bellagio, Howard found himself confronting an unpleasant crew, too. The first thing one of them said, scornfully, when Howard set and threw was, "Oh, another of the *Crapsguy*'s students!" Howard's first roll, a twenty-five-minute humdinger, had made us quite a bit of money. I had a decent roll as well. On Howard's second turn, the stickman passed him the dice with a seven on the side. Howard asked that the stickman not pass him the dice with any seven showing. The stickman argued with him. "It wasn't on top, was it? It was on the side!"

"I'm superstitious," said Howard.

Then Howard sneezed, a big, loud, man-sized sneeze.

"Jeez, Howard, I told you not to go to China," I said. That got a laugh out of many at the table who were well aware of the SARS epidemic occurring in that country.

That started it.

The dealer at Howard's SR side started to make all sorts of weird looking faces at my comment and then rolled his eyes and moved his lips as if to say, "Mimi, mimi, mimi." Then, when Howard rolled, Mr. Mimi started to make faux coughs every time Howard released the dice. Then when I rolled he did the same thing. He also kept repeating over and over under his breath, "Fancy shooter, fancy shooter!"

When Mr. Mimi came over to be the stick, he really got revved up. Another dealer told him, sarcastically, to remember to give "the big guy" (Howard) the dice without any sevens. Mr. Mimi replied: "Don't worry, when he rolls, watch how I take care of that prick."

That was it for me. I turned to Howard and said, "We're finished." Howard, Bob, Angela, Gary, and I colored up but this time I was so angry that I went over to the floorperson.

I asked him for the dealer's name and I informed him of what Mr. Mimi had said about Howard and how Mr. Mimi kept doing his phony cough whenever Howard shot the dice. The floorperson agreed that this wasn't the kind of behavior that Bellagio dealers should be exhibiting toward patrons.

What was happening at the MGM-Mirage properties? Stickpeople putting their sticks down almost in the middle of the tables; dealers not thanking you for tips; boxmen lambasting you even when you *hit* the back wall if you didn't hit it with the intention of putting a hole through it. And what had happened to turn Green Valley Ranch from a paradise for Dom into a place where scorn and sarcasm reigned in the pit?

And why were so many places asking us if we were students of the *Crapsguy*?

We went over to MGM next and had a fine session. Bob Swanson had the roll of the session and after he rolled it was time for us to go back to Treasure Island. Howard and I had dinner reservations at Moongate, the Chinese restaurant at Mirage. After dinner we played a little at Treasure Island. No ugly events occurred, I had a couple of good rolls, and then I called it a day and my playing for this trip was over. I never play on the day I am going to leave Las Vegas.

DAY 14 RESULTS: +48 units
GRAND TOTAL FOR TRIP: +558 units

· Day 15: Wednesday, April 30, 2003 ·

MY PLANE leaves at 10:55 A.M.

I had breakfast and then walked over to the host's desk at Treasure Island. I was curious to find out what my final rating was for this trip, but I also wanted to look at the individual days to see what had dropped me $40 overnight in my overall average-bet rating.

It wasn't hard to discover what happened. Mr. Power of the Pen had rated me as betting one-fourth what I actually was rated by other floorpeople. Translated into money, what this would mean is that a 10-unit player for all the other Treasure Island raters would suddenly became a 2.5-unit player for Mr. POP.

I decided that when I got home I would write a letter to my host and explain what had happened on this trip. In the past I have written many letters to casinos, all of them to highly praise individuals or crews for a job well done. I have *never* written a letter of complaint. I usually figure one or two bad dealers shouldn't overshadow all the good dealers. But the treatment at Treasure Island, especially the reduction of my average bet by three-fourths its worth, had me upset.

Interestingly enough, I had to change my ratings for Treasure Island in "the best casinos to stay and play" category for my *Casino Player* article as well. It wasn't just the individuals who had been nasty or unprofessional in the craps pits, it had been Howard Newman not getting a free room when Treasure Island had made the mistake in his reservation; it had been Dominator not getting a small meal charge taken off his room when that charge was less than one average bet; and it had been the installation of all those continuous-shuffle machines in an attempt to gouge more money from the players.

Usually when events such as these happen over a five-day period to different people, it's indicative of a pattern. And the pattern was clear. Treasure Island was no longer number one.

• Afterword •

NOW I'M back in New York. I received a response to my letter from the director of table games at Treasure Island. He was aghast that some of the dealers and pit personnel acted as they did and he told me he intends to rectify the situation. I hope so. I'd like to see Treasure Island return to number one, because I like the property and most of the personnel. AP loves the place. It suits her.

I don't know if the unpleasantness we experienced with some dealers and floorpeople at Treasure Island and elsewhere is a harbinger of more unpleasantness to come at the craps tables for careful shooters. I do know that on a one-day return trip to Treasure Island a few weeks after this diary, I met some wonderful dealers in the evening. One in particular, a young man named John, impressed me with his skill and his knowledge of the game. He had read all the leading authors in gambling and really understood the nature of casino games. He was a pleasure to talk to. I made it a point to avoid the individuals who had been surly the last time.

Perhaps Treasure Island will return to its former glory. Time will tell. But controlled shooting is here to stay. Unless the stupidest humans to walk the planet since Australopithecus run the casinos, the game of craps will see a renaissance as more and more players attempt to beat it—and ultimately fail. Instead of fearing and harassing those who take care with their rolls, the casinos should welcome them with open arms, because with each and every good roll, people get hooked on the game of craps.

Blackjack languished for years as the third-most-profitable table game, behind craps and roulette, until people read in 1963 that it could be beaten. Now, blackjack is number one—the table-game cash cow. Why? Because even people who can't beat the game, which is just about everyone, think they have a chance to do so! The same will hold true for craps. That is, unless the behavior of the few dealers, boxpeople and pit-people on this past trip foreshadows the behavior of the many in the future. Then craps play will continue to decline, and ultimately we'll see it take a backseat to such carnival games as Let It Ride, Three Card Poker, and Casino War. Before you know it, there will even be casinos that have no craps tables—and what casinos they will be! And those surly craps dealers, boxmen, and floorpeople will have, by their own actions, caused themselves to become unemployed as more and more machines take the place of people.

I don't want to see that happen. I want craps to survive and thrive.

Time will tell whether it will.

Epilogue

· · · ·

This story has no ending. It's a work in progress. Many of the people I wrote about in this book have won a million dollars at craps—and some have won much, much more. But even the non-million-dollar-winners are still *winners*.

And who knows; you might run into these greats at the tables, perhaps today or tonight.

The Lee brothers are still out there playing. GTC is going strong. And Dominator, Sharpshooter, Mr. Finesse, Howard "Rock 'n' Roller" Newman, Street Dog, Daryl "No Field Five" Henley, Dr. Richard "Samurai Shooter" McCall, Randy "Tenor" Rowsey, Doc Holliday, Billy the Kid, Jake from Pitt, Jerry "Stickman" Stich, and Bill Burton are all still playing, winning, and teaching. And, yes, Jerry Patterson is still marketing systems. And, yes, most gambling writers still dismiss the idea that craps can be beaten and thus few have looked into learning dice-control techniques. Even so, craps play is picking up slowly all over the country, due in large part, I believe, to the perception that it can be beaten. The fact that only a small nanopercent of the players can do so does not stop others from wishing, hoping, pretending, and playing . . . and playing some more.

And, yes, the Captain is still going strong, though he is now over eighty. My last meeting with him was at Wild Wild West in Atlantic City, where the Captain shot for forty-five minutes in the presence of GTC students! What a thrill for them to play with the legend himself.

As I finished writing the last chapter, I called the Captain. He had just come back from Bally's Park Place in Atlantic City, where he had had a one-hour-twelve-minute roll! "I was in the groove, Frank," he said. "I was hitting numbers like crazy. I was able to keep track of the time because the car was coming to pick me up at a certain time, so as the dice were passed over to me I checked my watch. I rolled for an hour and twelve minutes. This might be the greatest roll of my life. I just wish I had Jimmy and Russ and some of the old Crew with me to share it."

Well, Captain, a new Crew is forming and there's millions more to be made. But you started all this, so it's appropriate that I end this book by quoting you:

"The real struggle is not between you and the casino; the real struggle is between you and yourself."

I've taken that dictum to heart.

Thank you, Captain, for everything.